Thoughts
for
Good
Eating

Thoughts for Good Eating

HOUGHTON MIFFLIN COMPANY BOSTON
1975

Decorations by Tom Funk

Library of Congress Cataloging in Publication Data

Main entry under title:

Thoughts for good eating.

Includes index.
1. Cookery.   2. Menus.
TX715.T482   641.5   75-23062
ISBN 0-395-21891-8

Printed in the United States of America

V   10   9   8   7   6   5   4   3   2   1

Foreword

THIS BOOK has been the project of many knowledgeable cooks who share the belief that dining can be an enjoyable form of entertainment. It is another addition to our library of fine cook books: *Thoughts for Foods, Thoughts for Buffets* and *Thoughts for Festive Foods.*

We wish to thank those who used their creative skills to help write, test, plan and edit these menus.

A special thanks to our many friends and readers who requested a new "Thoughts" cookbook. We feel that we have replied with a unique and provocative book.

INSTITUTE PUBLISHING COMPANY

We may live without friends, we may live without
books. But civilized man cannot live without cooks.

OWEN MEREDITH

Contents

Introduction

BOTH THE EXPERIENCED COOK and the new cook will be able to find in this book menus that are suitable to their own particular talents. There are daring recipes, and some that are quite simple, and all have been tested for taste and accuracy. Advance preparation schedules have been included to help the cook budget time and enjoy the sharing of a meal with guests or family.

The number of people served is indicated on each menu. However, individual appetites vary, and you may find it advantageous to borrow a dish from one menu to put into another, or omit one from an existing menu.

Entertaining should be fun and anticipated with a great deal of pleasure. We know that *Thoughts for Good Eating* will help make it all happen. Some simple rules to follow are:

—Allow yourself time to plan.

—Read the recipe carefully before you start.

—Be certain to have all the ingredients.

—Preheat and know your oven.

—Cold foods should always be served properly chilled, and hot foods piping hot.

—Rely upon the hints that are furnished in the back of this book— they can prove helpful.

Brunches

A COMBINATION of breakfast and lunch, Brunch is a popular form of entertaining on Sundays and holidays. Menus can be extremely flexible, often ranging from a simple "Farmer's Breakfast" to an elaborate "Artichoke-Mushroom Omelette with Hollandaise Sauce."

Bountiful Brunch

(SERVES 4)

Champagne and Orange Juice Cocktail
Artichoke-Mushroom Omelettes
Blender Lemon Hollandaise Sauce (see Index)
Giant Popovers with Honey Butter
Watercress–Cherry Tomato Salad
Blueberry Coffee Cake
Coffee

1

Freezer   Early Morning

Blueberry Coffee Cake   *Hollandaise sauce*
                           Honey Butter
                           Watercress–Cherry Tomato Salad
                           Remove Blueberry Coffee Cake
                               from freezer

CHAMPAGNE AND ORANGE JUICE COCKTAIL

Combine equal parts of chilled orange juice and champagne in champagne glasses.

ARTICHOKE-MUSHROOM OMELETTES

8 eggs
Salt and pepper
4 teaspoons butter
1 14-ounce can artichoke hearts, halved
1 pound fresh mushrooms, thickly sliced

2 tablespoons butter
1 tablespoon lemon juice
1 recipe Blender Lemon Hollandaise (see Index)

With a fork, beat eggs with salt and pepper just until blended. For each omelette, melt 1 teaspoon butter in a 6- or 7-inch skillet. Melt over high heat, turning pan to coat sides with butter. Add one quarter of egg mixture (about 2 eggs) all at once. Stir rapidly with a fork while shaking pan back and forth over high heat. Let eggs set, but leave them slightly underdone. Slide each omelette out of pan onto a small oven-proof plate; top each with some of the artichoke hearts and mushrooms, which have been sautéed in the 2 tablespoons butter and lemon juice and sprinkled with salt and pepper. Cover each omelette with some of the Hollandaise sauce. Place omelettes under preheated broiler for a few minutes to brown Hollandaise. Serve at once.

GIANT POPOVERS WITH HONEY BUTTER

1 cup sifted all-purpose flour	1 tablespoon butter, melted
½ teaspoon salt	1 cup milk, at room temperature
1 teaspoon sugar	2 large eggs

Preheat oven for at least 15 minutes at 400°. Mix together flour, salt and sugar. Add butter, milk and eggs and beat with rotary beater until smooth. Butter large custard cups or spray with vegetable spray-on coating. Fill cups just under half full and bake for 40 minutes or until golden and sides are rigid to touch — *do not open oven until nearly baked.* Serve at once. This makes 5 or 6 giant popovers in oversized custard cups. If more are needed, mix each recipe separately. Serve with Honey Butter.

Honey Butter:

Mix ¼ pound butter or margarine, softened, with ½ cup honey and beat until well blended. Allow to stand at room temperature for ½ hour before serving.

WATERCRESS–CHERRY TOMATO SALAD

2 bunches watercress	1 pint cherry tomatoes

Wash and chill watercress and tomatoes. When ready to serve toss watercress and tomatoes with Vinaigrette Dressing.

BASIC VINAIGRETTE DRESSING

3 tablespoons olive oil	1 teaspoon Dijon mustard
1 tablespoon tarragon vinegar	Salt
Freshly ground pepper	

Combine Vinaigrette ingredients.

BLUEBERRY COFFEE CAKE

¼ cup butter, softened
¾ cup sugar
1 egg
½ cup milk
2 cups less 2 tablespoons sifted all-purpose flour

2 teaspoons baking powder
¼ teaspoon salt
2 cups frozen blueberries, well drained
2 tablespoons flour

Cream butter and sugar. Add egg and milk alternately with flour that has been sifted with baking powder and salt. Toss drained berries with 2 tablespoons flour and add to batter. Pour batter into a greased and floured 9-inch square pan. Bake cake in preheated 350 degree oven for 15 minutes. Remove from oven and cover with streusel topping. Return to oven and bake for 30 minutes or until cake tests done.

Streusel Topping:

½ cup sugar
⅓ cup all-purpose flour

¼ cup butter, softened
½ tablespoon cinnamon

Blend flour, butter and sugar until they crumble. Add cinnamon.

Sumptuous Sunday Brunch

(SERVES 8)

Cranberry Juice laced with Vodka and Soda, on ice
Chicken Livers en Brochette
Toasted Rice
Fruited Coleslaw
Cream Cheese Muffins
Coffee

Previous Day	Early Morning
Soak chicken livers	*Prepare chicken livers (up to point of broiling)*
	Coleslaw
	Muffins ready for baking

CHICKEN LIVERS EN BROCHETTE

Milk to soak livers
1 pound chicken livers
Seasoned bread crumbs for breading livers
Butter for frying livers

1 tablespoon bacon or chicken fat
½ pound fresh whole mushrooms
1 16-ounce can pineapple chunks, drained

Soak livers in milk overnight. Drain and pat dry. When ready to cook, roll livers in bread crumbs; fry in butter and fat until lightly browned but still pink inside. Remove from pan and alternate livers on skewers with mushrooms and pineapple chunks. Place skewers on broiler rack and place in preheated broiler 3 to 4 inches from heat. Broil about 2 minutes on each side. Serve immediately.

TOASTED RICE

1½ cups raw long-grain white rice
1 can beef consommé or bouillon
1⅔ cups water

1½ teaspoons instant minced onion
1 teaspoon curry powder
½ teaspoon salt

Spread rice in a baking pan, and toast in a preheated 400° oven for 25 minutes, stirring occasionally until rice is golden brown. Heat all remaining ingredients in a small saucepan. Place rice in a fine strainer and rinse with cold water. Place drained rice in a 6-cup baking dish, stir in hot consommé mixture. Cover and bake in a preheated 400° oven for 25 minutes.

FRUITED COLESLAW

1 cup unpeeled diced apple
Juice of 2 lemons
3 cups shredded cabbage
1 cup drained canned pineapple tidbits

½ cup diced celery
1 cup miniature marshmallows
½ cup mayonnaise
Salt

Combine apple with lemon juice; add remaining ingredients. Chill thoroughly before serving.

CREAM CHEESE MUFFINS

1 8-ounce package cream cheese, softened	pinch of salt
	2 eggs
½ pound Farmer's Cheese, softened	½ teaspoon vanilla
	½ cup prepared biscuit mix
½ cup butter, softened	⅓ cup sugar
3 tablespoons sour cream	½ teaspoon cinnamon (optional)

Combine cream cheese, Farmer's cheese and butter. Add sour cream, salt, eggs and vanilla; beat until smooth. Slowly mix in sugar, biscuit mix and cinnamon and mix all ingredients until smooth. Pour batter into greased muffin tins, filling each almost to the top. Bake in a preheated 350° oven for 35 to 40 minutes, until lightly browned. Makes 12 muffins; may be prepared in tins in the morning, refrigerated and baked before serving.

Western Brunch

(SERVES 6)

Sliced Oranges and Green Grapes
Bowl of Sour Cream   Brown Sugar
Chili-Topped Eggs on Toast
Banana Cake with Lemon Icing
Sangria (see Index)

ADVANCE PREPARATION SCHEDULE

Freezer

*Banana Cake with
Lemon Icing*

Early Morning

*Cut up oranges
Make Sangria
Remove Banana Cake
from freezer*

SLICED ORANGES AND GREEN GRAPES

6 navel oranges   1 cup sour cream
6 bunches green grapes   ½ cup firmly packed brown sugar

Peel and slice oranges and arrange them on individual plates, one per serving. Add a small but full bunch of grapes to each plate. Arrange decoratively. Serve sour cream and brown sugar in bowls on the side.

CHILI-TOPPED EGGS ON TOAST

1 16-ounce can chili without   ¼ cup shredded Cheddar cheese
   beans   Butter for frying eggs
12 eggs   6 slices white bread, toasted
¼ cup milk   4 tablespoons shredded Monterey
¼ cup chopped onion   Jack cheese
¼ cup chopped celery

Heat chili, keeping it warm while preparing eggs. Combine eggs with milk, onion, celery and Cheddar cheese. Mix well and fry in butter like scrambled eggs, until just set. Divide eggs among slices of toast placed on foil-lined pan; pour heated chili over eggs and sprinkle with Monterey Jack cheese. Heat in a preheated 350° oven for several minutes, until cheese is slightly melted and golden.

BANANA CAKE WITH LEMON ICING

½ cup butter, softened   1½ cups sifted all-purpose flour
1¼ cups sugar   Bananas (well-ripened) to make 1
2 eggs, well-beaten   cup pureé
1 teaspoon baking soda   1 teaspoon vanilla
4 tablespoons sour cream   ½ teaspoon salt

Cream butter with sugar; add eggs and stir in baking soda dissolved in sour cream. Beat well. Alternately stir in flour and mashed bananas. Add vanilla and salt, and mix well. Pour into an oblong 2-quart greased glass baking dish. Bake in a preheated 350° oven 30 minutes. When cake is barely warm, not hot, frost top with Lemon Icing.

Lemon Icing:

2 tablespoons butter, softened	1 tablespoon milk
1 cup confectioners' sugar	1 tablespoon lemon juice
1 teaspoon grated lemon peel	

Cream butter and confectioners' sugar. Gradually add milk, lemon juice and peel and beat ingredients well.

Farmer's Breakfast

(SERVES 4)

Bavarian Baked Apples
Farmer's Breakfast Eggs
Rye Toast
Orange-Cranberry Bread
Coffee

ADVANCE PREPARATION SCHEDULE

Freezer	Previous Day	Early Morning
Orange-Cranberry Bread	*Boil potatoes for Farmer's Breakfast Eggs*	*Baked Apples* *Cut up ingredients for Farmer's Breakfast Eggs* *Remove Orange-Cranberry Bread from freezer*

BAVARIAN BAKED APPLES

4 large baking apples	¼ cup firmly packed brown sugar
Sugar	Heavy cream (optional)
Juice of one large lemon (or ¼ cup lemon juice)	

Core apples; starting at stem, peel one third of the way down; reserve peelings. Place apples in a baking pan, stem side up, with peelings in bottom of pan. Fill apple center completely with sugar and squeeze lemon juice over sugar in each apple. This should form sufficient syrup for basting apples; if not, add a small amount of water to bottom of pan to make syrup. Bake apples in a preheated 325° oven for 60 minutes, basting every 10 to 15 minutes, until apples are golden brown. Sprinkle tops of apples with brown sugar and broil in preheated broiler, about 4 inches from heat until sugar carmelizes. Watch carefully, since sugar carmelizes and browns quickly. Serve apples warm or at room temperature. Serve with cream on the side, if desired.

FARMER'S BREAKFAST EGGS

8 slices bacon, cut into small strips
1 green pepper, diced
2 tablespoons finely chopped onion
3 large potatoes, boiled, peeled and cubed

Salt and pepper to taste
½ cup grated Swiss cheese (un-processed)
8 eggs

Over low heat, fry bacon pieces until slightly brown and crisp; drain off all but 3 tablespoons of bacon fat. Add vegetables, potatoes and seasonings to bacon. Cook for 5 minutes, over medium heat, stirring frequently until potatoes are golden. Sprinkle with cheese and stir; break eggs whole into pan. Cook over low heat until eggs are set; then stir and serve.

ORANGE-CRANBERRY BREAD

2 cups sifted all-purpose flour
½ teaspoon salt
1½ teaspoon baking powder
½ teaspoon baking soda
1 cup sugar

2 tablespoons melted butter
¾ cup orange juice
1 egg, well beaten
1 cup cranberries (in halves)
1 cup chopped nuts (optional)

Sift dry ingredients together. Combine melted butter and orange juice. Add to flour mixture. Add beaten egg. Mix well. Add nuts and cranberries. For a well rounded loaf, allow batter to stand 20 minutes in well-greased and floured 5″ x 9″ x 3″ loaf pan. Bake in a preheated 350° oven 60 minutes.

Sweet and Savory Brunch

(SERVES 6)

Salmon Ball
Chicken Livers with Mushrooms
Overnight Egg Soufflé
Sliced Fresh Fruit Platter
Sweet French Dressing
Pecan Tarts
Coffee

ADVANCE PREPARATION SCHEDULE

Freezer	Previous Day	Early Morning
Pecan Tarts	*Salmon Ball*	*Fruit Platter*
	Overnight Egg Soufflé	*Sweet French Dressing*
		Remove Pecan Tarts
		from freezer

SALMON BALL

1 16-ounce can red salmon, drained
1 8-ounce package cream cheese, softened
1 small onion, finely chopped
2 tablespoons lemon juice
½ cup finely chopped parsley
¼ cup chopped nuts

Remove and discard skin and bones from salmon; flake salmon. Add softened cream cheese; blend thoroughly. Add onion and lemon juice, mixing until well blended. Shape mixture into a ball and refrigerate until quite firm. Sprinkle parsley and nuts on waxed paper, mixing them together. Roll salmon ball in mixture until completely covered on all sides. Refrigerate until ready to serve. Place in center of bowl surrounded with crackers.

CHICKEN LIVERS WITH MUSHROOMS

2 pounds chicken livers	½ cup butter
Milk to soak livers	1 large onion, sliced
Flour seasoned with salt and pepper	1 pound fresh mushrooms, sliced
	Chopped parsley

Soak livers in milk for 1 hour. Drain livers and pat dry; dip lightly in seasoned flour. Melt ¼ cup of the butter in a skillet and sauté livers until browned and lightly crisped on all sides; turn only once. Meanwhile, sauté onions in the remaining ¼ cup butter in another skillet. Salt to taste and add mushrooms to onions. Sauté until lightly browned, about 5 minutes. Add mushrooms and onions to livers; heat together. Sprinkle with parsley and serve.

OVERNIGHT EGG SOUFFLE

8 slices day-old egg bread	1 teaspoon salt
1½ cups milk	Dash pepper
¼ cup butter, melted	6 eggs, well beaten
6 ounces Cheddar cheese, shredded	

Remove crusts from bread and cut bread into 1-inch cubes. Combine milk, butter, salt, pepper and eggs; beat well. Grease a 2-quart soufflé dish; layer bread, egg mixture and cheese, making 3 layers of each. Bread layer should be entirely covered with liquid when finished. Refrigerate overnight; this is a must! To prepare for serving, bake in a preheated 325° oven for 1 hour.

Variation:

Substitute Swiss cheese for Cheddar cheese and add ½ teaspoon dry mustard to egg mixture.

SWEET FRENCH DRESSING

1 cup vegetable oil	5 tablespoons sugar
1 teaspoon Worcestershire sauce	3 to 4 tablespoons vinegar
¾ teaspoon salt	¼ cup strained chili sauce
Pepper to taste	½ teaspoon dry mustard

Dash of Tabasco

Beat ingredients together until thick as honey. Refrigerate until ready to serve. Serve with your choice of chilled fresh fruits, such as grapefruit and orange sections, sliced bananas, apples and berries, arranged on a bed of lettuce.

PECAN TARTS

Crust:

1 3-ounce package cream cheese, softened	1 scant cup sifted all-purpose flour
½ cup butter, softened	

Cream cheese and butter together and mix in flour; cover dough and refrigerate for several hours or overnight. Press small pieces of dough into the cups of very small muffin tins, to line each cup. The dough will be enough to line about 24 cups.

Filling:

¾ cup firmly packed light brown sugar	½ cup chopped pecans
1 egg, beaten	1½ tablespoons butter, melted
	Confectioners' sugar

Combine filling ingredients; fill pastry-lined cups about half full. Bake in preheated 350° oven for 25 to 30 minutes. Remove tarts from cups immediately; cool and dust with confectioners' sugar after removing tarts from muffin tins. Tarts freeze well.

Heavenly Brunch

(SERVES 6)

Apricot Nectar Cocktail

Eggs and Chicken Apollo

Grapefruit Baskets

Assorted Cheeses   Thinly Sliced French Bread

Apple Ambrosia Pudding

Vanilla Sauce

Coffee

ADVANCE PREPARATION SCHEDULE

Previous Day

Make grapefruit shells and marinate fruit for Grapefruit Baskets

Early Morning

Cheese Platter
Apple Ambrosia Pudding

APRICOT NECTAR COCKTAIL

Apricot nectar   Light rum
Lime slices

Fill glasses with ice and apricot nectar. Add light rum to taste and float lime slices in glasses.

EGGS AND CHICKEN APOLLO

12 eggs, well beaten
Salt and pepper to taste
  6 tablespoons heavy cream
  6 tablespoons olive oil
  6 tablespoons sweet butter

3 cups cooked and diced chicken
6 tablespoons freshly grated
  Parmesan cheese
6 slices toasted French bread,
  buttered

Season eggs with salt and pepper according to taste. Stir in cream. Combine oil and butter in a skillet and heat; add chicken and cook until heated through. Pour egg mixture over chicken; stirring constantly, cook for 2 to 3 minutes, until eggs are just set. Sprinkle cheese over top and cook for 1 minute more. Spoon over toasted slices of French bread.

GRAPEFRUIT BASKETS

6 grapefruits   Port wine
Assorted fresh, in-season
    fruits cut up

Cut grapefruit in half and remove sections. Scallop edges of shells, if desired. Marinate cut-up fruits, including grapefruit sections, in port wine overnight. Scoop fruits into grapefruit shells to serve.

APPLE AMBROSIA PUDDING

6 tart apples, cored, peeled and   2 teaspoons grated lemon peel
    thinly sliced (about 6 cups)   1 cup firmly packed brown sugar
½ cup water   ¾ cup Grape-nuts
½ teaspoon cinnamon   6 tablespoons butter
                6 tablespoons all-purpose flour

Arrange sliced apples, overlapping, in a shallow, buttered 1½-quart baking dish. Pour water over apples, then sprinkle with cinnamon and lemon peel. Mix sugar, Grape-nuts, butter and flour until crumbly. Cover apples with mixture and bake in a preheated 350° oven for about 45 minutes, until apples are tender and crust is browned. Serve with Vanilla Sauce.

VANILLA SAUCE

1 cup confectioners' sugar   1 cup heavy cream, whipped
2 egg yolks, beaten until very light 2 egg whites, stiffly beaten

Gradually add sugar to well-beaten egg yolks. Then slowly fold in whipped cream and finally fold in egg whites. Serve at once.

Luncheons

MENU PLANNING and food tastes are changing to reflect the life style of today. Creamed tuna noodle shells and strawberry sundaes have been replaced by more challenging and exciting luncheons. Some old favorites have been liberated for this book, and our newcomers look very promising.

Formal Luncheon

(SERVES 6)

Asparagus Quiche
Trout Stuffed with Shrimp
New Potatoes Caviar
Watercress–Cherry Tomato Salad (see Index)
Peaches in Champagne
Forgotten Cookies
Coffee

15

Previous Day	**Early Morning**
Pastry shell for Quiche	*Prepare stuffing for trout*
Forgotten Cookies	*Prepare cherry tomatoes and*
	watercress for salad (see Index)
	Prepare peaches for Peaches in
	Champagne

ASPARAGUS QUICHE

1 9-inch unbaked pastry shell, chilled	½ cup milk
	½ cup light cream
4 ounces grated Swiss cheese, (1 cup)	3 eggs, slightly beaten
	¼ teaspoon nutmeg
4 ounces grated Gruyere cheese, (1 cup)	Salt and pepper to taste
	1 15-ounce can green, long tip asparagus, halved lengthwise
1 tablespoon flour	
1 large onion, thinly sliced	

Prepare pastry shell, chill. Mix cheeses with flour and spread in chilled pastry shell. Cover with onion slices. Heat milk and cream to just below boiling point. Gradually add eggs and season with salt and pepper. Pour mixture over cheese and onion. Arrange asparagus on top of pie like wheel spokes, with tips in center. Bake in a preheated 425° oven for about 35 minutes, until browned and knife inserted near center comes out clean.

TROUT STUFFED WITH SHRIMP

¾ cup finely chopped onion	¾ teaspoon salt
6 tablespoons finely chopped green pepper	Freshly ground pepper to taste
	Dash of ground thyme leaves
2 tablespoons butter	6 fresh brook trout, cleaned, boned and left whole, with heads and tails on
12 large shrimp, cleaned, cooked and finely chopped	
¾ cup chopped fresh mushrooms	Flour
¾ cup chopped parsley	¾ cup butter

Over medium heat, cook onion and green pepper in the 2 tablespoons butter for 5 minutes in a skillet. Add shrimp, mushrooms, parsley and seasonings; cook for 5 minutes more. Season insides of trout with more salt and pepper; divide stuffing among them. Handle fish carefully to avoid spills. Dip stuffed fish in flour and sauté in the ¾ cup butter for 5 minutes on each side, until done.

NEW POTATOES CAVIAR

12 small new potatoes, scrubbed	1 cup sour cream
Salt to taste	2 ounces black caviar
½ small onion, minced	Fresh parsley sprigs

Boil new potatoes for 15 to 20 minutes, until just done. Drain; scoop out a third of each potato and cut a small slice off bottom so it will stand up. Fill hollow in each potato with salt, minced onion, sour cream and caviar. Serve warm, garnished with fresh parsley.

PEACHES IN CHAMPAGNE

6 fresh peaches	Sugar
Lemon juice	Champagne

Dip peaches in boiling water for 10 seconds, until skins peel off easily. Roll skinned peaches in lemon juice and coat heavily with sugar. Cover and chill until ready to use. For each serving, place a peach in the bottom of a champagne glass and add champagne.

FORGOTTEN COOKIES

2 egg whites	1 6-ounce package semi-sweet
⅔ cup sugar	chocolate pieces
1 cup chopped nuts	

Beat 2 egg whites until stiff but not dry. Add sugar, nuts and chocolate pieces; mix well. Drop from a teaspoon about 1 inch apart onto two ungreased cookie sheets. Place sheets in a preheated 350° oven and immediately turn off heat and leave cookies overnight. Makes 3 to 4 dozen cookies.

Tropical Luncheon

(SERVES 6)

Curried Lemon Soup
Chicken Aloha
Chow Mein Noodles
Crispy Coleslaw
Frosty Daiquiri Soufflé
Oatmeal-Spice Cookies
Coffee
Tea

ADVANCE PREPARATION SCHEDULE

Previous Day

Frozen Daiquiri Soufflé
Oatmeal-Spice Cookies

Early Morning

Curried Lemon Soup
Cook chicken and slice vegetables
for Chicken Aloha
Crispy Coleslaw

CURRIED LEMON SOUP

2 10½-ounce cans cream of chicken soup	1 tablespoon water
2 cups light cream	¾ cup lemon juice
2 tablespoons curry powder	6 thin lemon slices
	6 blanched almonds
6 mint leaves	

Pour soup into container of an electric blender; add cream. Stir curry powder into water; add to blender and blend for 1 minute. Add lemon juice and chill soup. Serve very cold, garnished with a lemon slice topped with an almond and a mint leaf.

CHICKEN ALOHA

1½ cups thinly sliced celery
1 green pepper, cut into strips
3 tablespoons butter
3 cups cubed, cooked chicken
1 22-ounce can pineapple pie
 filling
⅓ cup water

¼ cup soy sauce
2 teaspoons granulated instant
 chicken bouillon
1 5½-ounce can chow mein
 noodles
Parsley
Kumquats

In a saucepan, cook celery and green pepper in butter until tender-crisp. Add chicken, pineapple pie filling, water, soy sauce and bouillon; cook over low heat, stirring, until heated through. Serve over chow mein noodles and garnish with parsley and kumquats.

CRISPY COLESLAW

1 medium head green cabbage,
 shredded
1 green pepper, finely chopped
1 onion, finely chopped
1 carrot, shredded

⅓ cup sugar
½ cup vinegar
½ teaspoon celery seed
½ teaspoon mustard seed
⅓ cup mayonnaise

Combine cabbage, green pepper, onion and carrot and chill for 3 hours. Combine sugar, vinegar, celery seed and mustard seed in a saucepan. Bring to boil and cook for 3 minutes. Chill thoroughly. Add mayonnaise. Combine slaw ingredients with dressing and chill until served.

FROSTY DAIQUIRI SOUFFLE

2 cups sugar
10 egg yolks, beaten until light
 and fluffy
½ cup lime juice
½ cup lemon juice
Grated peel of 2 lemons and 2
 limes
Pinch of salt

2 envelopes (2 tablespoons)
 unflavored gelatine
½ cup light rum
10 egg whites, stiffly beaten
2 cups heavy cream, whipped
1 cup heavy cream, whipped
Lime slices
Finely chopped pistachio nuts
Crystallized violets

Add sugar to beaten egg yolks; continue beating until smooth. Add lime and lemon juices, grated peels and salt; mix well. Pour mixture into a saucepan and cook over low heat, stirring constantly, until thickened. Remove from heat. Soften gelatine in rum and stir into hot custard; keep stirring until gelatine totally dissolves. Cool mixture to room temperature. Oil a 4-cup soufflé dish; tie an oiled paper collar around outside of dish to extend about 2 inches above top. Fold beaten egg whites into cooled custard, then fold in the 2 cups whipped cream. Pour into prepared soufflé dish and refrigerate several hours until firm. To serve, remove collar from soufflé dish; spread remaining 1 cup whipped cream over top; arrange lime slices over cream, sprinkle sides with pistachio nuts and decorate top with violets.

OATMEAL-SPICE COOKIES

1½ cups butter	2 teaspoons baking powder
2 cups sugar	1 teaspoon ground cloves
2 eggs	1 teaspoon ground ginger
3 cups sifted all-purpose flour	½ cup light molasses
1 teaspoon salt	1½ cups quick-cooking rolled oats

Melt butter in a large saucepan; cool slightly. Add sugar and beat with hand mixer. Add eggs and beat into mixture. Sift dry ingredients together and combine with mixture in saucepan. Stir in molasses; and finally, stir in rolled oats by hand. Drop batter by teaspoonfuls onto a cookie sheet. Bake in preheated 375° oven for 10 minutes. Store cookies in a tightly closed container.

Summer Luncheon

(SERVES 8)

Gin-Mint Fruit Cup
Seafood Over Rice
Caraway Crescent Rolls
Raspberry Mousse   Nut Sticks
Special Iced Tea   Coffee

ADVANCE PREPARATION SCHEDULE

Freezer	Previous Day	Early Morning
Caraway Crescent Rolls	*Gin-Mint Fruit Cup*	*Prepare ingredients for Seafood Over Rice*
Raspberry Mousse	*Iced Tea*	
Nut Sticks		

GIN-MINT FRUIT CUP

1 large fresh pineapple or 1 16-ounce can pineapple chunks
2 cups grapefruit sections, fresh or canned
¼ cup sugar, or to taste
8 fresh mint leaves, chopped, or 1 teaspoon dried mint leaves
Juice of 1 large lemon
8 ounces gin (1 cup)
8 fresh mint leaves
8 cherries

Dice fresh pineapple (or drain canned), reserving juice. Combine pineapple and juice with grapefruit sections, sugar, chopped or dried mint and lemon juice. Chill overnight or at least several hours. When ready to serve, divide among 8 champagne or sherbet glasses. Pour 1 ounce of gin over each serving and decorate each with a mint leaf and a cherry.

SEAFOOD OVER RICE

3 10½-ounce cans condensed
cream of chicken soup
2½ pounds shrimp, cleaned and
and cooked
2 6-ounce packages frozen crabmeat, thawed and drained
½ teaspoon pepper

1 5¾-ounce can black olives,
sliced
2 8-ounce cans water chestnuts,
chopped
¼ cup sherry or to taste
2 teaspoons salt
4 cups hot cooked rice

Combine all ingredients and heat through. Serve over hot rice.

CARAWAY CRESCENT ROLLS

1 cup crisp rice cereal, crushed
2 teaspoons salt
2 tablespoons caraway seeds

1 8-ounce package crescent
refrigerator rolls
½ cup milk

Mix crushed cereal with salt and caraway seeds. Remove rolls from container and cut each triangle in half to make 2 smaller triangles. Dip each piece of roll dough in milk, then in dry cereal mixture. Starting with narrow side, roll up dough and place on a cookie sheet. Bake rolls in a preheated 450° oven for 10 to 12 minutes. Makes 16 rolls.

RASPBERRY MOUSSE

2 10-ounce packages sweetened
frozen raspberries, defrosted and
drained
2 egg whites, unbeaten
1 pint heavy cream, whipped firm
but not stiff

2 10-ounce packages frozen
sweetened raspberries,
defrosted, for sauce

Beat the two drained packages of raspberries with egg whites until foamy. Add firmly whipped cream to mixture and combine well. Lightly oil an 8-cup mold or 8 individual custard cups. Pour mousse into cups or mold and freeze for 8 hours. Remove mousse 20 to 30 minutes before serving and serve with remaining thawed raspberries on the side, as sauce.

NUT STICKS

1 1-ounce cake yeast or 1 package active dry yeast
½ cup cold milk
1 cup butter, softened
½ cup sugar
3 cups sifted all-purpose flour

⅛ teaspoon salt
2 egg yolks
1½ cups chopped pecans
1 heaping teaspoon cinnamon
¾ cup sugar
½ cup butter, melted

Confectioners' sugar

Dissolve yeast in cold milk for 20 minutes. Mix the 1 cup softened butter, the ½ cup sugar, flour and salt with electric mixer at low speed. Add yeast mixture and egg yolks; mix again at low speed until well blended. Form 7 balls of dough and refrigerate for at least 1 hour. Roll out each ball of dough on a lightly floured board, into a large thin rectangle, about 6″ x 10″. Combine pecans with cinnamon and remaining ¾ cup of sugar. Brush dough with some of the melted butter and sprinkle some of the sugar-nut mixture over dough. Cut large rectangle lengthwise into 3 strips and then crosswise into small rectangles. Roll up rectangles so they look like long, narrow sticks. Place on baking sheet. Repeat with remaining dough. Let rise in a warm place 1 hour. Bake in preheated 350° oven for 15 minutes, until light brown. Cool the cookies and sprinkle with sifted confectioners' sugar. Makes about 75 cookies. May be frozen; will defrost in about 5 minutes.

SPECIAL ICED TEA

1 quart cold water   4 to 6 tea bags

Place tea bags in water and allow to stand in refrigerator a minimum of 6 hours. Squeeze out and remove tea bags. Tea is then ready to use. It does not become cloudy and will last 2 to 3 weeks with the flavor remaining stable. (Tea may be sweetened and kept the same length of time.)

Grand Slam Luncheon

(SERVES 8)

Clam-Tomato Soup
Bridge Club Salad
Whole Wheat Butterhorns
Fruit Pizza
Coffee

ADVANCE PREPARATION SCHEDULE

Freezer	**Previous Day**	**Early Morning**
Whole Wheat Butterhorns	*Club Dressing* *Fruit Pizza*	*Cook chicken and eggs and prepare vegetables for Bridge Club Salad* *Remove Whole Wheat Butterhorns from freezer*

CLAM-TOMATO SOUP

1 32-ounce bottle or can tomato juice

1 6½-ounce can minced clams, with juice

2 8-ounce bottles clam juice

Mix all ingredients together. Heat and serve. If available, 3 16-ounce bottles of clam broth and tomato juice may be substituted.

BRIDGE CLUB SALAD

1½ heads lettuce, shredded
3 whole chicken breasts, cooked and diced
3 medium tomatoes, diced
4 hard-cooked eggs, diced
10 slices bacon, crisply cooked and crumbled

5 ounces Roquefort cheese, crumbled
2 small or 1 large avocado, cut in wedges, soaked in lemon juice
Diced scallions or chives
Club Dressing

Cover bottom of salad bowl with lettuce. Arrange a row of chicken, a row of tomatoes, a row of eggs, a row of bacon and a row of cheese on lettuce. Place avocado decoratively around edge of bowl. Sprinkle with scallions or chives. Just before serving toss with Club Dressing.

CLUB DRESSING

¾ cup red wine vinegar	½ teaspoon dry mustard
Juice of 1 lemon	1½ teaspoons Worcestshire sauce
1 teaspoon salt	1 large clove garlic, minced
½ teaspoon sugar	½ cup salad oil
½ cup olive oil	

Combine and mix all ingredients well. Chill several hours or overnight.

WHOLE WHEAT BUTTERHORNS

2½ cups unbleached flour	2 tablespoons honey
2 packages active dry yeast	2 teaspoons salt
1¾ cups water	2 cups whole wheat flour
⅓ cup firmly packed brown sugar	6 tablespoons very soft butter
	½ cup finely chopped filbert nuts
3 tablespoons butter	Melted butter for brushing rolls

In a large mixing bowl, combine 1½ cups of the flour with yeast. Heat water, brown sugar, the 3 tablespoons butter, honey and salt until barely warm (about 125°) and add to dry mixture, beating slowly until smooth. Then, using an electric mixer, beat at high speed for 3 minutes. Stir in remaining white flour and whole wheat flour, kneading in last ½ cup by hand on a floured board; knead about 8 minutes until smooth and elastic. Place dough in a greased bowl, turning dough over to grease all sides. Cover; let rise in a warm place (85°) until doubled, about 90 minutes. Punch down and turn out on a lightly floured board. Divide into 3 parts and set aside for 10 minutes. Roll each third of the dough out into an extremely thin circle. Combine the 6 tablespoons soft butter with chopped filberts and spread one third of this filling over each circle of dough. Cut each circle into 12 wedges and roll wedges into crescents. Let rise on a buttered cookie sheet in a warm place (85°) until doubled. Brush with melted butter and bake in preheated 400° over for 10 to 12 minutes. Makes 36.

FRUIT PIZZA

1 18-ounce package refrigerated sugar cookie dough
1 8-ounce package cream cheese, softened
⅓ cup sugar
½ teaspoon vanilla

Sliced bananas, blueberries, strawberry halves, orange sections, raspberries
1 cup orange marmalade
¼ cup water

Cut dough into ⅛-inch slices. Line a 14-inch pizza pan with dough slices, overlapping and pressing them together to form a crust. Bake in preheated 375° oven for 12 minutes; cool. Blend cream cheese, sugar and vanilla and spread over crust. Arrange a layer of one or any combination of fruits over cream cheese layer. Combine marmalade and water. Brush fruit with marmalade mixture, making sure all fruit is covered. Chill and cut into wedges for serving. Fruit may be arranged by sections, or it may be arranged so that a combination of fruits will be on each slice when pizza is cut.

December Luncheon

(SERVES 8)

Tomato Bouillon
Crusty Rolls
Salmon Loaf
Marinated Artichokes   French-style Peas
Black-Bottom Rum Pie
Coffee

ADVANCE PREPARATION SCHEDULE

Previous Day **Early Morning**
Black-Bottom Rum Pie *Tomato Bouillon*
Marinated Artichokes

TOMATO BOUILLON

2 10½-ounce cans condensed
  tomato soup
2 10½-ounce cans condensed beef
  broth
  1 medium avocado, thinly sliced

2 soup cans of water
⅛ teaspoon garlic powder
⅛ teaspoon crushed oregano
  leaves

Combine soups, water and seasonings and bring to a boil. Lower heat and simmer 5 minutes. Serve in warmed bowls, with avocado slices floated on top. Serve with assorted crackers.

SALMON LOAF

2 tablespoons shortening
1 16-ounce can red salmon
3 eggs, separated
Pinch of salt
  1½ cups sour cream

Pinch of onion powder or ½ teaspoon instant minced onion
2 teaspoons parsley flakes
1 cup corn flakes, crushed

Preheat oven to 350°. Melt 2 tablespoons shortening in 9″ x 4½″ x 2¾″ loaf pan in oven. Remove from oven and with a brush coat bottom and sides of pan with the shortening. Remove and discard skin and bones from salmon; flake salmon. In large bowl mix salmon, egg yolks, salt, onion powder, parsley, crushed corn flakes and sour cream. Mix well. Beat egg whites until stiff, but not dry and fold into salmon mixture. Pour into loaf pan and bake at 350° for 1 hour.

MARINATED ARTICHOKES

6 medium artichokes, washed,
  stems and coarse outer leaves
  removed, and 1 inch cut off of
  tops
½ cup olive or salad oil

5 cloves garlic, minced
½ cup chopped parsley
¼ cup lemon juice
½ teaspoon salt
Dash pepper
  Sprigs of chicory or salad greens

Place artichokes, stem end down, in a large pot and cover with salted boiling water. Cook for 30 to 60 minutes, until base can be pierced easily with a fork. Pour out water and drain artichokes well. Slightly spread leaves and return artichokes to pot. Combine oil with garlic, parsley, lemon juice, salt and pepper; pour over artichokes to coat leaves well. Simmer over low heat for 10 minutes in oil mixture. Let stand at room temperature for at least one hour before serving. Arrange on individual salad plates garnished with sprigs of chicory or any other salad greens.

FRENCH-STYLE PEAS

2 10-ounce packages frozen peas, partially defrosted
6 lettuce leaves
¾ teaspoon sugar
½ teaspoon salt
⅛ teaspoon pepper
3 tablespoons butter
Chopped pimiento (optional)

Line a medium-size saucepan with 3 lettuce leaves. Add peas, sprinkle with sugar, salt and pepper and dot with butter. Cover the peas with remaining lettuce leaves. Cover saucepan and cook over low heat until peas are tender, about 15 minutes. Discard lettuce leaves. Spoon into serving dish and garnish with chopped pimiento, if desired. Serve at once.

BLACK-BOTTOM RUM PIE

Crust:

35 gingersnaps   4 tablespoons melted butter

Crush gingersnaps with a rolling pin, mix with butter and pat firmly on bottom and sides of a buttered 9-inch pie plate. Bake in a preheated 325° oven for 8 minutes. Remove to a rack and cool.

Basic Custard Filling:

½ cup sugar
4 teaspoons cornstarch
4 egg yolks, slightly beaten
2 cups milk, heated to boiling point

Combine sugar and cornstarch in a saucepan, slowly add about ½ cup of the hot milk to egg yolks, beating constantly. Stir egg mixture into sugar and then add the remaining hot milk. Cook and stir over medium heat until mixture thickens. Remove from heat.

Chocolate Layer:

1 cup hot Basic Custard Filling
1½ 1-ounce squares unsweetened chocolate, melted

1 teaspoon vanilla

To the hot custard add melted chocolate and vanilla. Spread mixture over bottom of baked gingersnap crust. Set aside.

Rum Layer:

1 envelope (1 tablespoon) unflavored gelatine
4 tablespoons cold water
Remaining hot Basic Custard Filling

4 egg whites
¼ teaspoon cream of tartar
½ cup sugar
1 tablespoon rum or bourbon

Soften gelatine in cold water. Add to remaining hot custard and stir over low heat until gelatine is dissolved. Remove from heat and cool. Beat egg whites and cream of tartar until soft peaks form. Gradually add sugar and beat until stiff. Fold meringue into cooled custard and add rum. Spread mixture over chocolate layer. Chill until firm.

Topping:

1 cup heavy cream
2 tablespoons confectioners' sugar
¼ teaspoon vanilla

½ 1-ounce square unsweetened chocolate, shaved or grated

Just before serving, whip cream until stiff; fold in confectioners' sugar and vanilla. Spoon cream over top of pie and sprinkle with chocolate.

Indian Summer Luncheon

(SERVES 6)

Crab Rangoon
Avocado Bombay with Assorted Condiments
Special Fruit Salad
Blackberry Cobbler

ADVANCE PREPARATION SCHEDULE

Freezer	Previous Day	Early Morning
Crab Rangoon	*Basic Vinaigrette Dressing*	*Avocado Bombay (except for Avocado) Condiments Section grapefruit for salad*

CRAB RANGOON

1 package frozen wonton skins (about 48)
1 6-ounce can crabmeat
1 8-ounce package cream cheese
2 dashes Tabasco
⅛ teaspoon garlic powder
1 tablespoon milk
2 tablespoons grated Parmesan cheese
1 egg, slightly beaten
Oil for frying

Place wonton skins on a tray. Cover with a damp cloth until ready to use. Combine crabmeat, cream cheese, Tabasco, garlic powder, milk and Parmesan cheese. Fill each wonton skin with some of the mixture. Moisten edges with beaten egg and fold into triangles, sealing edges with fingertips and making sure that no air bubbles are inside triangles. Next, moisten tips of 2 corners with beaten egg; fold toward center and press to seal. Add oil to a depth of about 3 inches in a deep saucepan and heat to a temperature of 375° on a deep-fat-frying thermometer. Add a few wontons at a time and fry until golden brown on each side. Remove with a slotted spoon; drain on paper towels. May be frozen and reheated in a 350° oven.

AVOCADO BOMBAY

1 small onion, chopped
1 small apple, peeled, cored and chopped
2 tablespoons butter
1 10½-ounce can condensed cream of chicken soup

Salt to taste
2 teaspoons curry powder
3 cups cooked and cubed chicken (or shrimp)
6 avocados, peeled and halved
3 cups hot cooked rice

Sauté onions and apples in butter. Stir in soup, salt to taste and add curry powder. Heat and stir over low heat until smooth. Add chicken or shrimp, and heat thoroughly. Place 2 avocado halves on a bed of rice on each plate, and fill with curry mixture. If desired, serve with assorted condiments: raisins, crisp bacon pieces, chopped nuts, chopped green pepper, chutney and toasted coconut.

SPECIAL FRUIT SALAD

Lettuce leaves
2 persimmons
Basic Vinaigrette Dressing (see Index)
1 large pomegranate
2 large grapefruits

Place lettuce leaves on individual salad plates as a base. Slice each persimmon into six wedges. Peel and section 2 grapefruits. Arrange grapefruit sections and persimmon wedges on lettuce leaves. Remove seeds from one large pomegranate and sprinkle some over each salad. Serve with Basic Vinaigrette Dressing.

BLACKBERRY COBBLER

5 cups fresh blackberries, or 5 cups frozen whole blackberries
1 cup sugar
3 tablespoons flour
1 tablespoon butter
2 cups sifted all-purpose flour
2 tablespoons sugar

4 teaspoons baking powder
½ teaspoon salt
½ teaspoon cream of tartar
½ cup butter
½ cup orange juice
2 tablespoons sugar for top of crust
Cream to serve on side

Toss berries with the 1 cup sugar. Pour into a well-buttered 1½-quart oblong baking dish. Sprinkle the 3 tablespoons flour over berries, dot with the 1 tablespoon butter and set aside. Sift the 2 cups flour, the 2 tablespoons sugar, baking powder, salt and cream of tartar. With a pastry blender or 2 knives, cut in the ½ cup butter until mixture is coarse and mealy. Stir in orange juice, and shape dough into a ball with the hands. Roll dough out on a floured board to the size of the baking dish. Cover berries with dough; trim edges, cut a vent in center and sprinkle top generously with sugar. Bake in preheated 400° oven for 40 minutes. Serve warm with cream on the side.

Dinners

THE FOLLOWING DINNER menus are distinctive and adventurous for both gourmet cook and daring novice. Although the table decor is determined by tastes, time limitations and budgets, these dinner recipes will create an elegant and gracious atmosphere for your guests.

London Dinner

(SERVES 6)

Salmon Mousse with Cucumber Sauce
Melba Toast
Perfect Roast Beef
Horseradish Sauce
Yorkshire Pudding   Glazed Beets
Caesar Salad
Trifle
English Tea

ADVANCE PREPARATION SCHEDULE

Previous Day	Early Morning
Salmon Mousse	*Cucumber Sauce*
Horseradish Sauce, covered tightly	*Prepare Romaine for salad*
	Cook beets
Croutons for Caesar Salad	*Prepare batter for Yorkshire*
Trifle	*Pudding*
	Cook Roast Beef

Note: *Because of the different temperatures of Perfect Roast Beef and Yorkshire Pudding this menu requires two ovens.*

SALMON MOUSSE WITH CUCUMBER SAUCE

1 envelope (1 tablespoon) un-flavored gelatine	1 16-ounce can red salmon, drained
2 tablespoons lemon juice	1 teaspoon dried dill weed
1 small onion, sliced	¼ teaspoon paprika
½ cup boiling water	½ cup heavy cream
½ teaspoon salt	1 lemon, sliced
½ cup mayonnaise	1 cucumber, sliced

Cucumber Sauce

Place gelatine, lemon juice, onion and water in the container of an electric blender and blend for 30 seconds. Add salt, mayonnaise, salmon, dill and paprika and blend another 30 seconds. Add cream; blend 15 seconds and pour into oiled 3-cup mold. Cover with plastic wrap and refrigerate. May be made 2 days in advance. Unmold on platter lined with lettuce leaves. Decorate with alternating lemons and cucumber slices. Serve with Cucumber Sauce.

Cucumber Sauce:

2 cups peeled, seeded and chopped cucumber	1 tablespoon dried dill weed
	1 tablespoon chopped chives
1 cup sour cream	½ teaspoon salt

Combine all ingredients. Serve as accompaniment to mousse. Chill until ready to serve.

PERFECT ROAST BEEF

1 8 to 9-pound beef rib roast	Pepper
Salt	Garlic salt

Season roast with salt, pepper and garlic salt. Preheat oven to 375°. Place roast on a rack in a shallow baking pan. Put roast in oven before 11 a.m. the day you are serving it. After baking roast for 1 hour, turn oven off and leave roast inside. Forty-five minutes before serving, turn oven to 375° and bake roast for remaining 45 minutes. *Do not open oven until time to remove roast except to remove drippings.* Serve with Horseradish Sauce.

HORSERADISH SAUCE

1 cup sour cream	¾ teaspoon white pepper
⅓ cup prepared horseradish	¼ teaspoon salt
2 tablespoons whipped cream	

Fold all ingredients together and chill. Serve with roast beef.

YORKSHIRE PUDDING

2 cups sifted all-purpose flour	1 cup milk
1 teaspoon salt	4 eggs
1 cup light cream	½ cup roast drippings or butter

Sift flour and salt together into a large mixing bowl. Slowly stir in cream and milk, beating vigorously with a rotary beater until smooth. Add eggs, one at a time, beating well after each addition to make a creamy batter. Cover with a cloth and chill in refrigerator for at least 2 hours. Thirty minutes before roast is done, spoon fat drippings or butter into a 9″ x 13″ baking pan. Set pan in preheated 375° oven until fat is sizzling hot. Beat chilled batter vigorously a few times and pour into the hot pan. Bake for 30 minutes, until pudding is light, crisp and brown. Cut into squares and place on platter surrounding roast beef.

GLAZED BEETS

½ cup butter
4 cups cooked whole
   baby beets

2 tablespoons sugar

Melt butter in saucepan, add beets and cook over low heat for about 3 minutes. Sprinkle with sugar, shake pan to coat beets evenly.

CAESAR SALAD

2 medium heads Romaine lettuce
  (1½ pounds), washed, dried
  and chilled
⅛ teaspoon salt
⅛ teaspoon freshly ground black
  pepper
1 teaspoon finely chopped garlic

8 tablespoons olive oil
2 Coddled Eggs
4 tablespoons lemon juice
¼ cup freshly grated Parmesan
  cheese
6 anchovy fillets, not rolled
10 to 12 Croutons

Chill salad forks and plates several hours before use. Break lettuce into serving size pieces in a large salad bowl. Add salt, pepper, garlic and oil and toss to coat lettuce well. Break Coddled Eggs into salad, add lemon juice, and mix again until lettuce is thoroughly coated. Add cheese and anchovies, mix once more, scatter Croutons over salad and serve at once on chilled plates.

Coddled Eggs:

Lower eggs (that have been brought to room temperature) into boiling water for 10 seconds only.

Croutons:

4 1-1½-inch thick slices white
  bread

4 tablespoons vegetable oil
1 clove finely chopped garlic

Trim crusts from bread and cut into ½ inch cubes. Heat oil in large heavy pan, add bread, and brown on all sides (more oil may be added if necessary). Remove pan from heat, add garlic, toss croutons lightly in pan and remove to paper towel to drain and cool. May be stored in airtight container.

TRIFLE

1 3½-ounce package vanilla pudding
2¼ cups milk
1 tablespoon butter
1 purchased orange chiffon cake
1 cup port wine
1 12-ounce jar raspberry jam

1 8-ounce can crushed pineapple, undrained
1 28-ounce can peeled apricot halves, drained
1 cup heavy cream, whipped
Maraschino cherries
Chopped pistachio nuts

Chocolate curls

Prepare pudding as directed on package using 2¼ cups milk and adding 1 tablespoon butter. Cut cake into 1-inch slices. In large glass serving bowl, layer ingredients twice, as follows: cake, wine, jam, pineapple, apricots and pudding. Cover and refrigerate overnight. Before serving, top with whipped cream and decorate with maraschino cherries, nuts and chocolate curls. (To make curls, have square of unsweetened chocolate at room temperature and shave in long, thin strokes with vegetable parer.) To serve trifle, just scoop out onto a dessert dish at the dinner table.

Fit-For-Your-King Dinner

(SERVES 8)

Scampi Hollandaise
Chicken Imperial
Mixed Wild and White Rice
Anytime Dinner Rolls   Brussels Sprouts Amandine
Dilly Carrot Salad
Lemon Butterfly Pie
Coffee

ADVANCE PREPARATION SCHEDULE

Freezer	Previous Day	Early Morning
Rice	*Anytime Dinner Rolls*	*Scampi (without Hollan-*
	Lemon Butterfly Pie	*daise)*
		Chicken Imperial, ready
		to bake
		Dilly Carrot Salad
		Remove rice from
		freezer

SCAMPI HOLLANDAISE

½ cup butter, melted
½ cup olive oil
1 tablespoon Worcestershire sauce
1 tablespoon chopped parsley
Juice of 1 lemon
2 cloves garlic, crushed

4 anchovy filets, finely chopped
2 stalks scallions, thinly sliced
Salt and pepper to taste
2 pounds shrimp
1 cup Blender Lemon Hollandaise (see Index)

Combine all ingredients except shrimp and Hollandaise sauce. Peel and devein shrimp, leaving tail attached. Split each shrimp down the back and spread it open to simulate a butterfly. Lay open shrimp, side by side, in a baking pan; pour butter sauce over shrimp. Bake in a 450° oven for 10 minutes, baste after 5 minutes. Remove shrimp from pan and arrange on heatproof serving platter. Cover shrimp with Hollandaise sauce. Place in preheated broiler 3 inches from heat and broil about 3 minutes until sauce is browned. Serve very hot with crusty French or Italian bread, if desired.

CHICKEN IMPERIAL

½ cup flour
½ teaspoon salt
⅛ teaspoon pepper
½ teaspoon paprika
½ teaspoon seasoned salt
8 whole chicken breasts, split
1 cup butter
¼ cup oil
1½ cups chicken broth
1 cup sherry
1 tablespoon soy sauce

2 tablespoons lemon juice
¾ teaspoon ground ginger
2 pounds mushrooms, thickly sliced
¼ cup butter
1 pint cherry tomatoes, washed
2 15-ounce cans artichoke hearts, drained
4 cups hot, cooked, mixed wild and white rice

Combine flour, salt, pepper, paprika and seasoned salt. Dredge chicken pieces in flour mixture. Sauté chicken in the 1 cup butter and oil until golden brown on all sides. Remove to a large ovenproof dish. Add broth, sherry, soy sauce, lemon juice and ginger to skillet, stirring to blend. Pour sauce over chicken; cover baking dish and bake in a 375° oven for 1 hour, basting twice. Sauté mushrooms in the ¼ cup butter and add to baking dish along with tomatoes and artichoke hearts. Bake, uncovered, for 20 minutes more. Serve on a bed of mixed wild and white rice.

ANYTIME DINNER ROLLS

½ cup butter, softened
3 tablespoons sugar
¾ teaspoon salt
½ cup boiling water
1 cup quick-cooking rolled oats

1 ⅗-ounce cake yeast, or 1 envelope active dry yeast
½ cup lukewarm water
1 egg
2½ cups sifted all-purpose flour

Mix butter, sugar, salt and boiling water; add oats, and cool to lukewarm. Soften yeast in lukewarm water and cool. Add to first mixture, along with egg; mix well. Stir in 1 cup of flour; beat with kneading hook of electric mixer or with wooden spoon. Add another cup of flour and beat in well. Turn dough out onto a floured board and knead about 8 minutes, until dough is smooth and elastic, adding remaining flour as needed to prevent sticking. Knead remaining flour into dough by hand on a lightly floured board. Put dough in a greased bowl, turning to grease top and bottom. Cover with waxed paper and refrigerate for up to 5 days. To bake, roll dough out and shape into any type of dinner roll; crescent rolls will work well, as will bow-knots. Let rolls rise in a warm place (85°) until doubled. Bake in a 450° oven for 15 to 20 minutes.

BRUSSELS SPROUTS AMANDINE

1 cup water
1 10¾-ounce can condensed chicken broth
½ teaspoon salt
⅛ teaspoon pepper
3 10-ounce packages frozen Brussels sprouts
½ cup butter
1 cup sliced, blanched almonds

Combine water, broth, salt and pepper in a large skillet; bring to a boil. Add Brussels sprouts; cover and simmer until fork-tender. Drain sprouts well. Arrange in a serving platter and keep warm. Over medium heat, melt butter in a skillet and add almonds. Stirring constantly, cook until almonds are golden brown. Pour over Brussels sprouts and serve at once.

DILLY CARROT SALAD

8 medium carrots, peeled and cut into sticks
½ cup water
¼ cup cider vinegar
1 teaspoon dried tarragon leaves
1 teaspoon dried dill weed
1 teaspoon seasoned salt
Lettuce

Bring all ingredients except lettuce to a boil in a saucepan. Cover, reduce heat and simmer for 30 minutes until carrots are crisp, but tender. Chill for several hours or overnight. Serve on bed of lettuce as relish.

LEMON BUTTERFLY PIE

Meringue Pie Shell:

4 egg whites, at room temperature
½ teaspoon cream of tartar
1 cup sugar

Beat whites until foamy; add cream of tartar and beat for 3 minutes, until nearly stiff. Add sugar by tablespoonfuls, blending after each addition; beat in sugar quickly, taking no more than 90 seconds to incorporate all sugar into whites. When sugar is beaten in, whites should be stiff; do not over-beat. Spread mixture gently over bottom and sides of a buttered 9-inch glass pie plate. Bake in a preheated 300° oven for 40 minutes. Cool completely.

Lemon Filling:

8 egg yolks	Grated peel of 1 large
1 cup sugar	or 2 small lemons
6 to 8 tablespoons lemon juice	

Beat yolks until thick and light-colored. Gradually beat in sugar and continue beating until light and smooth. Add lemon juice and peel and pour mixture into a saucepan. Cook over low heat, stirring constantly, for 10 to 15 minutes until thick and smooth. Remove from heat and cool completely.

Whipped Cream Filling:

1 cup heavy cream   1 tablespoon vanilla
¼ cup sugar

Whip cream with vanilla and sugar until stiff.

To Assemble Pie:

Spread half of Whipped Cream Filling over cooled Meringue Pie Shell. Spread cooled Lemon Filling over cream in shell, and top with remaining cream, so that lemon mixture is completely covered. Chill for at least 8 hours or overnight. Before serving, decorate with Lemon "Butterflies" from freezer.

Lemon "Butterflies"

Slice 1 lemon thinly; cut each slice from center to rim. Twist one half forward and one backwards, like a butterfly. Place on a cookie sheet and freeze.

Formal Dinner Party

(SERVES 8)

Cooked Shrimp Seviche
Lamb Wellington
Broccoli with Sesame Butter   Baked Tomatoes (see Index)
Green Salad with Roquefort Dressing
Strawberry Cream Sherbet
Chocolate-Filled Cookies
Coffee

ADVANCE PREPARATION SCHEDULE

Freezer	Previous Day	Early Morning
Strawberry Cream Sherbet	*Cooked Shrimp Seviche*	*Stuffing for Lamb Wellington*
Chocolate-Filled Cookies	*Roquefort salad dressing*	*Tomatoes, ready to bake*
		Prepare greens for salad

COOKED SHRIMP SEVICHE

⅔ cup olive oil
⅔ cup prepared mustard
⅔ cup fresh lime juice
2 hot chili peppers, chopped finely

2 cups finely chopped onion
4 cups cooked shrimp, cut into bite-size pieces
Salt and pepper to taste

Mix oil, mustard, lime juice, chili peppers and onion and stir into shrimp. Cover and marinate in the refrigerator for at least 8 hours, stirring occasionally. Add salt and pepper to taste, before serving. Should be made 1 day in advance, and may be prepared several days ahead.

LAMB WELLINGTON

½ pound ground, lean lamb	1 7-pound leg of lamb, boned
½ teaspoon seasoned salt	1½ teaspoons salt
⅛ teaspoon pepper	⅛ teaspoon pepper
1 egg white	1 package frozen patty shells
½ cup light cream	partially defrosted or 1 recipe
¼ cup fine, dry bread crumbs	pâté brisée (see Index)
½ cup cubed boiled ham	1 egg yolk
2 tablespoons shelled, peeled pistachio nuts	1 tablespoon water

About 3½ hours before serving make stuffing: Combine ground lamb, salt, pepper, egg white, cream and bread crumbs in a mixing bowl; then fold in ham and nuts. Cover and refrigerate.

Preheat oven to 325°. Cut all excess fat and skin from lamb and sprinkle inside and out with salt and pepper. Stuff with ground lamb mixture, and tie with string or secure with skewers. Place lamb on a wire rack in a shallow open roasting pan. Roast about 2 hours and 10 minutes, until medium rare (147° on a meat thermometer). Remove lamb from oven. Remove string or skewers. Increase oven temperature to 400°. Roll out each patty shell into a long thin strip; cover roasted lamb with strips, tucking ends in under roast. From leftover pastry, cut out decorative shapes. Beat 1 egg yolk with the 1 tablespoon water and brush pastry-covered lamb. Arrange decoration on lamb and brush once again. Set on wire rack in roasting pan and bake for 15 minutes at 400° until pastry is golden. With 2 broad spatulas, lift roast to serving platter.

BROCCOLI WITH SESAME BUTTER

¾ cup butter	3 tablespoons toasted sesame seeds
Salt and pepper to taste	
1½ tablespoons lemon juice	2 pounds fresh broccoli or 2 packages frozen broccoli, cooked
¾ teaspoon dried basil leaves	

Melt butter in a small saucepan. Add salt, pepper, lemon juice, basil and sesame seeds. Heat thoroughly. Pour over hot cooked broccoli and serve.

STRAWBERRY CREAM SHERBET

4 cups sour cream	2 tablespoons lemon juice
1 cup sugar	1 pint whole strawberries,
2 pints strawberries, washed, hulled and crushed	washed and hulled

Combine sour cream and sugar; mix into crushed strawberries and add lemon juice. Pour into a 6-cup mold; cover and freeze. Can be prepared up to 3 days in advance. Defrost mold in refrigerator for 45 minutes to 1 hour; unmold and serve. Garnish with 1 pint of strawberries in center of mold.

CHOCOLATE-FILLED COOKIES

1 cup butter	2½ cups sifted all-purpose flour
1 cup sugar	¼ teaspoon cream of tartar
1 egg	Rum-flavored or plain thin choco-
1 teaspoon vanilla	late candy wafers

Cream butter and sugar until light and fluffy. Add egg and vanilla and beat thoroughly. Sift flour and cream of tartar together and add to butter-sugar mixture, beating until blended. Chill dough until firm enough to handle. Form dough into two long rolls, each about 10 inches in length. Wrap each roll in waxed paper; chill for several hours or overnight. Slice dough into ⅛-inch-thick rounds. Place rounds of dough on an ungreased cookie sheet. Place a chocolate wafer on top of each round. Top each with another round of dough and press edges together gently to completely cover chocolate layer. Bake cookies in preheated 375° oven for 10 minutes until delicately browned. Makes about 5 dozen cookies. Can be frozen.

Spicy Dinner

(SERVES 6)

Mushroom Morsels
Anchovy Rolls
Chicken Parmesan
Tortellini della Casa
Asparagus Salad Royale
Nectarine Pie
Coffee

ADVANCE PREPARATION SCHEDULE

Freezer	Previous Day	Early Morning
Anchovy Rolls	*Asparagus Salad Royale*	*Stuff mushrooms, ready to bake*
		Nectarine Pie
		Remove Anchovy Rolls from freezer

MUSHROOM MORSELS

1 pound mushrooms, washed
3 tablespoons grated Parmesan cheese
1 clove garlic, minced
2 tablespoons olive oil

1 small onion, chopped
1 tablespoon chopped parsley
2 to 4 tablespoons butter, melted
Salt, pepper, seasoned salt to taste

Separate mushroom caps and stems; finely chop stems. Mix stems with cheese, garlic, onion, parsley, butter and seasonings. Fill mushroom caps with mixture. Pour oil into bottom of a large, shallow pan, arrange mushrooms in pan; bake in preheated 350° oven for 20 minutes.

ANCHOVY ROLLS

1 loaf fresh thin-sliced white bread
8 ounces cream cheese, softened

Anchovy paste to taste (mixture should be salty)

Cut crusts off bread slices and roll each thin and flat with a rolling pin. Combine cheese with anchovy paste. Spread mixture on bread slices, and roll up, secure with wooden picks. At this point, rolls may be frozen and defrosted when ready to use. To serve, place anchovy rolls seam-side down on a cookie sheet. Place in preheated broiler about 3 inches from heat and broil until golden brown, turn and broil other side. Cut in half and serve at once.

Variation:

Substitute 1 3¾-ounce can mashed sardines for anchovy paste, or 1 small grated onion and 2 tablespoons caraway seeds.

CHICKEN PARMESAN

4 large whole chicken breasts, split, boned and skinned
2 eggs, slightly beaten
¾ cup fine dry bread crumbs
¾ cup grated Parmesan cheese
1 15-ounce can tomato sauce

1 teaspoon salt
1 teaspoon paprika
½ cup butter, melted
1 6-ounce package Mozzarella cheese, grated

Dip chicken in eggs. Combine bread crumbs with Parmesan cheese and seasonings; coat chicken with crumb mixture. Melt butter in a large skillet and brown chicken on all sides in butter. Place chicken in a 13″ x 9″ x 2″ pan and either freeze at this point or cook to serve. To finish cooking, top chicken with Mozzarella cheese and pour tomato sauce over all. Cover with foil and bake in preheated 350° oven for 45 minutes, until almost tender. Uncover and bake for 20 minutes longer.

TORTELLINI DELLA CASA

6 quarts water
1 tablespoon salt
1 tablespoon oil
1 pound fresh or frozen meat-filled
  tortellini
2 cloves garlic, crushed
6 tablespoons butter

⅓ cup minced parsley
4 teaspoons mashed anchovy
  filets
1 tablespoon fresh basil, minced,
  or 1 teaspoon dried basil
  leaves
¾ cup heavy cream

In a large kettle, bring water to a rolling boil with salt and oil. Drop in tortellini and boil for 10 minutes, until just tender. Remove with a slotted spoon and drain on paper towels. In a large skillet, sauté garlic in butter until golden. Remove garlic with a slotted spoon and add tortellini to skillet, along with parsley, anchovy filets and basil. Stir in cream and cook mixture several minutes over moderate heat, stirring just until hot. Do not let mixture boil. Serve immediately.

ASPARAGUS SALAD ROYALE

1½ pounds fresh asparagus,
   washed
1 14-ounce can hearts of palm,
  drained and sliced
½ cup strong Italian dressing

1 tablespoon bottled dill sauce
Lettuce
Red pepper rings or hard-cooked
  eggs, sliced

Cut each stalk of asparagus crosswise into thirds. Cook asparagus in boiling water until crisp-tender, not soft. Drain. Mix asparagus with hearts of palm, toss with dressing and dill sauce. Cover and marinate in refrigerator for at least 6 hours or overnight. Serve on a bed of lettuce and garnish with red pepper rings or hard-cooked egg slices, if desired.

NECTARINE PIE

3 pounds nectarines, unpeeled
    and sliced
1 cup firmly packed light brown
    sugar
¼ cup butter, melted
2 tablespoons flour

1 teaspoon vanilla
⅛ teaspoon salt
⅛ teaspoon nutmeg
1 thin pie crust; a frozen pie
    crust, slightly defrosted and
    flattened, is perfect

1 tablespoon butter, melted

Toss nectarines, sugar, the ¼ cup butter, flour, vanilla, salt and nutmeg together. Pour into an 8-inch round ovenproof glass dish, 3 inches deep. Cover top with pie crust and trim it to fit dish. Brush crust with melted butter and bake in a preheated 400° oven for 30 minutes, until golden. Serve warm.

International Dinner

(SERVES 8)

Sausage Quiche

Russian Shish-Kabob   Butter-Baked Rice

California Green Salad

French Cream Cheese Pound Cake

Turkish Coffee

ADVANCE PREPARATION SCHEDULE

Previous Day

Marinate meat for Shish-Kabob
Italian Salad Dressing (see Index)

Early Morning

Sauté sausage and prepare pastry
    for Quiche
Prepare vegetables for Shish-
    Kabob
Prepare rice (do not bake)
Refrigerate prepared fruit and
    vegetables for salad (except
    avocado)
Make French Cream Cheese
    Pound Cake

SAUSAGE QUICHE

4 sweet or mild Italian sausages,
  casings removed
1 teaspoon fennel seed
Pepper to taste
3 eggs
2 cups heavy cream
⅓ cup grated Parmesan cheese
¼ teaspoon freshly grated nutmeg

Salt and pepper to taste
2 tablespoons Parmesan cheese,
  grated
1 recipe Pâté Brisée, or 1 package
  patty shells, partially defrosted
  and rolled into one large pastry
  shell

In a skillet, sauté sausages, breaking up meat with a fork, until well-browned. Remove from skillet with a slotted spoon and drain on paper towel. Put meat in a bowl and toss with fennel and pepper; cool. In a second bowl, beat together eggs, heavy cream, the ⅓ cup Parmesan cheese and nutmeg. Add salt and pepper to taste and pour egg-cream mixture into sausage. Pour filling into lightly baked pastry shell and top with the 2 tablespoons Parmesan cheese. Bake in upper third of a preheated 400° oven for 30 to 35 minutes, or until quiche is brown and set. Cool five minutes and serve.

PATE BRISEE

1¼ cups sifted all-purpose flour
6 tablespoons cold butter, cut
  into bits
2 tablespoons vegetable
  shortening

¼ teaspoon salt
3 tablespoons ice water
Raw rice

Mix flour, butter, shortening and salt until well blended; add ice water and toss dough until water is incorporated. Form into a ball. With heel of hand, gently knead dough on a lightly floured board for several minutes and reform into a ball. Dust with flour, wrap in waxed paper and chill for one hour. Roll chilled dough into a circle about 12 inches in diameter and ⅛-inch thick on a lightly floured board. Drape dough over a rolling pin, and fit it into a 10-inch quiche pan with fluted edges and a removable bottom. Press dough firmly into pan; cut off excess. Prick bottom of shell with fork and chill for 1 hour. Line shell with aluminum foil; fill with raw rice and bake in bottom third of a preheated 400° oven for 10 to 15 minutes. Carefully remove rice and foil and bake shell for an additional 10 minutes, until lightly colored. Transfer to a rack; cool.

RUSSIAN SHISH-KABOB

Marinade:

2 teaspoons salt	1 cup water
3 tablespoons Worcestershire sauce	2 tablespoons dried dill weed
	1 teaspoon dried oregano leaves
¼ cup sugar	½ teaspoon garlic powder
¼ cup wine vinegar	½ teaspoon onion powder
1 cup catsup	

Combine all ingredients in a saucepan; bring to a boil and then simmer for 40 minutes. Cool.

Shish-Kabob:

4 pounds beef tenderloin, or top quality chuck steak, cut into 32 large squares	6 medium white onions, peeled and quartered
24 large whole fresh mushrooms	4 large green peppers, seeded and each cut into 6 pieces
24 whole cherry tomatoes	

Place meat squares in a large shallow pan; pour marinade over meat, cover and refrigerate for at least 8 hours or overnight. When meat has marinated, oil 8 long skewers, and alternate meat and vegetables, beginning and ending with meat; each skewer should have 4 pieces of meat. Place skewer on broiler rack and place in a preheated broiler 3 to 4 inches from heat. Broil 8 to 10 minutes on one side; turn and broil on other side about 5 minutes. Brush frequently with some of the marinade. If desired, marinade may be doubled, and half served hot as a sauce with Shish-Kabob.

BUTTER-BAKED RICE

4 teaspoons salt	Dash of garlic salt
4 cups water	3½ cups chicken broth
2 cups raw long-grain rice	Finely snipped parsley
⅔ cup butter	½ cup toasted almonds

Add salt to water. Bring to boil and pour over rice; let stand for 30 minutes. Rinse rice with cold water and drain well. Melt butter in skillet; add rice and cook over medium heat, stirring constantly, for about 5 minutes, until butter is almost absorbed. Turn rice into a 1-quart casserole; sprinkle with garlic salt and pour chicken broth over rice. If cooking immediately, bake, covered, in a preheated 325° oven for 45 minutes. Add parsley and fluff rice with fork. Sprinkle with almonds and bake, uncovered, for 10 more minutes. If preparing ahead, refrigerate rice in casserole until ready to cook. Bake 1 hour before adding parsley and almonds. Cooked rice may also be frozen; allow several hours for defrosting. Reheat, covered, in a slow oven.

CALIFORNIA GREEN SALAD

2 pounds of fresh lettuce, washed and chilled
1 head curly endive, washed and and chilled
2 medium-size red onions, sliced into rings

2 11-ounce cans mandarin orange sections, drained, or 4 navel oranges, peeled and sliced
Italian Dressing (see Index)
1 large avocado, sliced and dipped into lemon juice

Break lettuce and endive into bite-size pieces in a salad bowl. Add onion rings and orange sections. Toss with dressing. Just before serving, add avocado slices and toss again.

FRENCH CREAM CHEESE POUND CAKE

½ cup butter, softened
¾ cup sugar
3 eggs
1 teaspoon vanilla
2 cups sifted cake flour

1 teaspoon baking powder
1 teaspoon baking soda
1 cup sour cream
Cream Cheese Filling
Sliced strawberries

Cream butter and sugar. Add eggs, one at a time beating well after each addition. Stir in vanilla and mix ingredients thoroughly. Sift flour with baking powder. Add baking soda to sour cream. Alternately, add flour and sour cream to butter-sugar mixture. Grease a Bundt pan. Pour half of cake batter into pan; top with Cream Cheese Filling and pour in remaining cake batter. Bake in a preheated 350° oven for 45 minutes. Cool completely. Serve with sliced strawberries.

Cream Cheese Filling:

2 8-ounce packages cream cheese, softened	1 egg yolk
¾ cup sugar	1 tablespoon vanilla
	1 teaspoon lemon juice

Combine all ingredients and mix well.

TURKISH COFFEE

4 tablespoons ground expresso coffee	12 lumps of sugar
	4 cups of water

Place coffee, sugar, and water in a small saucepan, bring to a boil and remove from heat. Cool slightly. Repeat heating and cooling process twice more. Strain and serve in small cups.

Winter Dinner

(SERVES 6)

Hot Spiced Wine

Liver Pâté

Melba Toast (see Index)

Roast Loin of Pork

Spicy Noodle Bake   Applesauce Brûlée

Cold Vegetable Medley

Dill Dressing

Fruit Kuchen

Coffee

ADVANCE PREPARATION SCHEDULE

Previous Day

Spice Wine (heat before serving)
Liver Pâté
Marinate Roast Loin of Pork
Applesauce Brûlée
Cold Vegetable Medley
Dill Dressing

Early Morning

Spicy Noodle Bake
Fruit Kuchen

HOT SPICED WINE

2 pints cranberry juice
1 cup water
1½ cups sugar
1 4-inch stick cinnamon
12 whole cloves

Grated peel of ½ lemon
¼ cup lemon juice
2 ⅘-quart bottles red wine
    (claret or port)

Combine cranberry juice, water, sugar, cinnamon, cloves and lemon peel; bring to a boil and simmer for 15 minutes. Add wine and lemon juice; heating gently. Do not boil. Serve hot. Keeps well in the refrigerator.

LIVER PATE

1½ pounds chicken livers
Flour
2 tablespoons oil
¼ cup butter
1½ tablespoons unflavored gelatine, dissolved in ½ cup cold water

1 cup sour cream
½ teaspoon salt
¼ teaspoon pepper
¼ teaspoon seasoned salt
½ onion, grated
2 tablespoons brandy (optional)
Fresh Melba Toast (see Index)

Coat chicken livers with flour and sauté over moderate heat in butter and oil until no longer pink inside. Dissolve gelatine in water. Add gelatine, sour cream, seasonings and onion to livers. Put mixture in container of an electric blender, one third at a time, blend until smooth. Add some of the brandy, or a small amount of hot water if mixture is too thick to blend. Put pâté in an oiled 3-cup mold or crock and refrigerate until set. Serve with Melba Toast.

ROAST LOIN OF PORK

1 4-pound boneless pork loin roast	1 cup beef broth
Buttermilk	2 tablespoons flour
Salt and pepper	2 tablespoons butter
2 tablespoons butter	Strip of lemon peel
1 cup dry white wine	¼ cup currant jelly
	3 tablespoons sour cream

Place meat in a deep container just large enough to hold it easily. Cover meat with buttermilk, cover and refrigerate for 24 hours. Turn roast several times. Drain and wipe roast with paper towel and rub with salt, pepper and 2 tablespoons of butter. Place roast on a rack in a shallow roasting pan; roast in a preheated 350° oven for 30 minutes per pound. Combine wine and broth and baste meat frequently with mixture. When done, remove meat from pan, keeping it warm. Skim fat from pan; blend flour and 2 tablespoons of butter with drippings in pan. Add lemon peel and cook on top of range until thick. Add jelly and sour cream; heat through and serve with roast.

SPICY NOODLE BAKE

½ cup finely chopped onion	2 teaspoons Worcestershire sauce
1 large clove garlic minced	
2 tablespoons butter	2 dashes Tabasco
8 ounces medium noodles, cooked and drained	4 teaspoons poppy seeds
Pinch of pepper	½ teaspoon salt
3 cups cream-style cottage cheese	Paprika
2 cups sour cream	Grated Parmesan cheese (optional)

Cook onions and garlic in butter until tender. Add noodles to onion mixture and combine with pepper, cottage cheese, sour cream, Worcestershire sauce, Tabasco, poppy seeds and salt. Turn into a greased 10" x 6" x 1½" baking dish. Sprinkle top with paprika. Bake in preheated 350° oven for 25 minutes. May be served with grated Parmesan cheese on the side.

APPLESAUCE BRULEE

1 20-ounce jar applesauce
3 tablespoons seedless raisins
1 teaspoon cinnamon

½ cup lemon juice, or to taste
Brown sugar, sifted

Combine applesauce, raisins, cinnamon and lemon juice in a sauce-pan. Cook together a few minutes until flavors are blended (it should be quite tart). Pour into a deep heat-proof 3-cup casserole and chill well. Before serving, cover top of applesauce with a thin layer of brown sugar. Place in preheated broiler about 3 inches from heat until sugar melts. Watch carefully.

COLD VEGETABLE MEDLEY

1 10-ounce package frozen artichoke hearts, cooked and cut
into smaller pieces
1 cup thinly sliced scraped raw
carrots
2 cups thinly sliced raw
cauliflower

½ cup finely chopped red onion
½ cup thinly sliced raw celery
1 16-ounce can green beans,
drained and cut into halves or
thirds
½ cup bottled Italian salad
dressing

Mix all the vegetables together; add Italian dressing and mix well. Chill vegetables in the dressing at least 2 hours, stirring occasionally. Before serving, drain vegetables quite thoroughly and add Dill Dressing.

DILL DRESSING

⅔ cup mayonnaise
2 tablespoons chili sauce
½ teaspoon salt

1 tablespoon lemon juice
1 tablespoon dried dill weed

Combine all the ingredients and chill thoroughly.

FRUIT KUCHEN

1 cup butter, softened	½ teaspoon baking powder
¼ cup sugar	1½ pints fresh blueberries
5 tablespoons heavy cream	1 cup sugar, or to taste
2¼ cups sifted all-purpose flour	Pinch of cinnamon
1 tablespoon flour	

Cream butter with the ¼ cup sugar until light; add cream, then the 2¼ cups flour sifted together with the baking powder. With the fingers pat dough into a 9″ x 13″ pan. Combine blueberries with the 1 cup sugar, cinnamon and the 1 tablespoon flour. Top dough with berry mixture. Bake in a preheated 350° oven for 45 minutes until brown.

Variation:

Substitute fresh, sliced apples or peaches for blueberries.

Happy Holiday Dinner

(SERVES 8)

Crabmeat Imperial
Glazed Leg of Lamb
Fabulous Rice Ring   Carrots with Grapes
Five-Greens Salad
French Vinaigrette Dressing
Double-Chocolate Viennese Torte
Viennese Coffee

ADVANCE PREPARATION SCHEDULE

Freezer	Previous Day	Early Morning
Double-Chocolate Viennese Torte	*Salad dressing Fabulous Rice Ring, ready to heat*	*Crabmeat Imperial, ready to heat Season lamb Cook carrots, ready to add grapes Seed grapes Prepare salad greens*

CRABMEAT IMPERIAL

1 pound cooked peeled and de-veined shrimp	¼ cup dry sherry
1 cup butter	½ teaspoon salt
⅓ cup flour	¼ teaspoon white pepper
1 quart half-and-half	5 dashes Tabasco
½ cup grated Parmesan cheese	1 pound fresh, frozen or canned crabmeat
2 egg yolks, well beaten	½ cup fine dry bread crumbs

In a skillet heat cooked shrimp in ¼ cup of the butter. Melt ½ cup of the butter in a sauce pan, add flour and cook for 5 minutes. Remove from heat and gradually add half-and-half, stirring constantly. Cook, stirring constantly, until mixture thickens. Add cheese, egg yolks, sherry, seasonings, shrimp and crabmeat. Mix well until just heated through. Place in a large serving dish or individual shells. Sprinkle with bread crumbs and dot with the remaining ¼ cup butter; bake in a preheated 350° oven for 15 to 20 minutes for one large dish or 10 minutes for individual shells.

GLAZED LEG OF LAMB

1 7-pound leg of lamb	¼ teaspoon pepper
2 teaspoons salt	1 onion, sliced
1 teaspoon dry mustard	½ cup currant jelly, melted
½ teaspoon ground ginger	1 tablespoon lemon juice

Rub lamb with dry seasonings. Place lamb, fat side up, on a rack in a shallow roasting pan. Add onion to bottom of pan. Roast, uncovered, in a preheated 325° oven for about 2½ hours (allow 20 minutes per pound). Combine currant jelly and lemon juice. About 20 minutes before lamb is done, brush with the jelly-lemon glaze. Roast until glaze is set.

FABULOUS RICE RING

1½ cups raw brown rice
2 pounds fresh mushrooms, finely chopped
2 10½-ounce cans condensed onion soup

1 cup butter, metled
2 soup cans of water
Carrots with Grapes

Combine rice, mushrooms, soup, butter and water in a shallow baking pan or 2-quart casserole. Cover and bake in a preheated 350° oven for 2 hours, stirring occasionally. When rice is cooked, pack it into a well-buttered 6½-cup ring mold. To serve, place ring mold in a pan of water, cover with foil, and bake in a preheated 325° oven about 30 minutes until heated through. Unmold and fill center with Carrots with Grapes.

CARROTS WITH GRAPES

2 pounds carrots, peeled and cut into thick diagonal slices
2 tablespoons butter
⅛ teaspoon sugar

½ cup water
1 tablespoon vodka
1½ cups dark purple grapes, seeds removed

Salt to taste

Saute carrots in butter for a few minutes. Sprinkle sugar over carrots and cook for 2 to 3 minutes. Add water and vodka and cook until carrots are almost tender. Add grapes; cover pan and cook until carrots and grapes are both tender. Add salt to taste.

FIVE-GREENS SALAD

Choose 5 different greens from the following list:

Spinach	Boston lettuce	Endive
Iceberg lettuce	Bibb lettuce	Escarole
Romaine lettuce	Leaf lettuce	Watercress

1 garlic clove   Seasoned salt
1 teaspoon salt   Freshly ground pepper
French Vinaigrette Dressing

Wash greens thoroughly; wrap in towels and chill well. Season salad bowl with garlic mashed with salt; shake out residue. Add equal amounts of 5 greens, torn into bite-size pieces, to bowl; sprinkle with seasoned salt and pepper. Pour on French Vinaigrette Dressing just before serving.

FRENCH VINAIGRETTE DRESSING

Freshly ground black pepper and
  salt to taste
2 tablespoons wine vinegar
1 tablespoon Dijon mustard
6 tablespoons olive oil

2 tablespoons minced fresh herbs
  (basil, parsley, chervil, tarragon), or ½ teaspoon each, if
  dried leaves are used

Blend pepper, salt, vinegar and mustard. Slowly add oil and herbs. Beat well with a rotary beater.

DOUBLE-CHOCOLATE VIENNESE TORTE

1 cup sweet butter
1 cup sugar
1 teaspoon vanilla
8 1-ounce squares sweet cooking
  chocolate, melted

8 egg yolks
8 egg whites, at room temperature
  and stiffly beaten
Semi-sweet chocolate, grated

Place butter, sugar, vanilla and chocolate in a mixing bowl; with electric mixer, beat together at slow speed. Gradually add egg yolks, one at a time, beating well after each addition. Beat at slow speed for at least 25 minutes, or at medium speed for 15 minutes. Fold in beaten egg whites. Butter only the bottom of a 9-inch spring form pan. Pour ¾ of the mixture into pan. Reserve remaining batter for later use. Cover but do not refrigerate. Bake cake in a preheated 325° oven for 30 minutes, until a straw inserted in center of cake comes out clean. Let stand until completely cooled (cake will sink in middle). Remove side of spring form pan, leaving cake on pan bottom. Spread reserved batter on top as an icing and grate extra semisweet chocolate on top. Cover well and place in refrigerator or freezer overnight. Must be made day before.

VIENNESE COFFEE

Make coffee extra strength, ¼ cup of coffee to each ¾ cup of water. Sweeten to taste, top with whipped cream and garnish with chocolate sprinkles.

Trout Dinner

(SERVES 8)

Cheese-Stuffed Brussels Sprouts
Almond-Chutney Spread   Melba Toast (see Index)
Broiled Trout
Glazed Carrots   Noodle Pudding Soufflé
Double O Green Salad
Garlic-Lime Dressing
Caramel Cake

Freezer	Previous Day	Early Morning
Caramel Cake	Garlic-Lime Dressing	Cheese-Stuffed Brussels Sprouts
		Almond-Chutney Spread
		Melba Toast (see Index)
		Prepare fish with mustard butter (do not broil)
		Cook carrots for glazing
		Combine ingredients for noodle pudding (do not bake)
		Marinate onions and oranges for salad
		Prepare greens for salad
		Remove Caramel Cake from freezer

CHEESE-STUFFED BRUSSELS SPROUTS

2 pints Brussels sprouts   ⅓ cup Roquefort cheese
⅔ cup cream cheese, softened

Wash sprouts and remove discolored leaves; leave them whole. Parboil until tender-crisp and quickly cool in ice water. Drain sprouts thoroughly; scoop out a small hollow in center of each sprout. Combine cheeses, and stuff sprouts with mixture. Refrigerate until serving.

ALMOND-CHUTNEY SPREAD

¼ cup butter
2 cups chopped blanched almonds
2 drops Tabasco
6 tablespoons chopped chutney
Melba Toast, made from cocktail rye bread (see Index)

Melt butter in skillet over low heat and slowly brown almonds, stirring frequently. Add Tabasco to chutney and mix thoroughly with nuts. Serve spread on slices of rye Melba toast.

BROILED TROUT

½ cup butter, softened
¼ cup chopped parsley
2 tablespoons lemon juice
2 tablespoons Dijon mustard

¼ cup butter, melted
4 pounds fresh brook trout,
   filleted

Combine the ½ cup softened butter with parsley and lemon juice; set aside. Combine mustard with the ¼ cup melted butter. Place trout skin side down in preheated broiler pan. Brush fish with some of the mustard-butter; broil in preheated broiler, 3 inches from heat, for 10 to 12 minutes, occasionally brushing with the mustard-butter. Remove fish to serving platter and top with parsley-butter mixture.

GLAZED CARROTS

2 bunches small young
   carrots, peeled
Salt

½ cup butter
½ cup chopped parsley
Dash sugar

Boil whole carrots in salted water until just barely tender. Cool and leave whole or cut into 1-inch pieces. Melt butter in a large skillet, add carrots and sprinkle with parsley and sugar. Shake skillet to coat carrots with butter and parsley. Serve hot.

NOODLE PUDDING SOUFFLE

4 ounces medium noodles,
   cooked according to package
   instructions
1 3-ounce package cream
   cheese, softened

½ cup sugar
4 eggs
1½ cups milk
1 teaspoon vanilla
½ cup butter, melted

Crushed corn flakes

Combine noodles with all ingredients except corn flakes; mix well. Pour mixture into a 9″ x 13″ buttered glass baking dish and top with crushed corn flakes. Bake in a preheated 350° oven for 1 hour, until brown and crispy.

Note: Use only 4 ounces of noodles.

DOUBLE O GREEN SALAD

1 medium red onion, thinly sliced
3 large navel oranges, peeled and
  sectioned

2 pounds mixed torn, crisp
  greens, spinach, romaine and
  watercress

Pour Garlic-Lime Dressing over onions and oranges; refrigerate for
at least one hour. Toss mixture with greens just before serving.

GARLIC-LIME DRESSING

1 clove garlic, crushed
½ cup olive oil

¼ cup cider vinegar
¼ cup lime juice

Salt and pepper

Mix together all ingredients and beat until blended. Cover and refrigerate.

CARAMEL CAKE

½ cup butter
½ cup margarine
2 cups sugar
4 eggs, separated
1 teaspoon vanilla

3 cups sifted cake flour
3 teaspoons baking powder
1 cup milk
¼ teaspoon salt
Caramel Frosting

Cream butter, margarine and 1½ cups of the sugar; add egg yolks
and vanilla. Beat thoroughly. Sift flour with baking powder; add
alternately with milk to creamed mixture. Beat egg whites and salt
until soft peaks form. Gradually add the remaining ½ cup sugar
while continuing to beat egg whites. Fold beaten egg whites gently
into batter. Pour into three greased and floured 8-inch layer cake
pans; bake in preheated 350° oven for 25 to 30 minutes. Cool thoroughly. Frost between layers, top, and sides with Caramel Frosting.

CARAMEL FROSTING FOR LAYER CAKE

1½ cups firmly packed dark
      brown sugar
1 cup granulated sugar

½ cup water
¼ cup heavy cream
¼ cup butter

Boil sugars and water until mixture will form a thread when poured from a spoon; add cream and cook 5 minutes or to 232° on candy thermometer. Add butter; cool without stirring to 110° or until comfortable to touch. Beat until creamy and of spreading consistency.

Penthouse Dinner

(SERVES 6)

Tuna Antipasto
Cheese Hors d'Oeuvres
Steak Diane
Chip Potatoes
Asparagus Hollandaise
Green Salad with Vinaigrette Dressing (see Index)
Peach Mousse
Coffee

ADVANCE PREPARATION SCHEDULE

Freezer	Previous Day	Early Morning
Peach Mousse	*Tuna Antipasto*	*Cheese mixture for*
	Prepare Vinaigrette	*hors d'oeuvres*
	Dressing	*Toast bread strips for*
		hors d'oeuvres
		Prepare greens for salad

TUNA ANTIPASTO

2 or 3 carrots, shredded
½ cup French dressing
1 3½-ounce jar pearl onions, drained
1 7-ounce can pitted ripe olives, drained
1 2-ounce jar green pimento-stuffed olives, drained, chopped
1 cup chopped celery
1 13-ounce can water-pack tuna, drained

1 cup coarsely chopped: sweet pickles, dill pickles (not garlic) or a combination of both
1 cup raw cauliflower buds
1 cup canned button mushrooms
1 2-ounce tin anchovies, cut-up
½ cup mayonnaise
¾ cup chili sauce
Dash Worcestershire sauce

Marinate carrots in ¼ cup of the French dressing for one hour. Add remaining ingredients and just enough of the remaining ¼ cup French dressing to make mixture moist. Mix ingredients thoroughly. Keeps well in refrigerator.

CHEESE HORS D'OEUVRES

1 cup grated Parmesan cheese
1 large scallion, finely cut
Dash of seasoned salt
½ cup half-and-half

15 slices thin-sliced white bread, each cut into 4 strips and toasted on one side

Mix together cheese, scallions, seasoned salt and half-and-half. Spread cheese mixture on untoasted side of bread strips and bake in preheated 350° oven for several minutes until lightly browned. Makes five dozen hors d'oeuvres.

STEAK DIANE

3 pounds beef steak, cut ¾" thick
8 tablespoons butter
4 tablespoons chopped scallions
2 tablespoons Worcestershire sauce
1 tablespoon dry mustard

½ cup sliced mushrooms (optional)
Salt and freshly ground pepper to taste
4 tablespoons Cognac
Chopped parsley

Cut steak into 6 individual portions. Put steaks between sheets of waxed paper and pound with a meat mallet to ½-inch thickness.

Put 2 tablespoons of the butter into a large hot skillet, add steaks and quickly brown on both sides. Remove steaks and set aside. Melt the remaining 6 tablespoons of butter in same skillet, and add scallions, Worcestershire, dry mustard, mushrooms, salt and pepper. Simmer slowly until thick. Return steak to skillet; cook in sauce for 1 to 2 minutes on each side. Heat Cognac, flame and pour over meat. Remove steaks and sauce to a serving platter, garnish with chopped parsley, serve at once.

CHIP POTATOES

4 to 6 baking potatoes, scrubbed but unpeeled, sliced crosswise into ¼-inch slices
Salt

Soak sliced potatoes in cold water for 15 minutes. Dry thoroughly on a towel. Place slices in a single layer on a cookie sheet and bake in a preheated 450° oven until crisp and puffy, about 30 minutes. Sprinkle with salt and serve hot.

ASPARAGUS HOLLANDAISE

2 pounds fresh Asparagus

Wash asparagus and cook in boiling salted water until crisp-tender. Drain well. Serve with Blender Lemon Hollandaise poured over it or served on the side.

BLENDER LEMON HOLLANDAISE

3 egg yolks   ½ teaspoon salt
Juice of ½ lemon   Dash of cayenne pepper
½ cup hot, melted butter

Place egg yolks, lemon juice, salt and cayenne pepper in the container of an electric blender and blend at low speed. Remove center piece from blender top and pour hot melted butter into blender in a slow steady stream. When butter is completely added to other ingredients, sauce is ready. Makes 1 cup.

PEACH MOUSSE

1 cup sugar
1 tablespoon lemon juice
5 large whole fresh freestone
  peaches, peeled and mashed

1 cup heavy cream, whipped
½ cup coarse macaroon crumbs

Add sugar and lemon juice to mashed peaches. Fold in whipped cream and spoon into a 4-cup mold. Freeze until firm, 3 to 6 hours. Unmold; press macaroon crumbs around base of mousse and sprinkle a few crumbs on top. Let mousse stand at room temperature for 20 minutes before serving.

Note: If using canned drained peaches do not add sugar.

Festive Dinner

(SERVES 10)

Cocktail Pâté   Crab Fingers with Mustard Mayonnaise
Roast Duckling with Orange Sauce
Baked Apples with Sweet Potato Stuffing
Watercress–Cherry Tomato Salad (see Index)
Pots de Crème
Lace Cookies
Coffee
Brandy

ADVANCE PREPARATION SCHEDULE

Freezer	Previous Day	Early Morning
Pots de Crème	*Cocktail Pâté*	*Mustard Mayonnaise*
	Lace Cookies	*Baked Apples with Sweet Potato Stuffing (do not bake)*
		Prepare watercress

COCKTAIL PATE

1 cup softened butter
1 pound liver sausage
2 3-ounce packages cream cheese, softened
2 tablespoons minced parsley
2 tablespoons minced chives

2 tablespoons minced scallions with tops
2 tablespoons dry vermouth
2 teaspoons Worcestershire sauce
2 dashes Tabasco
Salt and pepper to taste

Mash butter, liver sausage and cream cheese together; add remaining ingredients and beat with fork until thoroughly blended. Place in a mold or crock; cover tightly and refrigerate. Serve with Melba toast or crackers.

CRAB FINGERS WITH MUSTARD MAYONNAISE

Buy 2 cans fresh crab fingers at fish market; drain. Arrange decoratively, with shell side along rim of platter. In center of platter, place bowl of Mustard Mayonnaise for dipping.

Mustard Mayonnaise:

½ cup prepared mustard
½ cup mayonnaise

½ teaspoon dry mustard (optional; use for stronger flavor)

Combine ingredients and serve as a dip with crab fingers.

ROAST DUCKLING WITH ORANGE SAUCE

4 4- to 5-pound ready-to-cook ducklings, quartered
4 teaspoons salt
½ teaspoon pepper
2 bouillon cubes, crushed
2 cups hot water
2 cups orange juice

½ cup currant jelly
½ cup firmly packed brown sugar
1½ tablespoons cornstarch, combined with ¼ cup cold water for each cup of sauce

Arrange duckling quarters on rack in a large roasting pan. Roast in preheated 325° oven about 2 hours. Remove fat from pan while cooking. Remove duckling from pan. Spoon off fat and place remaining drippings in a sauce pan, add salt, pepper, bouillon, water and orange juice. Set aside. Return duckling to pan. Cover and bake at 325° for 1½ to 2 hours, or until tender. Remove duckling from pan and return it to oven to keep warm in another pan. Skim any fat from sauce; add jelly and brown sugar and stir. Measure sauce and add correct amount of cornstarch and water. Pour into saucepan and cook until thick and clear, about 5 minutes. Serve with duckling.

BAKED APPLES WITH SWEET POTATO STUFFING

10 large firm, green apples
2 16-ounce cans sweet potatoes
Juice of 2 large lemons
2 ripe bananas, mashed well
½ cup dry sherry
½ teaspoon salt
¼ teaspoon pepper
¼ cup butter
16 minature marshmallows

To prepare apple shells, cut off tops of apples and scoop out pulp until apple walls are ½-inch thick. Combine sweet potatoes and juice from can with lemon juice, bananas, sherry, salt and pepper. Beat until well blended. Stuff apples generously with sweet potato filling. Place apples in a large buttered baking dish; dot tops with butter and marshmallows and bake in a preheated 325° oven for 30 minutes, or until mixture bubbles and top is brown.

POTS DE CREME

8 1-ounce squares sweet cooking chocolate
3 tablespoons water, rum or strong coffee
4 egg yolks, beaten
2 tablespoons confectioners' sugar
1 cup heavy cream, whipped
4 egg whites, beaten stiff
Whipped cream
Chocolate sprinkles or curls of bitter-sweet chocolate

Melt chocolate in top of double boiler over hot, not boiling, water; add water, rum or coffee and mix until smooth. Remove from heat. Gradually beat in yolks until mixture is smooth. Cool; add sugar and blend. Fold in whipped cream and then beaten egg whites. Pour into individual pots de crèmes; top with extra whipped cream and chocolate sprinkles or chocolate curls. Cover and refrigerate overnight. May be frozen. Defrost in refrigerator 1 hour.

LACE COOKIES

⅔ cup slivered blanched almonds ½ cup butter
½ cup sugar 3 tablespoons flour
2 tablespoons milk

Combine all ingredients in saucepan and cook, stirring constantly, until well-blended. Drop level teaspoonfuls of mixture onto greased and floured cookie sheets, with 6 cookies per sheet. Bake, 1 sheet at a time, in preheated 350° oven for 5 to 6 minutes, until lightly browned. Watch closely to avoid burning. Remove pan from oven and allow to stand for 1 minute, until easily removable. Remove with broad spatula and cool on wire cake racks. Makes about 40 cookies. Store in an airtight container.

Note: This cookie is difficult to make in humid weather.

Fort Knox Dinner

(SERVES 8)

Oysters Midas
Beef Fillet with Madeira Sauce
Wild Rice and Mushrooms
Green Salad with Lorenzo Dressing
Chocolate Mousse Cake
Coffee

ADVANCE PREPARATION SCHEDULE

Freezer

*Wild Rice and
  Mushrooms*
*Chocolate Mousse
  Cake*

Previous Day

Lorenzo Dressing
Brown Sauce

Early Morning

*Oysters Midas (ready to
  bake)*
Madeira Sauce
Prepare greens for salad
*Remove Wild Rice and
  Mushrooms and
  Chocolate Mousse
  Cake from freezer*

OYSTERS MIDAS

1 cup butter
½ cup flour
1 medium onion, finely chopped
2 cloves garlic, minced
1 teaspoon chopped fresh thyme
  or ¼ teaspoon dried thyme
  leaves
1 pint oysters, fresh, frozen or

canned, drained and liquid
  reserved
1 teaspoon brown bouquet sauce
1 teaspoon chopped parsley
4 large whole artichokes, cooked
½ cup fine dry bread crumbs
¼ cup butter
8 lemon slices

Melt the 1 cup butter, add flour, and mix well. Add onions and garlic. Simmer over low heat until onion is soft. Stir in thyme and oysters. Add enough water to reserved oyster liquid to make ½ cup and add to oyster mixture with bouquet sauce and parsley. Heat through. Cook artichokes, remove and reserve leaves; remove chokes and cut hearts into chunks. In bottoms of 8 individual heat-proof serving dishes, place chunks of artichoke hearts and cover with oyster mixture. Sprinkle with bread crumbs; dot with the ¼ cup butter and top each with a lemon slice. Bake in a preheated 400° oven about 10 minutes until bubbly. Place dishes on individual serving plates and arrange artichoke leaves on plates to dip into mixture.

BEEF FILLET WITH MADEIRA SAUCE

¼ cup butter
1 8-pound fillet of beef, well
  trimmed

Salt and freshly ground pepper
2 tablespoons butter

Preheat oven to 450°. Heat the ¼ cup butter in a shallow roasting pan. When just melted, turn fillet in pan to coat meat with butter. Sprinkle with salt and pepper. Bake for 25 to 35 minutes, or until a meat thermometer inserted in center of meat registers 140° for rare or 160° for medium rare. Baste frequently with pan drippings. Transfer meat to a large serving dish, and keep warm. Pour off most of fat from pan and pour in Madeira Sauce. Dissolve brown particles clinging to sides and bottom of pan. Swirl in the remaining 2 tablespoons of butter. Heat. Slice fillet; spoon some of the hot Madeira Sauce over beef and serve remaining sauce on side.

Madeira Sauce:

1 tablespoon butter	⅓ cup Madeira wine
4 large mushrooms, sliced	1½ cups Brown Sauce (recipe
Salt and pepper	below) or 1 10¾-ounce can
2 tablespoons finely chopped	beef gravy
shallots	

Heat butter in a skillet and add mushrooms. Sprinkle with salt and pepper, and cook until mushrooms give up their liquid. Add shallots, and cook until most of liquid evaporates, stirring. Add wine, and cook for 1 minute. Add brown sauce or beef gravy; simmer for 15 minutes. Serve hot.

Brown Sauce:

2 tablespoons butter	2 cups canned beef consommé
1 tablespoon flour	⅛ teaspoon pepper
2 tablespoons minced onion	1 tablespoon tomato paste
1 bay leaf (optional)	

Heat butter in pan, add flour and cook until bubbly. Blend in minced onion and cook, stirring, until light brown. Add consommé slowly and bring to a boil; add pepper, tomato paste and bay leaf. Simmer 20 minutes, strain and cool.

WILD RICE AND MUSHROOMS

1 cup finely chopped onion	1 pound mushrooms, sliced
1 cup finely chopped celery	2 cups cooked wild rice
½ cup butter, melted	1½ cups cooked white rice
Salt and pepper to taste	

Sauté onion and celery in ¼ cup of the butter; add mushrooms.

Add vegetables to cooked rices. Add salt, pepper and remaining ¼ cup melted butter. Pack mixture into a greased 2-quart ring mold. Place mold in pan of water, cover with foil and bake in a preheated 350° oven for 1 hour. Unmold on serving platter. May be frozen and reheated before serving.

GREEN SALAD WITH LORENZO DRESSING

Lorenzo Dressing:

½ cup salad oil	¼ teaspoon Worcestershire
⅓ cup water	Dash of paprika
⅓ cup white vinegar	½ cup chili sauce
1 teaspoon salt	¼ cup chopped watercress

Combine all ingredients and blend well; cover and refrigerate. Serve dressing over mixed salad greens, or over chilled asparagus, topped with pimiento and sliced hard-cooked egg.

CHOCOLATE MOUSSE CAKE

1 1-pound package chocolate sandwich cookies with fudge filling, crushed	½ cup water
	½ cup sugar
	4 egg yolks, well beaten
1 12-ounce package semi-sweet chocolate pieces	4 egg whites
	½ cup sugar
1 tablespoon instant coffee powder	3 cups heavy cream, whipped

Press cookie crumbs onto the bottom of 9-inch greased spring form pan. Bake in a preheated 325° oven for 10 minutes; cool. In top of a double boiler, melt chocolate chips over hot, not boiling, water; blend in coffee, water and the ½ cup sugar; cool. Blend in egg yolks. Beat egg whites until soft peaks form, gradually add the ½ cup sugar and beat until stiff. Fold egg whites, and then whipped cream into chocolate mixture. Spread evenly over crumb crust. Cover and freeze overnight or longer. Defrost in refrigerator for 8 hours before serving.

Chicken Caper Dinner

(SERVES 6)

Jellied Tomato Soup
Crackers
Chicken in Caper Sauce
Creamed Corn Pudding
Green Peas and Water Chestnuts
Danish Fruit Mold
Fruit Sauce
Coffee

ADVANCE PREPARATION SCHEDULE

Previous Day	Early Morning
Jellied Tomato Soup	*Cook peas*
Danish Fruit Mold	*Fruit Sauce*

JELLIED TOMATO SOUP

2 envelopes unflavored gelatine	2 tablespoons lemon juice
2½ cups canned tomatoes	2 tablespoons grated lemon peel
2 beef bouillon cubes	2 teaspoons minced onion
2¼ cups water	1 teaspoon salt

Sprinkle gelatine over ½ cup of the tomatoes and let soften 5 minutes. Combine rest of tomatoes with bouillon cubes, water, lemon juice and peel, onion and salt. Simmer 5 minutes. Add gelatine and stir to dissolve. Cool slightly and strain into 6 bouillon cups. Refrigerate until set. Just before serving, break up slightly with fork.

CHICKEN IN CAPER SAUCE

2 2-pound broiler chickens quartered	1 tablespoon flour
3 tablespoons butter, or more	¾ cup dry white wine
1 teaspoon salt	4 anchovy fillets, mashed
	2 tablespoons drained capers

2 tablespoons lemon juice

Wash and dry chicken quarters. Melt half the butter in a deep skillet and brown chicken very well. Add a little more butter if needed to prevent sticking. Season with salt and stir in the flour; stir until flour is lightly browned. Add wine, anchovies, capers and lemon juice. Stir in remaining butter. Cover and cook over low heat 30 to 45 minutes, or until chicken is fork-tender. Turn once or twice during cooking time. (Chicken and sauce may be placed in a casserole and baked, covered, in a preheated 325° oven for about 45 minutes.)

CREAMED CORN PUDDING

2 tablespoons butter	Pinch of salt
1 tablespoons flour	Pinch of pepper
1 16-ounce can (2 cups) cream-style corn	⅓ cup sugar
	4 eggs, slightly beaten

1 cup milk

Preheat oven to 325°. Melt butter in a 1-quart casserole in oven, add flour and stir until smooth. Combine remaining ingredients and pour into pie plate. Carefully place plate in a pan of water and bake 1 hour, or until set.

GREEN PEAS AND WATER CHESTNUTS

¼ cup melted butter or margarine	2 10-ounce packages frozen peas, cooked and drained
1 5-ounce can water chestnuts, drained and sliced	
½ teaspoon chopped fresh dillweed	

Melt butter in a skillet over moderate heat. Add water chestnuts and cook about 5 minutes, or until lightly browned. Stir in dill. Add peas and heat about 5 minutes.

DANISH FRUIT MOLD

4 egg yolks	½ pound marshmallows
1 teaspoon sugar	1 pound red-skinned grapes
¼ teaspoon salt	⅓ cup drained green maraschino
2 tablespoons lemon juice	cherries
1 cup heavy cream	8 slices canned pineapple
1 teaspoon unflavored gelatine	1 cup pecans
softened in 2 tablespoons cold	Fruit Sauce
water	

Beat egg yolks till lemon-colored and add sugar, salt, lemon juice and ½ cup of the cream, beating only until blended. Cook this mixture in a 1-quart saucepan over a very low heat until thickened, stirring constantly; allow to simmer for 2 minutes. Add softened gelatine, and stir until gelatine has melted. Pour into a large bowl and allow to cool but not to set. While this mixture is cooling, cut marshmallows, grapes, cherries, pineapple and nuts into small pieces and combine. When custard is cool, beat the remaining ½ cup cream until stiff and fold it into the custard. Mix only until blended, add fruit mixture and blend well. Pour into a well-oiled bowl or mold. This mold must stand at least 8 hours before unmolding. It is not advisable to make this mold more than a day in advance. When ready to unmold, loosen around top edge with a thin spatula. Dip mold into a pan of lukewarm water for a few seconds and turn out onto large round platter. Serve with Fruit Sauce.

FRUIT SAUCE

2 tablespoons melted butter	2 tablespoons sugar
2 tablespoons flour	1¼ cups lukewarm strained pine-
½ cup sugar	apple juice
2 egg yolks, slightly beaten	1 cup heavy cream, beaten until
½ cup pineapple juice	thickened but not stiff
⅛ teaspoon salt	
2 egg whites beaten until soft	
peaks form	

Combine melted butter and flour and mix until smooth. Add the ½ cup sugar and egg yolks combined with the ½ cup pineapple juice and salt. Mix thoroughly. To the beaten egg whites add the

2 tablespoons sugar and beat only until blended. Blend egg whites gently into first mixture. Slowly add the 1½ cups lukewarm strained pineapple juice. Cook in upper part of double boiler or in heavy saucepan until thick and smooth, stirring constantly. Watch carefully to see that it does not curdle, keeping heat low. If it curdles, beat a few seconds with egg beater. Chill mixture and fold in slightly beaten cream. Serve very cold.

Springtime Dinner

(SERVES 8)

Lobster Cutlets
Marinated Vegetables
Butterfly Leg of Lamb with Blender Lemon Hollandaise (see Index)
Eggplant Experience   Noodle-Rice Casserole (see Index)
Green Salad with Anchovy Dressing
Feathery Cheesecake
Coffee

ADVANCE PREPARATION SCHEDULE

Previous Day

Marinate Vegetables
Marinate Lamb
Feathery Cheesecake

Early Morning

Lobster Cutlets
Prepare Eggplant Experience (do not bake)
Prepare rice and noodles for casserole (do not bake) (see Index)
Prepare salad greens
Anchovy Salad Dressing

LOBSTER CUTLETS

1 16-ounce can lobster, drained	1½ cups milk
Salt and cayenne pepper	2 eggs
1 tablespoon lemon juice	2 cups fine dry bread crumbs
2 tablespoon butter	Vegetable oil for frying
3 tablespoons flour	Mayonnaise

Cut lobster into very small pieces; season with salt, pepper and lemon juice and set aside. Put butter in a skillet to melt. When butter melts, add flour and stir until smooth, remove from heat. Beat milk with one of the eggs; slowly stir mixture into butter-flour mixture. Bring to a boil and stir until thickened and smooth; add lobster and remove from heat. Spread mixture 1-inch thick on a well-buttered platter and let cool. Cut and shape into 8 chop-shaped pieces. Beat the remaining egg well. Dip lobster cutlets in egg and then coat with bread crumbs. Heat oil to a depth of about 2 inches in a deep sauce pan to a temperature of 375° on a deep-fat-frying thermometer. Add a few cutlets at a time and fry until golden brown on each side. Remove with a slotted spoon and dry on paper towels. Serve hot with mayonnaise. If made ahead of time, reheat in a 325° oven.

MARINATED VEGETABLES

1 head cauliflower, broken into flowerettes	1 cup mayonnaise
1 cup sliced celery	1 tablespoon lemon juice
1 cup bottled Italian dressing	2 tablespoons chili sauce
1 6-ounce jar marinated artichoke hearts	2 tablespoons fresh dill
	1 teaspoon salt

Soak cauliflower and celery in ice water for 2 hours. Drain; add Italian dressing and marinate overnight. Next morning drain vegetables. Combine all remaining ingredients and add to cauliflower. Refrigerate 6 hours.

BUTTERFLY LEG OF LAMB
WITH BLENDER LEMON HOLLANDAISE

Marinade:

⅔ cup vinegar	¾ teaspoon dried oregano leaves
⅓ cup dry red wine	½ teaspoon dried basil leaves
1¼ cups salad oil	½ teaspoon black pepper
2 teaspoons salt	2 cloves garlic, slivered
	3 small lemons, thinly sliced

Combine all ingredients except garlic and lemon slices. Beat with a rotary beater for 1 minute. Add garlic and lemon slices.

1 6-pound leg of lamb, butterflied	Blender Lemon Hollandaise (see Index)
½ teaspoon coarse salt	

Pour Marinade over meat; cover and refrigerate overnight. When ready to cook, drain meat and reserve marinade. Sprinkle meat with coarse salt. Place on broiler rack. Place in preheated broiler 4 inches from heat. Broil 15 minutes. Turn; baste with some of the reserved marinade and broil on other side for 12 minutes. Serve Blender Lemon Hollandaise on side.

EGGPLANT EXPERIENCE

1 large eggplant, peeled and cut into 1-inch cubes	½ teaspoon Worcestershire sauce
1 large onion, sliced	2 small cloves garlic, minced
½ cup shredded sharp Cheddar cheese	10 soda crackers, crushed
	½ cup light cream
	Salt and pepper to taste
1 tablespoon butter	

Cook eggplant and onion in a small amount of salted boiling water until tender. Drain; add all remaining ingredients, except butter, to vegetables. Spoon into a greased 1-quart casserole, dot top with butter. Bake in a preheated 350° oven for 15 minutes. May be made in advance and refrigerated. Bake just before serving.

ANCHOVY DRESSING

¾ cup salad oil
¼ cup tarragon, or white wine vinegar
1 2-ounce can anchovy fillets, drained
⅛ teaspoon black pepper
3 to 4 scallions, coarsely chopped
½ cup chopped fresh parsley

Blend all ingredients in the container of an electric blender. Serve over crisp salad greens. Refrigerate.

FEATHERY CHEESECAKE

1 cup sugar
12 ounces cream cheese, softened
1 3-ounce package lemon-flavored gelatin
1 cup boiling water
Shaved chocolate for garnish

2 teaspoons vanilla
2 cups heavy cream, stiffly whipped
Graham Cracker Crust to line a 9-inch springform (see Index)

Blend sugar into softened cream cheese. Dissolve gelatin in boiling water; cool slightly. Add gelatin to sugar-cheese mixture, blending well. Add vanilla; fold in whipped cream. Pour into a 9-inch spring form pan lined with a Graham Cracker Crust. Chill overnight. Before serving, garnish with shaved chocolate.

Special Saturday Dinner

(SERVES 6)

Cherry Tomato Treats
Shrimp Marinade
Steak and Pea Pods
Rice
Spinach–Bean Sprout Salad
Sour Lemon Cream Pie

CHERRY TOMATO TREATS

1 7-ounce can tuna, drained
1 tablespoon mayonnaise
1 tablespoon chopped parsley
1 tablespoon finely chopped celery
Pinch cayenne pepper
1 pint cherry tomatoes, washed
Mayonnaise

Blend tuna and mayonnaise. Add parsley, celery and pepper. Cut a slice from tops of tomatoes and scoop out pulp with a very small spoon, leaving a hollow shell. Drain tomatoes and fill with tuna mixture. Top with small dab of mayonnaise. Refrigerate.

Variation:

Fill tomatoes with caviar and decorate with a dab of sour cream. Tomatoes may be filled with a mixture of cream cheese beaten with grated onion and topped with sour cream and caviar.

SHRIMP MARINADE

3 tablespoons sugar
2 cups mayonnaise
2 large onions, sliced and separated into rings
⅔ cup lemon juice
Lemon pepper to taste
3 pounds shrimp, cooked, shelled and deveined

Dissolve sugar in mayonnaise. Add onion rings, lemon juice and lemon pepper. Finally, combine with shrimps and marinate, covered, in refrigerator at least 3 days, stirring occasionally.

STEAK AND PEA PODS

8 beef tenderloin steaks, cut 1-inch thick
8 tablespoons butter
1 pound fresh mushrooms
1 large onion, sliced
1 clove garlic, crushed
1 teaspoon salt

2 teaspoons freshly ground pepper
1 ounce Maggi seasoning
¼ cup dry sherry
½ pound fresh Chinese snow peas (peapods)

Quickly brown steaks on all sides in 4 tablespoons of the butter; do not overcook. Remove from heat. Cut stems from mushrooms, keeping the caps whole. Slice stems, and brown mushroom stems and caps in the remaining 4 tablespoons butter with onion and garlic. Combine steaks with vegetables, salt, pepper, Maggi seasoning, sherry and pea pods. Heat just until pea pods turn shiny, about 5 minutes or less.

SPINACH–BEAN SPROUT SALAD

1 pound spinach, washed, dried and chilled
½ pound fresh bean sprouts, chilled

8 slices bacon, cooked crisp and crumbled
1 5-ounce can water chestnuts, drained and thinly sliced

Tear spinach into bite-size pieces in a salad bowl. Add bean sprouts, bacon and water chestnuts. Just before serving toss with Red French Dressing.

RED FRENCH DRESSING

1 cup salad oil
2 tablespoons sugar
1 onion, finely chopped
⅓ cup catsup

½ cup cider vinegar
1 tablespoon Worcestershire sauce
Pinch of salt

Combine all ingredients and blend well. Chill until ready to use.

SOUR LEMON CREAM PIE

1 9-inch Graham Cracker pie
    shell
1 cup sugar
1 tablespoon cornstarch
¼ cup lemon juice

2 tablespoons grated lemon peel
3 egg yolks, beaten
1 cup milk
1 cup sour cream
1 lemon, thinly sliced, for garnish

Whipped cream, for garnish

Prepare and chill Graham Cracker Crust. Cook sugar, cornstarch, lemon juice and peel, egg yolks and milk in top of double boiler over boiling water, stirring until thick. Fold in sour cream and let mixture cool. Pour into prepared Graham Cracker Crust and cool in refrigerator several hours.

Cut each thin lemon slice halfway through, from center to outside edge. Twist one half forward, and one half backward, so each lemon slice is almost "butterfly-shaped." Place the "butterflies" on a cookie sheet and place in freezer for several hours. Just before serving, cover entire surface of pie with a thin layer of whipped cream and top with frozen lemon slices.

Graham Cracker Crust:

1¼ cups finely crushed graham
    crackers

½ cup sugar
⅓ cup melted butter

Mix well. Press in bottom and sides of a 9-inch pie plate. Chill until set.

Old World Dinner

(SERVES 6)

Stuffed Mushrooms
Red Caviar and Sour Cream
Rye Rounds
Hungarian Pork Chops
Tiny Caraway Potatoes
Pickled Beets and Onions
New World Strudel
Coffee

ADVANCE PREPARATION SCHEDULE

Freezer	Previous Day	Early Morning
New World Strudel	*Pickled Beets*	*Stuffed Mushrooms (ready to broil)*
		Toast bread rounds for Red Caviar and Sour Cream
		Peel potatoes and cover with water
		Marinate onion rings

STUFFED MUSHROOMS

18 large mushrooms, caps and
    stems separated
Onion-flavored crackers,
    finely crushed

1 clove garlic, minced
½ cup butter

Finely chop mushroom stems; measure and add an equal amount of crushed crackers. Add minced garlic and combine thoroughly. In ¼ cup of the butter, sauté mushroom caps for a few minutes until lightly browned. Remove from skillet and set aside. Add the remaining ¼ cup butter and sauté mushroom-cracker mixture about

2 minutes, stirring frequently. Fill mushroom caps with cracker mixture. Place mushrooms on a cookie sheet and place in a pre-heated broiler about 3 inches from heat; broil for several minutes until hot. Serve at once.

RED CAVIAR AND SOUR CREAM

1 4-ounce jar red caviar	Thinly sliced rye bread
1 cup sour cream	Butter
Paprika	

Carefully fold caviar into sour cream. Cut rounds from bread with a small cookie cutter. Place rounds on a cookie sheet and toast on both sides in a preheated broiler; butter while warm. Place a generous mound of caviar-sour cream mixture on toast rounds. Sprinkle each with paprika and serve at once.

HUNGARIAN PORK CHOPS

6 rib pork chops, cut ¾ inch thick	½ teaspoon salt
1½ cups sliced onions	¼ teaspoon garlic powder
½ cup water	1 cup sour cream
2 teaspoons dill seed	1 tablespoon flour
1 teaspoon caraway seed	1 teaspoon paprika

In a large skillet over medium heat, brown pork chops on both sides. Pour off excess fat; add onions, water, dill, caraway, salt and garlic powder to chops in skillet. Cover and simmer for 35 to 45 minutes, until chops are tender. Remove chops to a warm platter. Combine sour cream, flour and paprika. Stir mixture into drippings in skillet. Cook over low heat, stirring constantly, until sauce is heated through. Pour over chops and serve at once.

TINY CARAWAY POTATOES

20 small peeled new potatoes	2 tablespoons caraway seed
¼ cup butter, melted	Salt and pepper

Cook potatoes in a small amount of boiling salted water until fork-tender. Drain and return to hot pan. Add butter, caraway seed and salt and pepper to taste; toss to coat potatoes with butter.

PICKLED BEETS AND ONION RINGS

1 16-ounce can sliced beets, drained and juice reserved
½ cup cider vinegar
2 tablespoons sugar
½ teaspoon salt
3 peppercorns
2 whole cloves
1 bay leaf

1 garlic clove, halved
¾ cup salad oil
½ cup tarragon vinegar
¼ teaspoon garlic salt
Dash white pepper
4 medium onions, thinly sliced and separated into rings
1 tablespoon sour cream
Freshly ground black pepper

Boil ½ cup of the beet juice with the cider vinegar for 5 minutes. Add sugar, salt, peppercorns, cloves, bay leaf and garlic. Simmer for 15 minutes; strain, and pour over sliced beets. Store in refrigerator overnight in a covered container. Combine oil, tarragon vinegar, garlic salt and white pepper. Pour over onion rings and refrigerate for 3 to 4 hours.

Drain beets and onions. Arrange in circle design on lettuce leaf on individual plates. Garnish each with a little sour cream and sprinkle with pepper.

NEW WORLD STRUDEL

Dough:

5 cups sifted all-purpose flour
1 pound creamed small curd cottage cheese

1 pound softened butter
1 egg white, slightly beaten

Mix flour, cheese and butter together, blend well. Shape into a ball, cover and refrigerate overnight. Next day divide dough into 6 portions. Roll dough out into 14″ x 3″ rectangle. Brush dough with melted butter and spread with any of the following fillings.

Apricot Jam: Spread dough with a thin layer of apricot jam. Sprinkle lightly with coconut, chopped nuts and raisins.

Prune: Spread dough with puréed prunes or canned prune filling and sprinkle with chopped nuts.

Apple: Spread dough with chopped, peeled, uncooked apples, sprinkled with cinnamon, sugar, raisins, nuts and coconut.

Poppyseed: Sprinkle dough generously with poppyseed.

Each of the rolls may be made with a different filling, if desired. When dough is covered with a filling mixture, roll up starting with a wide side. Place on a cookie sheet; brush with egg white and bake in a preheated 350° oven about 45 minutes or until lightly browned. Cut into thin slices while still warm. Makes a flaky and delicious dessert, at least 100 pieces. Freezes perfectly.

V.I.P. Dinner

(SERVES 8)

Artichokes with Shrimp Stuffing
Half-Minute Steaks
Potato Soufflé
Beefsteak Tomatoes with Herbs
Vinegar and Oil
Royal Ice Cream Torte
Coffee

ADVANCE PREPARATION SCHEDULE

Freezer	**Early Morning**
Royal Ice Cream Torte	*Shrimp Stuffing for artichokes*
	Cook artichokes, ready for stuffing
	Beefsteak Tomatoes with Herbs

ARTICHOKES STUFFED WITH SHRIMP

8 artichokes	Shrimp Stuffing
Pinch of salt	2 tablespoons lemon juice
Juice of 1 lemon	Oil
½ cup melted butter	

Trim base of artichokes so they will stand up straight; cut ½ inch off of tops to remove prickles; cut off small base leaves, and trim ends of leaves, if desired. Stand artichokes side by side in a roasting pan, so that they fit closely together. Add salt, juice of 1 lemon and two to three inches of boiling water to pan. Cook, covered, over medium-high heat for 20 minutes, until partially tender. Remove from pan, and turn upside down to thoroughly drain. Let cool before stuffing. Spread leaves of artichokes; remove yellow leaves from center. With a large spoon, scrape out choke, removing all fuzzy and prickly sections from heart. Spoon shrimp stuffing mixture into cavity of artichokes; if desired, some stuffing may be placed between leaves. Place artichokes in a baking pan to fit tightly. Add one inch of boiling water to pan; add the 2 tablespoons lemon juice, and generously brush artichokes with oil. Cover with aluminum foil and bake in a preheated 350° oven for 30 minutes. Serve with melted butter to pour into center of artichokes and dip leaves into.

Shrimp Stuffing:

2 cups cooked shrimp, cut into small pieces	½ cup onion, finely chopped
2½ cups bread crumbs	2 tablespoons lemon juice
	2 eggs, beaten

Combine ingredients and blend well. Cover and refrigerate until ready to use.

HALF-MINUTE STEAKS

32 *very* thinly sliced club steaks	1 cup butter
½ cup parsley or chives, chopped	

Steaks must be cut on a slicing machine to the thickness of sliced roast beef from a delicatessen. Have slices laid on sheets of waxed paper, about 3 raw slices per sheet to prevent sticking. In a large skillet, melt butter and add parsley or chives, or both. Lay a few slices of meat in butter, fry quickly over moderately high heat barely long enough for meat to change color. Turn and fry other side. As steaks are done, put on a serving platter in a warm oven. When all steaks are fried, pour butter and herbs from skillet over steaks. Serve at once, allowing at least 3 slices per person.

POTATO SOUFFLE

4 cups mashed potatoes Salt and white pepper
½ cup heavy cream 3 egg yolks, well beaten
3 egg whites, stiffly beaten

Blend mashed potatoes with cream. Season very well with salt and white pepper. Stir in egg yolks. Just before baking fold in beaten egg whites. Pour mixture into a 1-quart soufflé dish; mixture should reach to one finger-width from top of dish. Bake in a preheated 350° oven for 20 to 25 minutes.

BEEFSTEAK TOMATOES WITH HERBS

1 Spanish onion, thinly sliced and separated into rings ¾ teaspoon salt
 Freshly ground black pepper
4 large ripe, beefsteak tomatoes, peeled and cut into ½-inch thick slices 1 tablespoon fresh basil, chopped
 ¾ teaspoon celery seed
 1 tablespoon chopped fresh chives or scallion tops
¼ teaspoon sugar
1 tablespoon chopped fresh dill

Place onion rings on a large flat serving dish. Top with tomato slices. Sprinkle with sugar, salt and pepper; then sprinkle with all the remaining ingredients. Cover and store in refrigerator for several hours before serving. Arrange on individual serving plates. Serve with cruets of vinegar and oil and let each guest dress his own salad at the table.

ROYAL ICE CREAM TORTE

1 8½-ounce package chocolate wafer cookies	2 pints raspberry sherbet
2 pints chocolate ice cream	¼ to ½ pound chocolate-covered English toffee, crushed
1 8-ounce bottle fudge sauce	

Oil an 8-inch spring form pan. Crush chocolate wafers and spread half the crumbs over bottom of pan. Let chocolate ice cream soften slightly; spread it over the crushed wafers in pan, and dribble 2 tablespoons of the fudge sauce over ice cream. Spread remaining crushed wafers over sauce and top with raspberry sherbet and 2 tablespoons fudge sauce. Crush toffee and sprinkle over entire torte. Freeze for 4 to 5 hours. Remove from freezer 30 minutes before serving. Heat remaining fudge sauce and serve with the torte.

Divine Indulgence Dinner

(SERVES 6)

Crabmeat Cocktail

Artichoke Wedges

Chicken with Chutney Sauce

Buttered Rice

Romaine-Tarragon Salad

Dobosch Torte

Coffee

ADVANCE PREPARATION SCHEDULE

Previous Day	Early Morning
Artichoke Wedges	*Sauce for Crabmeat Cocktail*
Dobosch Torte	*Chutney Sauce for chicken*
	Prepare salad greens and dressing for salad

CRABMEAT COCKTAIL

¾ cup mayonnaise
1 clove garlic, finely minced
   (optional)
Juice of ½ lime
4 teaspoons hot mustard

2 teaspoons steak sauce
½ teaspoon dried tarragon leaves
4 dashes Angostura bitters
1 teaspoon brandy
1 pound fresh crabmeat

Crisp lettuce leaves

Blend mayonnaise with garlic, lime juice, seasonings and brandy; cover and chill. Also keep crabmeat refrigerated until ready to use. Before serving, gently mix sauce and crabmeat. Spoon mixture into 6 lettuce-lined dishes.

ARTICHOKE WEDGES

½ bunch scallions, finely chopped
1 tablespoon butter
¼ pound sharp Cheddar cheese,
   grated

3 saltine crackers, crushed
Salt, pepper and Tabasco to taste
1 14-ounce can artichoke hearts,
   drained

2 eggs, well beaten

Lightly sauté scallions in butter. Combine with cheese, crackers and seasonings. Arrange artichoke hearts in a greased 8-inch glass pie pan, cutting hearts in half if too large. Sprinkle cheese mixture over artichokes and pat down firmly. Pour beaten eggs on top. Bake in a preheated 350° oven for 35 minutes. May be frozen or refrigerated and reheated for 20 minutes in a 350° oven. Remove from oven and cool slightly. To serve, cut into wedges.

CHICKEN WITH CHUTNEY SAUCE

3 2½- to 3-pound frying chickens,
   quartered or in parts

Salt and pepper
Butter
Chutney Sauce

Place chicken pieces in a shallow baking pan; season with salt and pepper and dot with butter. Bake in a preheated 425° oven 15 minutes or until golden brown. Reduce oven temperature to 350°. Pour

Chutney Sauce over browned chicken and bake for 1 hour and 15 minutes. While baking, baste chicken occasionally with Chutney Sauce.

Chutney Sauce:

1½ cups orange juice	½ teaspoon curry powder
¼ cup chopped chutney	½ cup dry white wine
½ teaspoon cinnamon	1½ teaspoons salt
½ cup raisins	½ teaspoon pepper
½ cup blanched almonds, slivered	3 tablespoons butter

Combine ingredients in a saucepan and simmer for 10 minutes.

ROMAINE-TARRAGON SALAD

2 heads romaine lettuce (use pale inner leaves), washed and dried	1 teaspoon dry mustard
4 to 5 plump endive, cleaned with leaves separated	1 teaspoon Dijon mustard
2 handfuls fresh spinach, washed, dried, stems removed	1 tablespoon lemon juice
3 teaspoons salt	⅓ cup tarragon vinegar
2 teaspoons freshly ground pepper	2 cups combination vegetable and olive oils
	1 clove garlic, minced
	1 hard-cooked egg

Arrange greens in large salad bowl. In a separate bowl, combine salt, pepper, the mustards, lemon juice and vinegar and stir vigorously. Slowly add oil, and beat until dressing is smooth and creamy. Add garlic. Sieve egg yolk and white separately. Toss salad with dressing. Sprinkle sieved egg yolk and white over salad.

DOBOSCH TORTE

10 egg yolks	Pinch of salt
1 cup sugar	10 egg whites
2 teaspoons vanilla	1 cup sifted cake flour
Frosting	

With an electric mixer beat yolks until foamy; gradually add ½ cup of the sugar, beating until yolks become light in color. Add vanilla. Add salt to egg whites and beat (with clean beaters) until whites form moist peaks. Slowly add the remaining ½ cup sugar and beat until quite stiff. Gently fold egg whites and flour into yolk mixture. Divide batter among 4 ungreased 8-inch layer cake pans. Bake in preheated 350° oven for 20 minutes. Cool pans on a cake rack. Cakes will drop from pans easily once cooled. When cool, use a knife with serrated blade to carefully split each cake in half, so that there are 8 layers in all. Spread Frosting between all layers and on sides and top of torte.

Frosting:

9 1-ounce squares unsweetened chocolate, melted and cooled	3 cups confectioners' sugar
3 tablespoons butter	3 teaspoons vanilla
	¾ cup milk

3 eggs

Melt chocolate and butter together; cool. Combine sugar, vanilla, milk and eggs. Beat with an electric mixer until smooth. Add chocolate-butter mixture and beat until creamy and thick.

Mediterranean Dinner

(SERVES 6)

Antipasto   Garlic Fingers
Classic Veal Roast
Green Noodles   Baked Tomatoes
Rum Cake
Coffee

ADVANCE PREPARATION SCHEDULE

Freezer	Previous Day	Early Morning
Garlic Fingers	*Olive Salad for*	*Salads for Antipasto*
Veal Roast (uncooked)	*Antipasto*	*(except Artichoke*
	Rum Cake	*Salad)*
	(undecorated)	*Decorate Rum Cake*
		Tomatoes (do not bake)

ANTIPASTO

To build an antipasto, cover a large platter with leaf lettuce. Mound Ricotta Salad in the center, place Olive Salad (which may be purchased in an Italian grocery) on one side, and Pepperoni Salad on the other side. Surround the platter with the Melon and Prosciutto, sliced meats, Cheese Wedges and Artichoke Salad. Serve with oil and vinegar and Garlic Fingers.

Ricotta Salad:

1 pound ricotta cheese	¼ teaspoon salt
2 tablespoons finely chopped scallions	⅛ teaspoon white pepper
	¼ teaspoon dried oregano
1 tablespoon freshly grated Parmesan cheese	leaves
	1 egg yolk

Combine ingredients and refrigerate.

Pepperoni Salad:

½ pound thinly sliced pepperoni	1 medium red onion, thinly sliced
1 large tomato, cut into small wedges	¼ cup Italian salad dressing

Toss ingredients lightly and refrigerate.

Olive Salad:

1 pound green Sicilian olives	½ cup olive oil
3 ribs of celery, diced	½ teaspoon freshly ground pepper
½ cup drained capers	1 small carrot, thinly sliced
1 clove garlic, sliced	¼ teaspoon fennel seed
1 small onion, sliced	1 tablespoon red wine vinegar
1 large pepperoncini pepper cut in pieces	

Pound olives with cleaver or hammer until broken, but leaving pits intact. Place in large bowl, add celery, capers, garlic, onion, pepperoncini, olive oil, pepper, carrot, fennel and vinegar. Mix well and let stand in a cool place for 24 hours. Refrigerate. This keeps for weeks in the refrigerator.

Melon and Prosciutto:

1 small honeydew cut into wedges	¼ pound prosciutto, thinly sliced

Wrap small wedges of melon with ham slices.

Assorted Meats:

| ¼ pound sliced capacollo | ¼ pound sliced Italian salami |

Fold meats in half.

Cheeses:

| ¼ pound Provolone | ¼ pound Gorgonzola |

Cut cheeses into small wedges.

Artichoke Salad:

| 1 14-ounce can artichoke hearts, drained | 1 2-ounce can flat anchovies |
| 1 4-ounce jar whole pimientos | Italian salad dressing |

Place half an artichoke heart on a slice of pimiento, criss-cross 2 anchovies over the top. Drizzle with Italian salad dressing.

GARLIC FINGERS

| 1 loaf Italian bread | 1 large clove garlic, minced or ¼ |
| ¼ pound melted butter | teaspoon garlic powder |

Slice bread lengthwise in half and then in half again. Cut into 4-inch fingers. Brush each finger with melted butter combined with garlic. Bake in a preheated 250° oven for 15 to 20 minutes.

CLASSIC VEAL ROAST

1 4-pound leg of veal, boned and rolled (frozen)	¼ cup butter, melted
Salt and pepper	½ teaspoon cornstarch
Flour	1 tablespoon water
¼ cup olive oil	½ small onion, grated
	1 tablespoon Madeira (optional)

Season frozen veal with salt and pepper and sprinkle on all sides with flour. Mix olive oil and butter and heat in roasting pan. Roll roast in oil-butter mixture. It will form a wax-like coating over meat. Place on a rack in a roasting pan and roast in preheated 475° oven for ½ hour. Reduce temperature to 375°; roast an additional 1¼ hours. Turn off oven; and let roast rest in oven one hour. Remove drippings from pan. Mix cornstarch and water. Heat with drippings to make gravy. Stir in onion and Madeira and serve with veal roast.

Note: This is the best method to cook any frozen roast. If roast is not frozen reduce time at 475° to 15 minutes, and at 375° to 1 hour.

GREEN NOODLES

1 16-ounce package green spinach noodles
½ cup butter, cut in small pieces
1 cup freshly grated Parmesan cheese

4 tablespoons unsweetened whipped cream

Cook noodles until just tender not soft, and toss with remaining ingredients. Serve at once.

BAKED TOMATOES

3 large firm-ripe tomatoes, halved, crosswise
½ cup butter
1 large garlic clove, crushed
1 teaspoon fresh or ½ teaspoon dried rosemary leaves (optional)

Salt
Freshly ground pepper
½ cup fine dry bread crumbs
½ cup chopped parsley

Arrange tomato halves in broiler pan to fit snugly. Melt butter and mix with all other ingredients. Top tomatoes with butter mixture, and bake in preheated 350° oven for 10 to 15 minutes, until topping is brown and tomatoes are heated through.

RUM CAKE

5 egg whites, at room temperature	Juice of 3 large oranges
1 cup sugar	¾ cup light rum
5 egg yolks, at room temperature	Few drops rum extract
1 cup sifted cake flour	6 tablespoons sugar
1¼ teaspoons baking powder	2 cups whipped cream
½ teaspoon salt	2 16-ounce cans Bing cherries, drained and juice reserved
1 teaspoon vanilla	2 16-ounce cans apricot halves, drained
2 teaspoons cornstarch	

Beat egg whites until stiff and gradually add ½ cup of the sugar. Beat yolks and the remaining ½ cup sugar until thick. Fold into egg whites. Stir in vanilla. Sift flour, baking powder and salt together. Fold into egg mixture. Pour into an ungreased 12-inch spring-form pan and bake in preheated 325° oven for 30 minutes. Cool. Prick cake all over with a fork, piercing it down to the bottom. Mix orange juice, rum, rum extract and the 6 tablespoons sugar; gradually pour mixture over cake until most of liquid is absorbed. Keep cake in pan several hours or overnight.

Remove cake from pan and decorate a few hours before serving: Cover cake with whipped cream. Thoroughly drain cherries and apricots, reserving cherry juice. Place 1 apricot half (cut side down) in center of cake and surround with a circle of Bing cherries. Alternate rings of cherries and apricots until cake is covered. Refrigerate while making glaze. Cook reserved cherry juice with 2 teaspoons cornstarch until clear and thickened. Cool glaze and pour over fruit and cake. Keep cake refrigerated until serving time.

Roast Capon Dinner

(SERVES 6)

Sweet-and-Tart Trout

Roast Capon

Celery Amandine   Eastern Zucchini

Blueberry Mold

Boston Cream Pie

Coffee

ADVANCE PREPARATION SCHEDULE

Previous Day	Early Morning
Sweet-and-Tart Trout	*Prepare capon for roasting*
Blueberry Mold	*Prepare celery for Celery Amandine*
	Prepare vegetables for Eastern Zucchini
	Boston Cream Pie

SWEET-AND-TART TROUT

3 apples, cored and quartered
2 large onions, sliced
3 to 4 pounds trout cleaned and cut into thick slices (reserve heads)
2½ cups water
½ cup firmly packed brown sugar (or to taste)
6 ginger snaps
1 teaspoon salt
Lemon juice to taste
2 small bay leaves
½ teaspoon allspice

In a large sauce pan, cook apples, onions and trout heads, with eyes removed, in water until apples are soft. Remove trout heads and mash apples. Add sliced fish and brown sugar. Take a small amount of juice from saucepan and add to ginger snaps; mash ginger snaps and add to saucepan. Add salt, lemon juice to taste, bay leaves and allspice. Simmer mixture for 1 hour, until fish is tender. Remove fish with spatula. Strain sauce and pour over fish. May be prepared and refrigerated up to a week in advance. May be used as luncheon dish.

ROAST CAPON

1 7-pound capon	½ teaspoon salt
5 slices white bread	½ teaspoon pepper
½ cup water	1 small onion, grated
½ cup finely chopped parsley	½ cup butter, softened
4 eggs, slightly beaten	1 teaspoon coarse salt

Loosen skin of capon by inserting hand under skin over breast meat and around thighs, carefully tearing connective tissue. Sprinkle bread with water; let soak 3 minutes. Squeeze out excess moisture; mix with parsley, eggs, ½ teaspoon salt, ¼ teaspoon of the pepper and grated onion. Preheat oven to 375°. Stuff dressing between meat and skin of capon, over breast and forcing it into leg pockets. Place capon, breast up, on a rack in a shallow roasting pan. Spread with soft butter and sprinkle with coarse salt and the remaining ¼ teaspoon pepper. Roast for 45 minutes, basting often with pan drippings. Reduce oven temperature to 350° and roast for 1 hour longer, basting every 20 minutes.

CELERY AMANDINE

4 cups diagonally sliced celery	½ teaspoon sugar
1 chicken bouillon cube, crumbled	⅛ teaspoon garlic powder
(or 1 teaspoon powdered	⅛ teaspoon ginger
chicken bouillon)	⅓ cup blanched almonds
1 tablespoon instant minced onion	2 tablespoons butter

Put celery in a large saucepan with a small amount of water. Simmer over low heat, stirring frequently until almost tender. Mix together bouillon cube, onion, sugar, garlic powder and ginger; toss with celery and continue cooking for 7 to 8 minutes, until crisptender. Sauté almonds in the butter until lightly toasted; add to celery mixture.

EASTERN ZUCCHINI

1½ pounds small zucchini, uniform in size
1 pint cherry tomatoes, halved
3 tablespoons butter
2 teaspoons fresh lemon juice

1 teaspoon salt
¼ teaspoon sugar
⅛ teaspoon freshly ground black
  pepper

Wash zucchini; do not peel. Cut crosswise into ½-inch-thick slices; place in a large skillet and add boiling water to cover. Cover and cook for about 10 minutes, until barely tender. Drain well. Return zucchini to skillet and add remaining ingredients. Toss gently to mix. Cover and simmer until tomatoes are just heated through, about 3 minutes.

BLUEBERRY MOLD

3 3-ounce packages lemon-flavored
  gelatin
2 cups hot water
1 pint sour cream, at room temperature

2 15-ounce cans blueberries,
  undrained

Mix gelatin, water and sour cream with a spoon or egg beater until gelatin is dissolved. Set aside until mixture is the consistency of unbeaten egg whites. Add blueberries and juice; pour into a 6-cup mold and chill until ready to serve. Unmold before serving.

BOSTON CREAM PIE

¼ cup shortening
¼ cup butter
1½ cups sugar
2 large eggs

2½ teaspoons baking powder
2¼ cups sifted all-purpose flour
½ teaspoon salt
1 cup milk

1 teaspoon vanilla

Cream shortening, butter and sugar and add eggs. Combine dry ingredients and add alternately with milk to creamed mixture; then add vanilla. Pour batter into a 10-inch pie pan and bake in a preheated 350° oven for 45 minutes. Cool and remove from pan. Split cake into 2 layers. Fill with Custard Filling and frost with Chocolate Icing.

Custard Filling:

1 tablespoon cornstarch	2 egg yolks, slightly beaten
¼ cup sugar	½ teaspoon vanilla
1 cup milk, scalded	

Mix cornstarch and sugar; add hot milk and gradually pour mixture over egg yolks. Cook in top of double boiler over hot water, stirring constantly, until thickened. Cool, and add vanilla.

Chocolate Icing:

½ cup heavy cream	8 ounces semi-sweet chocolate
2 tablespoons orange flavored	bits
liqueur	

Heat cream; add chocolate pieces, stirring constantly until chocolate is melted. Remove from heat and add orange-flavored liqueur. Let cool for 15 minutes, stirring occasionally; then frost top of cake.

Something-to-Celebrate Dinner

(SERVES 4)

Oysters in Crab-Sauce
Filet Mignon Concordia
Broccoli in Lemon-Butter Sauce   Straw Potatoes
Treasure Chest Salad
Sour Cream–Shrimp Dressing
Black-Bottom Ice Cream Pie
Coffee

Freezer

Black-Bottom Ice Cream Pie

Early Morning

Prepare Broccoli, ready to cook
Straw Potatoes
Prepare salad dressing (do not add
shrimp)

OYSTERS IN CRAB-SAUCE

¼ cup butter
¼ cup minced onions
3 tablespoons flour
1 pint oysters, drained with
   liquor reserved
1 cup half-and-half (about)
1 cup flaked crabmeat
2 teaspoons Worcestershire sauce
¼ cup sherry wine

Generous dash Cayenne pepper
½ teaspoon salt
¼ teaspoon pepper
¼ teaspoon paprika
2 tablespoons minced parsley
8 toast points
¼ cup finely grated Parmesan
   cheese
¼ cup fine dry bread crumbs

In a 10-inch frying pan, sauté onions in butter until limp. Stir in flour and cook until bubbly. Measure oyster liquor, add enough half-and-half to measure 2 cups liquid. Add liquids to pan, stirring until thickened. Add oysters and cook over low heat until edges curl. Add crab, seasonings and parsley; heat thoroughly. Pour over toast points; sprinkle with cheese and bread crumbs and serve immediately.

FILET MIGNON CONCORDIA

½ pound fresh mushrooms, sliced
3 tablespoons butter
1 tablespoon each brandy,
   Madeira and dry sherry
             4 8-ounce filets mignons

1 teaspoon flour
¼ cup sweet butter
1 tablespoon French mustard
Salt

Sauté mushrooms in the 3 tablespoons butter for 5 minutes. Warm brandy and wines. Ignite and let flames die down. Add to mushrooms, sprinkle flour over mushrooms; stir in sweet butter until melted, then add mustard. Continue to stir until sauce thickens slightly. Keep warm over very low heat. Heat a cast iron skillet until very hot and sprinkle it lightly with salt. Panbroil filets for 4 minutes on one side and 3 minutes on the other, for medium rare. Spoon mushroom-mustard mixture over filets and serve on hot plates.

BROCCOLI IN LEMON-BUTTER SAUCE

1 large bunch fresh broccoli	½ cup butter melted

Juice of 1 lemon (medium sized)

Wash broccoli in cold water. Remove large leaves and cut off about 1½″ of the fibrous portion of the stems. It is not necessary to remove base from thin, tender stalks. Cut larger stalks into uniform pieces. Place in a saucepan with 1½″ boiling water. Cover and steam 10 to 12 minutes until crisp-tender. Drain, place in serving dish and pour melted butter and lemon juice over broccoli. Serve at once.

STRAW POTATOES

Peel, rinse and dry 1½ pounds potatoes. Slice potatoes very thin; stack slices and slice again into thinner-than-matchstick strips. As potatoes are cut, drop them into a bowl of cold water. After soaking, to remove starch, drain and dry potatoes. Heat 3 inches of shortening or oil in a deep saucepan to a temperature of about 370° on a deep-fat-frying thermometer. Add potatoes by handfuls and cook until golden brown. When done, remove with a slotted spoon and drain on paper towel. Spread potatoes on a cookie sheet. At this point, they may be set aside or frozen. Just before serving, bake potatoes on cookie sheet in preheated 300° oven until hot and crisp.

TREASURE CHEST SALAD

1 pint cherry tomatoes	1 14½-ounce can white
1 6-ounce jar marinated artichoke	asparagus, drained
hearts, drained	1 avocado, sliced thin

Roquefort cheese, crumbled, for garnish

Decoratively arrange salad ingredients in salad bowl or on individual plates. Pour Sour Cream–Shrimp Dressing over salad; toss and garnish with Roquefort cheese.

SOUR CREAM–SHRIMP DRESSING

1 8-ounce package cream cheese, softened
2 scallions, finely chopped
½ cup sour cream
¼ teaspoon garlic salt
¾ teaspoon salt
2 tablespoons lemon juice
¼ cup Sauterne
1 5-ounce can shrimp, drained

Prepare dressing by combining all ingredients, except shrimp. Just before serving, add shrimp. (Shrimp may be omitted, if desired).

BLACK-BOTTOM ICE CREAM PIE

1½ cups cream-filled chocolate cookie crumbs
¼ cup butter, melted
1 quart coffee ice cream
1 11½-ounce can fudge sauce, refrigerated
Whipped cream and pecan halves to garnish

Crush cookies with rolling pin or in blender to make crumbs. Combine with butter. Press firmly onto bottom and sides of a 9-inch pie pan. Freeze or refrigerate crust several hours, until firm. Fill shell with softened coffee ice cream and return to freezer. When frozen, spread ice cream layer with refrigerated fudge sauce; freeze until fudge has set, and cover pie with whipped cream. Garnish with pecan halves. Pie may be made several days in advance and removed from freezer 30 minutes before serving.

Family Dinners

A GATHERING OF THE CLAN, Family Dinners, can easily fall into dull or trite patterns. However, with a little imagination the main meal of the day can be both interesting and delicious. By careful planning, boring and repetitive meals can be avoided.

December Dinner

(SERVES 6)

Mushroom-Barley Soup
Brisket of Beef
Potatoes   Carrots
Mixed Green Salad
Apple Cake
Coffee

105

ADVANCE PREPARATION SCHEDULE

Freezer	Previous Day	Early Morning
Mushroom-Barley Soup	*Brisket of Beef*	*Prepare greens for salad* *Apple Cake*

MUSHROOM-BARLEY SOUP

2 quarts water
2 carrots, peeled and diced
3 celery stalks, diced
½ cup medium barley
½ teaspoon salt
¼ teaspoon pepper

1 8-ounce package onion soup mix
Soup bones
2 pounds lean beef, cubed
2 1-ounce packages of dried mushrooms

Wash mushrooms, cover with water and soak 1 hour, drain. Combine all ingredients in a large kettle. Simmer, covered, for at least two hours. Remove soup bones before serving. Freeze, if desired, and reheat to serve.

BRISKET OF BEEF

2 large onions, sliced
1 5-pound fresh brisket of beef
½ cup chili sauce
1 teaspoon caraway seed
¼ cup flour mixed with 2 teaspoons seasoned salt

1½ cups water
3 carrots, peeled and thickly sliced
18 small potatoes, peeled and halved

Place meat over onions in roasting pan. Spread chili sauce over meat and sprinkle with caraway seed and flour mixture. Add water in bottom of pan. Cook covered in preheated 350° oven until tender, approximately 30 minutes per pound. Uncover for last half hour to brown. Water may be added while cooking for more gravy. When meat is tender, remove from gravy and cool. Add carrots and potatoes to gravy in pan and cook until tender. Slice meat thinly and return to pan with carrots, potatoes and gravy. Heat and serve.

APPLE CAKE

4 large eggs
1¾ cups sugar
1 cup vegetable oil
2 cups sifted all-purpose flour
1 teaspoon baking soda
1 teaspoon cinnamon

1 teaspoon salt
3 cups peeled, cored and thinly
   sliced tart apples
1 cup chopped nuts
Confectioners' sugar
Ice cream or whipped cream

Beat eggs and sugar well. Add oil; continue beating until thoroughly blended. Sift flour, soda, cinnamon and salt together; stir into egg mixture. Fold in apples and nuts. Spread in a greased 9" x 13" pan. Bake in a preheated 350° oven for 45 to 60 minutes. Top with confectioners' sugar and serve with ice cream or whipped cream.

Sweet-and-Simple Dinner

(SERVES 8)

Party Herring
Sweet-and-Sour Stuffed Cabbage
Hearty Rye Bread   Applesauce-in-a-Wink
Noodle Fruitcake
Coffee

ADVANCE PREPARATION SCHEDULE

Freezer	Previous Day	Early Morning
Sweet-and-Sour *Stuffed Cabbage* *Hearty Rye Bread*	*Applesauce-in-a-Wink* *Noodle Fruitcake* *(do not bake)*	*Party Herring* *Remove stuffed cabbage* *from freezer*

PARTY HERRING

2 5½-ounce cans Matjes Herring, drained (reserve liquid), and cut into 1-inch pieces
1 bunch radishes, sliced
1 large green pepper, chopped
1 pint cherry tomatoes, halved
1 large red onion, sliced
2 to 3 scallions, chopped
¼ cup vinegar
¼ cup herring liquid

Combine all ingredients in a bowl. Cover and refrigerate several hours. Serve chilled.

SWEET-AND-SOUR STUFFED CABBAGE

1 large head cabbage
2 pounds ground beef, seasoned with salt and pepper
3 tablespoons catsup
3 eggs
¼ cup quick-cooking rolled oats, softened with 4 teaspoons water
2 onions, coarsely chopped
2 apples, coarsely chopped
Juice of 2 lemons
3 tablespoons catsup
6 gingersnaps
3 lemons, sliced
½ cup firmly packed brown sugar
3 bay leaves
Pinch of allspice

Trim cabbage; remove core. Place in boiling water and simmer gently about 10 minutes until leaves separate easily; remove from water and cool. Separate and reserve larger leaves. Shred enough of the inner leaves to make ½ cup. Combine seasoned ground beef, the 3 tablespoons catsup, eggs and rolled oats; set aside. In a saucepan, combine onions, apples, the ½ cup shredded cabbage, lemon juice and the remaining 3 tablespoons catsup; bring to a boil and pour into a 9″ x 13″ pan. Place 1 heaping tablespoon ground beef mixture on each leaf; tuck ends in and roll up. Place stuffed cabbage rolls in pan over apple-onion mixture. Cover with foil and bake in a preheated 325° oven for 30 minutes. Remove pan from oven. Soften gingersnaps in a little of the sauce from the pan. Combine gingersnaps with sliced lemons, brown sugar, bay leaves and allspice; add to sauce. Bake for 30 minutes longer, basting cabbage rolls often with the sauce. Can be prepared in advance, frozen and reheated. Makes 16 rolls.

HEARTY RYE BREAD

2 packages active dry yeast	1 tablespoon salt
¾ cup warm water	2 tablespoons caraway seeds
1 tablespoon sugar	1½ cups sour milk or buttermilk
1 cup sifted all-purpose flour	1 cup whole wheat flour
3 to 3½ cups rye flour	

In a large bowl dissolve yeast in warm water; add sugar; gradually stir in all-purpose flour, and mix well. Cover and let rise in a warm place (85°) for 20 minutes, until quite spongy. Add remaining ingredients, reserving 1 cup of the rye flour. Blend with mixer or a wooden spoon. Sprinkle some of reserved 1 cup rye flour on a wooden board and knead dough for about 8 minutes, until smooth and elastic, adding enough additional flour to board to prevent dough from sticking. Place dough in a greased bowl, turning dough over to grease top. Cover with a towel and let rise in a warm place (85°) until double in size, about 90 minutes. Punch dough down; return to floured board and cut in half. Shape each half into a round loaf and place each loaf in a greased pie plate. Cover and let rise in a warm place until doubled, about 45 minutes. Brush tops of loaves with cold water and bake in a preheated 400° oven for 10 minutes. Reduce temperature to 350° and bake for 45 minutes longer.

APPLESAUCE-IN-A-WINK

1 16-ounce jar applesauce	½ teaspoon cinnamon
Juice of 1 large lemon, or to taste	Dash of nutmeg

Mix all ingredients well and chill until ready to serve.

NOODLE FRUITCAKE

Brown sugar
1 1-pound can pineapple slices, drained and cut in half
Red and green cherries (optional)
1 16-ounce package medium noodles, cooked, drained and rinsed well with cool water
¼ cup butter, melted
1 16-ounce container large curd cottage cheese

1 pint sour cream
Cinnamon and suger to taste
1½ cups pre-sweetened corn flakes, crushed
3 eggs, beaten well
1 tablespoon vanilla
¼ cup apricot preserves
1 16-ounce can crushed pineapple, well drained

Pack a ⅛-inch thick layer of brown sugar into bottom of a well-greased 9- or 10-inch spring form pan. Lay halved pineapple rings on top of brown sugar in spring form, placing one inside the other to form attractive pattern. Combine noodles and the remaining ingredients; blend well. Carefully spoon noodle mixture over pineapple slices. Bake in a preheated 375° oven for 1 hour until golden brown. Cool in pan for 10 minutes, unmold and serve. If prepared day before, cover and refrigerate until ready to bake.

Sunday Dinner

(SERVES 6)

Creamy Italian Dip   Raw Vegetables
Corned Beef with Tangy Sauce
Carrots, Potatoes, Cabbage
Caraway Crescent Rolls (see Index)
Glazed Grapefruit
Pecan-Dream Bars
Coffee

Freezer

*Caraway Crescent
Rolls (see Index)*

Previous Day

Pecan-Dream Bars

Early Morning

*Creamy Italian Dip
Prepare and refrigerate
raw vegetables
Boil corned beef (do not
bake)
Glazed Grapefruit*

CREAMY ITALIAN DIP

2 16-ounce containers small-curd
cottage cheese

1 package Italian salad dressing
mix

Place cheese and salad dressing mix in the container of an electric blender and blend at high speed until thoroughly mixed and smooth. Cover and chill. Serve with assorted raw vegetables for dipping.

CORNED BEEF WITH TANGY SAUCE

6 pounds corned beef, rolled and
tied
Several peppercorns
1 clove garlic
4 to 5 bay leaves
12 whole cloves
⅓ cup catsup

1 tablespoon prepared mustard
⅓ cup firmly packed brown sugar
3 tablespoons vinegar
3 tablespoons water
4 carrots, peeled and quartered
4 potatoes, peeled and quartered
1 large head cabbage, quartered

Put corned beef in a large kettle and cover with water. Drop in peppercorns, garlic and bay leaves and bring water to a boil. Reduce heat and simmer gently until meat is tender when pierced with a fork. Allow about 30 minutes per pound. Reserve cooking liquid. Transfer beef to a shallow baking pan and stud fat side with cloves. Mix catsup, mustard, brown sugar, vinegar and water and pour over meat. Bake in preheated 350° oven with fat side up for 1 hour, basting occasionally. Thirty minutes before meat is done, put carrots, cabbage and potatoes in the kettle with reserved cooking liquid from beef. Cook for 15 minutes until tender. Place beef on a large platter and surround with the vegetables.

GLAZED GRAPEFRUIT

4 whole grapefruit   ½ cup grape jelly

Peel grapefruit, divide into segments and remove membranes. Melt jelly in a saucepan, stirring until smooth and slightly bubbling. Pour jelly over grapefruit segments and refrigerate. During the day, stir fruit occasionally. Serve segments with their juice.

PECAN-DREAM BARS

Crust:

½ cup firmly packed light brown sugar

½ cup butter, softened
1 cup sifted all-purpose flour

Topping:

2 eggs
1½ cups firmly packed light brown sugar
2 tablespoons flour

½ teaspoon salt
½ teaspoon baking soda
1 teaspoon vanilla
1 cup chopped pecans

Combine crust ingredients until crumbly. Pat crumbs firmly into bottom of a greased 10″ x 10″ pan. Bake in preheated 350° oven for 15 minutes. Cool while preparing topping. Beat eggs well, mix in remaining ingredients. Pour mixture over cooled crust and bake in a 350° oven for 20 minutes. Cool and cut into bars.

All American Dinner

(SERVES 8)

Old-Fashioned Vegetable Soup
Oven-Fried Chicken   Country Baked Potatoes
Tomato Aspic
Chocolate-Bar Bundt Cake   Brandy Sauce
Coffee

OLD-FASHIONED VEGETABLE SOUP

1½ quarts water
2 pounds lean beef short ribs
3 center marrow bones (no knuckle bones)
½ cup dried lima beans
3 teaspoons salt
3 tablespoons medium barley
1 cup diced vegetables (such

as carrots or celery, do not use turnips or cabbage)
1 whole onion
1 whole green pepper (optional)
Pepper to taste
1 20-ounce can tomatoes (2½ cups)

Bring water to boil in a large kettle and add meat, bones, beans, salt and barley. Cook, covered, over low heat for about 2 hours, until beans are tender. Add cut up vegetables, onion, green pepper and pepper; cook over low heat for 1 hour longer. Add tomatoes and simmer soup until meat is very tender. Remove onion and green pepper and bones.

Note: It is best to make soup the day before; cool and refrigerate. The next day skim fat from top and reheat before serving. Soup may be frozen.

OVEN-FRIED CHICKEN

4 2½- to 3-pound chickens, cut up
Pepper
Paprika
½ teaspoon garlic powder

1 cup butter, melted
4 cups crushed corn flakes
4 cups very finely crumbled potato chips

Season each piece of chicken with pepper and paprika and roll each piece in melted butter. Combine corn flakes, potato chips and garlic powder. Roll pieces in crumb mixture, coating them thickly. Lay chicken in shallow roasting pan, skin side up. Bake in preheated 375°

oven for 90 minutes, without turning chicken. Serve with Country Baked Potatoes.

COUNTRY BAKED POTATOES

8 washed, unpeeled baking potatoes, cut into ¼-inch thick rounds

¼ cup grated or finely chopped onion

¼ cup butter

Salt and pepper

Place potato rounds on a cookie sheet. On each potato round, place a pinch of grated onion, a dot of butter and a dash each of salt and pepper. Bake in a preheated 425° oven for 20 minutes. Then place in preheated broiler, about 4 inches from heat, and broil for 8 to 10 minutes, until crisp and curled at the edges. Serve hot.

Note: Rounds may be baked earlier in day and broiled just before serving.

TOMATO ASPIC

4 cups tomato juice

2 3-ounce packages lemon-flavored gelatin

1 small onion, grated

⅛ teaspoon ground cloves

¼ teaspoon pepper

¼ teaspoon salt

¼ teaspoon paprika

⅔ cup vinegar

Parsley sprigs

Cherry tomatoes

Heat tomato juice and dissolve gelatin in hot tomato juice. Add onion, cloves, pepper, salt, paprika and vinegar; pour into 6-cup ring mold. Refrigerate until firm. Unmold and garnish with parsley and cherry tomatoes.

CHOCOLATE-BAR BUNDT CAKE

1 cup butter, softened

2 cups sugar

4 eggs

1 5½-ounce can chocolate syrup

1 teaspoon vanilla

½ teaspoon baking soda

1 cup buttermilk

2½ cups sifted cake flour

4 1½-ounce chocolate bars, melted

Confectioners' sugar

Cream butter and sugar. Add eggs, one at a time beating well after each addition. Beat in chocolate syrup and vanilla. Add baking soda to buttermilk; alternately add flour and buttermilk to butter-chocolate mixture. Stir melted chocolate bars into batter, combining all ingredients thoroughly. Pour into well-greased and floured 9-inch Bundt pan. Bake in a preheated 325° oven for 1 hour. Cool about 5 minutes before removing from pan. Sprinkle with confectioners' sugar. If desired, cake may be served warm with Brandy Sauce.

BRANDY SAUCE

1 egg yolk	3 tablespoons brandy
1 cup sugar	1 cup heavy cream, whipped

Combine yolk, sugar and brandy; beat well and fold into whipped cream. Serve with Chocolate-Bar Bundt Cake.

Accent on Lamb Dinner

(SERVES 6)

Mushroom Spread
Orange-Raisin Lamb Roll
Spinach Pie
Broccoli-Tomato Salad
Blueberry-Nut Meringue
Greek Coffee (see Index)

Previous Day   **Early Morning**

Mushroom Spread   *Bake crust for Spinach Pie*
Blueberry-Nut Meringue,   *Prepare Broccoli-Tomato Salad,*
(without topping)   *   omitting tomatoes*
                                    Bone, butterfly, flatten and season
                                    *   leg of lamb*
                                    Put topping on Blueberry-Nut
                                    *   Meringue*

MUSHROOM SPREAD

½ medium onion, minced   1 tablespoon lemon juice
1 tablespoon butter   ½ teaspoon Worcestershire sauce
½ pound fresh mushrooms, finely   Mayonnaise
    chopped   Salt and pepper
                    Chopped parsley

In a skillet, sauté onion in butter until golden. Add mushrooms and continue to sauté for 5 minutes, stirring lightly to mix. Add lemon juice and Worcestershire; mix ingredients and remove from heat. When cool, add enough mayonnaise to bind ingredients; add salt and pepper to taste. Mound mixture on a serving platter and garnish with parsley. Chill thoroughly and serve with Melba toast or crackers. Keeps well in refrigerator.

ORANGE-RAISIN LAMB ROLL

⅔ cup chopped onion   1 egg, beaten
⅔ cup chopped celery   1 6-pound leg of lamb, boned,
3 tablespoons butter   butterflied, flattened with a mal-
10 slices cinnamon-raisin bread,   let, and seasoned with salt and
    cut into cubes   pepper
2 tablespoons grated orange peel   Orange-Mint Sauce

In a skillet, sauté onion and celery in butter until soft. Toss with bread cubes, orange peel and egg. Spread mixture over lamb and roll up, jelly-roll style, securing lamb with string. Place on a rack in a shallow roasting pan. Roast in a preheated 350° oven for approximately 1½ hours, or 20 minutes per pound, for medium rare. Transfer lamb to hot platter and keep warm. Prepare Orange-Mint Sauce in pan with lamb drippings. Slice lamb and spoon sauce over slices or serve it on the side.

Orange-Mint Sauce:

1¾ cups orange juice
¼ cup firmly packed brown sugar
¼ cup melted butter
1 tablespoon cornstarch, dissolved in 2 tablespoons water
1 tablespoon dried mint flakes, crushed

1 tablespoon grated orange peel
1½ teaspoons ground ginger
¼ teaspoon ground cloves
2 teaspoons salt
2 oranges, peeled and sectioned

Combine all ingredients, except orange sections. Pour mixture into pan with lamb drippings. Cook and stir over medium heat until thickened. Add orange sections and beat.

SPINACH PIE

6 frozen patty shells
6 eggs, beaten
1 3-ounce package cream cheese, softened
¼ pound sharp cheese, grated
1 9-ounce package frozen chopped spinach, defrosted and well drained

2 tablespoons chopped scallion tops
1 tablespoon chopped parsley
2 tablespoons grated Parmesan cheese

Defrost patty shells and roll them together to form a pie crust. Put dough in a 9-inch pie plate, prick entire surface, and bake in a preheated 425° oven until lightly browned. Reduce oven temperature to 325°. Combine eggs, cream cheese and sharp cheese, mixing all ingredients thoroughly. Add spinach, scallions, parsley and Parmesan cheese. Pour filling into lightly baked pie crust and bake for 15 minutes at 325°. Pie is done when spinach-custard is well set.

BROCCOLI-TOMATO SALAD

1 small bunch uncooked broccoli ½ cup bottled Italian dressing
1 pint cherry tomatoes, halved Salt and pepper

Cut broccoli in 1-inch pieces from stems through flowerettes, discarding only the tough base. Toss uncooked broccoli and tomatoes with Italian dressing. Season with salt and pepper to taste and serve. Salad may be prepared, omitting tomatoes, several hours before serving. Toss in halved tomatoes no more than 1 hour before serving time to prevent wilting.

BLUEBERRY-NUT MERINGUE

6 eggs whites, at room
  temperature
2 cups sugar
2 teaspoons baking powder
24 single saltines or soda crackers,
  crushed

1½ cups walnuts or pecans,
  crushed
2 teaspoons vanilla
2 teaspoons vinegar
1 21-ounce can blueberry pie
  filling
Whipped cream for decoration

Beat egg whites until soft peaks form; gradually add sugar and baking powder, beating until stiff peaks form. Combine crackers and nuts and fold into beaten egg white mixture. Add vanilla and vinegar and pour into greased 9-inch spring form pan. Bake in a preheated 350° oven for 35 minutes. Cool; leave cake in spring form; cover and refrigerate. Early in day that cake is to be served, cover top with pie filling. Before serving remove rim of pan and decorate cake with whipped cream.

Cornish Hen Dinner

(SERVES 4)

Carrot Vichyssoise
Rock Cornish Hen with Wild Rice
English Baked Asparagus
Herbed Tomatoes
Easy Chocolate Cream
Coffee   Tea

ADVANCE PREPARATION SCHEDULE

Freezer	**Previous Day**	**Early Morning**
Easy Chocolate Cream	*Carrot Vichyssoise*	*Defrost Cornish Hens* *Herbed Tomatoes*

CARROT VICHYSSOISE

2 tablespoons butter	½ teaspoon salt
2 bunches scallions, sliced	⅛ teaspoon pepper
2 cups seasoned chicken broth	½ cup heavy cream
2 cups cooked carrots	1 tablespoon snipped chives

Melt butter in saucepan; add scallions and cook about 5 minutes.
Add 1 cup of the broth, bring to a boil; cover and simmer over low
heat 15 minutes longer. Pour scallions and broth into the container
of an electric blender. Add remaining 1 cup broth, carrots, salt and
pepper; cover and blend until smooth. Stir in cream and chill thoroughly. Serve topped with chives. May also be served hot.

ROCK CORNISH HEN WITH WILD RICE

2 1½-pound frozen rock cornish hens, defrosted
Fresh lemon juice
Salt and pepper to taste

1 6-ounce package long-grain and wild-rice mix
4 tablespoons melted butter
Dry white wine

Split hens into halves. Sprinkle with lemon juice, salt and pepper and rub seasoning into hens. Place hens in well-buttered, shallow baking dish, breast sides up; bake in a preheated 450° oven for 15 minutes. Cook rice mix as directed on the package but for only 15 minutes. Remove hens from oven and reduce temperature to 350°. Turn hens over and spoon partially cooked rice into cavities. Spoon 1 tablespoon butter over each and sprinkle generously with white wine. Bake for 30 minutes longer, or until hens are tender.

ENGLISH BAKED ASPARAGUS

1½ pounds fresh asparagus, washed, drained and trimmed of tough ends
¼ cup melted butter or olive oil

1 tablespoon chopped fresh parsley or mint
Freshly ground black pepper
Salt

Preheat oven to 400°. Arrange asparagus spears close together in a 9″ x 13″ pan. Top with butter, parsley, pepper and salt. Cover pan with foil and bake 15 to 20 minutes, until asparagus is tender but still firm to the bite.

HERBED TOMATOES

3 to 4 tomatoes, peeled and cut into ½-inch slices
1 small onion, thinly sliced
Parsley sprigs
⅓ cup vegetable oil

3 tablespoons vinegar
½ clove garlic, minced
⅛ teaspoon each of basil, thyme and marjoram
½ teaspoon salt

Fresh ground pepper

In a shallow dish, layer tomato slices, onion and parsley sprigs. Mix remaining ingredients and pour over tomatoes. Cover and refrigerate for several hours; occasionally spoon dressing over tomatoes.

EASY CHOCOLATE CREAM

1 pint heavy cream   1 16-ounce can chocolate syrup
3 tablespoons Grand Marnier

Whip cream, add chocolate syrup and Grand Marnier. Pour into a 1½-quart mold and freeze until firm. Before serving, allow to stand at room temperature for ½ hour.

Sauerbraten Dinner

(SERVES 8)

Lentil Soup
Pumpernickel Slices
Sauerbraten
Blender Potato Pancakes
Applesauce
Parsley-Buttered Carrots
Raspberry Chiffon Pie
Coffee

ADVANCE PREPARATION SCHEDULE

Freezer	Previous Day	Early Morning
Lentil Soup	*Sauerbraten must be*	*Finish Sauerbraten*
Potato Pancakes	*started 3 to 4 days*	*Raspberry Chiffon Pie*
	in advance	*Remove Lentil Soup*
	Applesauce	*from freezer*

LENTIL SOUP

1 16-ounce package of lentils
2 quarts water
Meaty hambone from leftover ham,
   or ham hock
2 large carrots
4 or 5 celery stalks, without tops

2 bay leaves
1 onion
2 or 3 whole cloves
2 small cans skinless all-meat
   cocktail frankfurters (if mild
   ones are used, add salt to taste)

Soak lentils in water, in a large pot, 6 to 8 hours or overnight. Add ham bone, carrots, celery, bay leaves and onion stuck with cloves, bring to boil, cover tightly and reduce heat. Cook about 2 hours, stirring occasionally. Remove ham bone and dice meat. Dice carrots and onion and celery, if desired. Remove bay leaves and cloves. Allow to cool and refrigerate tightly covered. Reheat before serving and add frankfurters. If thinner consistency is desired, thin soup with water.

SAUERBRATEN

1 onion, sliced
3 bay leaves
1 teaspoon whole black peppercorns
4 pounds beef (chuck, rump or
   round)
2 teaspoons salt

2 cups water
2 cups cider vinegar
1 cup sugar
¼ cup firmly packed brown sugar
4 to 6 gingersnaps, crushed
¼ cup seedless raisins
Flour

Place onion, bay leaves and whole peppercorns on bottom of Dutch oven or crock. Sprinkle meat with salt and place on top of onions. Heat water and vinegar and add sugar; stir to dissolve. Let cool and pour over meat. Place in refrigerator and let meat stand in brine for 3 to 4 days, turning meat each day. Remove meat and reserve marinade. Pat meat dry on paper towels. Place meat in a deep pot, add onions and enough marinade to cover meat. Simmer slowly for 2½ to 3 hours, adding marinade as necessary. Liquid should cover the meat, and if it is not enough, add water. Add brown sugar to sweeten. During last hour of cooking, add gingersnaps and raisins. When ready to serve, thicken liquid, as desired, with a little flour mixed with a little water.

BLENDER POTATO PANCAKES

2 eggs	¼ teaspoon baking powder
½ small onion	2 tablespoons flour
1¼ teaspoons salt	3 cups cubed peeled raw potato
Dash of pepper	Corn oil for frying

Put first 6 ingredients plus ½ cup of the potato cubes in the container of an electric blender. Blend at "chop" until potatoes have gone through the blades. Add remaining potatoes and blend at "chop" only until the last potato cube has gone through blades. (If blended too long, pancakes will not have the right texture). In a large skillet heat corn oil. Drop batter by spoonfuls into skillet. Cook until golden brown. Turn to brown on both sides; remove from frying pan and drain on paper toweling. Serve at once or keep warm in 200° oven. This recipe makes 15 thin, crisp pancakes. If necessary to double recipe make each batch of 3 cups of potato separately. If pancakes have been frozen: place, frozen, on cookie sheet and heat in 375° oven until hot.

APPLESAUCE

8 medium tart cooking apples	1 teaspoon ground cinnamon
1 cup water	¼ teaspoon salt
2 tablespoons flour	½ cup sour cream
1½ cups sugar	

Wash, peel and core apples and cut into chunks. Place in saucepan with water to barely cover. Cook until soft. Mix flour and sugar and add to apples. Cook until it thickens, stirring constantly. Stir in the rest of the ingredients. Chill.

RASPBERRY CHIFFON PIE

1 baked 9-inch pastry shell	¼ cup lemon juice
1 envelope unflavored gelatine	½ teaspoon salt
¼ cup cold water	1 16-ounce can raspberries,
4 eggs, separated	drained
¾ cup sugar	1 cup heavy cream, whipped

Prepare, bake and cool pastry shell. Soften gelatine in cold water.

Beat egg yolks slightly and mix with ½ cup of the sugar, lemon juice, salt and raspberries in top of double boiler. Cook over hot water, stirring, until thickened. Add gelatine and stir until dissolved. Cool until the consistency of unbeaten egg whites. Beat egg whites until soft peaks form and gradually beat in the remaining ¼ cup of sugar. Continue beating until stiff but not dry. Fold into first mixture. Turn into pastry shell and chill for several hours. Before serving, garnish with whipped cream.

Baked Turbot Dinner

(SERVES 6)

Tomato Cream Soup
Cheese Snacks (see Index)
Oven Baked Turbot
Zucchini   Noodle Pudding
Radish-Cheese Salad
Applesauce-Soufflé Cake
Coffee

ADVANCE PREPARATION SCHEDULE

Freezer	Previous Day	Early Morning
Tomato Soup (without sugar and cream)	*Cheese Snacks* *Radish-Cheese Salad* *dressing*	*Turbot (up to point of baking)* *Sauce for Zucchini* *Noodle Pudding* *Prepare radishes and cheeses for Salad* *Applesauce-Soufflé Cake* *Remove Tomato Soup from freezer*

TOMATO CREAM SOUP

½ cup butter	3 tablespoons tomato paste
2 tablespoons olive oil	1 35-ounce can Italian tomatoes
2 cups thinly sliced onions	¼ cup flour
½ teaspoon dried thyme leaves	3¾ cups chicken broth
Salt and pepper to taste	1 teaspoon sugar
1 cup heavy cream	

Heat butter and oil. Add onions and seasonings, and cook until onions are wilted. Add tomato paste and tomatoes; simmer 10 minutes. Place flour in a small bowl; add 6 tablespoons chicken broth, and blend. Stir into tomato mixture. Add remaining broth and simmer for 30 minutes, stirring frequently. Put mixture through a sieve or food mill. Return to heat; add sugar and cream and simmer for 5 minutes.

OVEN BAKED TURBOT

3 pounds turbot fillets	3 tablespoons mayonnaise
¾ cup dry white vermouth	½ teaspoon onion salt
¾ teaspoon lemon pepper	¼ cup sour cream

Marinate fish in vermouth and lemon pepper for 1 hour or longer. Drain; spread mayonnaise on both sides of fillets. Place in a large shallow roasting pan; sprinkle with onion salt and spread sour cream over top. Bake in a preheated 400° oven for 25 minutes.

ZUCCHINI

3 large zucchini	1 teaspoon grated lemon peel
2 tablespoons fresh lemon juice	2 teaspoons grated onion
¼ cup melted butter	

To cook zucchini, wash but do not peel. Remove stem and blossom ends and cut into slices or cubes. Place in about 1 inch of boiling water in saucepan, adding salt to taste. Cook covered for 8 to 10 minutes, or until tender but still crisp. Drain. Add lemon juice, lemon peel and onion to melted butter. Pour over zucchini and serve.

NOODLE PUDDING

8 oz. medium noodles	1 cup sour cream (½ pint)
1 tablespoon butter	½ cup raisins
3 eggs, separated	Orange Marmalade
½ cup melted butter	Butter
1 16-ounce container cream-style cottage cheese	

Cook noodles as directed on package; drain, add the 1 tablespoon butter. Beat egg yolks, add the ½ cup of melted butter and fold in the cottage cheese, sour cream and noodles. Beat egg whites until stiff, but not dry, and fold into the noodle mixture. Stir in raisins. Place in a buttered, deep, round 2-quart casserole and bake in a preheated 350° oven, for 45 minutes until set. Spread a thin layer of orange marmalade on top and return to oven for 5 to 10 minutes until glazed.

RADISH-CHEESE SALAD

5 cups sliced radishes	1 cup finely cubed Swiss cheese

Dressing:

2 tablespoons tarragon vinegar	1 small clove garlic, minced
6 tablespoons olive oil	2 tablespoons minced scallions
1 teaspoon Dijon mustard	Salt
1 teaspoon anchovy paste	Freshly ground black pepper

Place radishes in a salad bowl; sprinkle with cheese, set aside. Combine dressing ingredients, mixing until thick and creamy. Pour over radishes and mix well. Add salt and pepper to taste.

APPLESAUCE-SOUFFLE CAKE

4 egg yolks, beaten	2 cups well drained applesauce
Juice of 1 lemon	4 egg whites, beaten stiffly
Grated peel of 1 lemon	Graham Cracker Crust
1 15-ounce can sweetened condensed milk	

Combine egg yolks with lemon juice, peel, condensed milk and applesauce. Mix well. Finally, add beaten egg whites. Pour apple-

sauce mixture into Graham Cracker Crust. Bake in preheated 350°
oven for 45 minutes. Let cake cool completely in oven. Remove
rim of pan before serving.

Graham Cracker Crust:

20 graham crackers, crushed	½ teaspoon cinnamon
⅓ to ¼ cup butter, softened	1 tablespoon sugar

Combine ingredients and pat firmly onto bottom of 9-inch spring
form pan.

Mandarin Orange Roast Dinner

(SERVES 6)

Stuffed Snow Peas
Mandarin Orange Roast
Buttered Noodles
Broccoli-Cheese Casserole
Green Salad
Peach-Caramel Ice Cream Pie
Coffee

ADVANCE PREPARATION SCHEDULE

Freezer	Previous Day	Early Morning
Peach-Caramel Ice Cream Pie	*Prepare Broccoli-Cheese Casserole, refrigerate but do not bake*	*Stuffed Snow Peas Prepare greens for salad*

STUFFED SNOW PEAS

24 fresh snow peas, young and   Fillings
    tender

Pour boiling salted water over 24 small, unopened, snow pea pods
and soak for 1 minute only. Drain and dry pea pods. Make a ¼"
long incision across the width of the flat side of each pod. Use a
sharp knife and do not cut through. Cool pods. Fill with one of the
Fillings.

Cream cheese filling:

8 ounces cream cheese, softened   ¼ teaspoon dry mustard
1 tablespoon mayonnaise   ¼ teaspoon salt
3 tablespoons tomato purée   ⅛ teaspoon white pepper

Blend cream cheese with mayonnaise, tomato purée, mustard, salt
and white pepper. With a pastry tube or metal cake decorator, pipe
mixture into pea pods. Chill 1 hour before serving.

Crabmeat filling:

1 6½- or 7-ounce can crabmeat or   1 teaspoon horseradish
    ½ pound fresh crabmeat   ¼ teaspoon salt
2 tablespoons mayonnaise   ⅛ teaspoon white pepper

For crabmeat filled snow peas, simply slit each pea pod on the flat
side and stuff with crabmeat mixed with mayonnaise, horseradish,
salt and pepper.

Note: If you cannot obtain fresh snow peas do not attempt to
make this recipe.

MANDARIN ORANGE ROAST

1 4-pound boneless beef chuck   segments, drained and liquid
    roast   reserved
2 tablespoons butter or margarine,   1 cup catsup
    softened   1 tablespoon Worcestershire
1 teaspoon seasoned salt   sauce
1 teaspoon seasoned pepper   2 tablespoons vermouth
2 sliced onions   ½ cup reserved liquid from
1 sliced green pepper   orange segments
1 11-ounce can mandarin orange

Place roast in a shallow roasting pan and spread with softened butter. Sprinkle with salt and pepper and cover with onion slices, green pepper and 1 cup of the drained orange segments. Combine catsup, Worcestershire, vermouth and the ½ cup reserved orange liquid; pour over roast. Cover tightly and bake in a preheated 350° oven about 2 hours or until tender. Add remaining orange segments about 10 minutes before serving so they are warm but have not lost their bright color. Serve sauce with roast. Serve with buttered noodles.

BROCCOLI-CHEESE CASSEROLE

2 tablespoons butter
2 tablespoons flour
1 3-ounce package cream cheese, softened
¼ cup grated Cheddar cheese
1 cup milk

2 10-ounce packages frozen chopped broccoli, cooked and well drained
⅓ cup crushed round buttery crackers (about 10)

Melt butter in a saucepan; blend in flour and cheeses until smooth. Add milk and cook, stirring, until mixture boils. Stir in broccoli. Place mixture in a 1-quart casserole and top with crushed cracker crumbs. Bake in preheated 350° oven for 30 minutes.

Note: Blue cheese may be substituted for Cheddar cheese.

PEACH-CARAMEL ICE CREAM PIE

1 9- or 10-inch graham cracker crust, chilled (see Index)
1 cup frozen peach slices, thawed
2 pints vanilla ice cream, slightly softened

¾ cup firmly packed light brown sugar
½ cup butter
¾ cup chopped pecans

Drain peaches, reserving syrup. Stir one pint ice cream to soften and stir in half of the peaches. Spread on crust and freeze for several hours.

In a saucepan combine brown sugar, butter, 2 tablespoons of the reserved peach syrup and bring to a boil; cook about 8 minutes to thicken. Remove from heat and stir in half the pecans. Cool, but do not let mixture harden. Spread over ice cream in crust. Return to freezer for an hour.

Soften second pint of ice cream, stir in other half of the peaches and spread over caramel layer. Top with remaining pecans. Freeze.

Treasure in the Freezer

(SERVES 8)

Mushroom-Bacon Bites   Little Chicken Drums

Lamb Ragout

Butter-Wheat Bread

Sesame-Lettuce Salad

Apricot Crumb Cake

Coffee

ADVANCE PREPARATION SCHEDULE

Freezer

Mushroom-Bacon Bites (do not broil)
Little Chicken Drums (do not bake)
Lamb Ragout
Butter-Wheat Bread
Dough for Apricot Crumb Cake

Early Morning

Prepare lettuce, vegetables and dressing for Sesame-Lettuce Salad
Remove Mushroom-Bacon Bites and Little Chicken Drums from freezer

MUSHROOM-BACON BITES

1 loaf thin-sliced white bread
1 10½-ounce can cream of mushroom soup

⅓ pound bacon, each strip cut into thirds

Remove crusts from bread and cut each slice into 3 strips. Spread each strip with undiluted soup; roll up. Wrap one third of a slice of bacon around each roll. Secure rolls with toothpicks. Place on a cookie sheet. Broil in preheated broiler, about 3 inches from heat, turning once, until crisp. May be frozen before broiling. Defrost and broil as directed.

LITTLE CHICKEN DRUMS

8 chicken wings	1 cup Italian-flavored fine dry
1 egg	bread crumbs
¼ cup milk	½ cup flour
Pinch garlic salt	1 teaspoon barbecue spice
Salt and pepper to taste	½ teaspoon pepper

Use only large "drumstick" after separating it from tip and center section of wings. Beat egg with milk; add garlic salt, salt and pepper. Mix bread crumbs with flour, barbecue spice and pepper in a shallow dish. Dip chicken pieces first in egg-milk mixture, then roll in crumb mixture. Arrange in a greased baking dish and bake in a preheated 350° oven for 30 minutes or until golden. Serve hot.

LAMB RAGOUT

5 cups cold water	6 to 8 peppercorns
2 pounds lamb bones	4 pounds boneless lamb shoulder,
2 carrots	cut into 1½-inch cubes
2 stalks celery	18 small white onions, peeled
2 leeks	2 tablespoons butter
Bouquet garni (3 sprigs parsley, 1	½ pound whole mushrooms
bay leaf, ½ celery stalk with	Salt and freshly ground pepper to
leaves)	taste
1 tablespoon salt	

In a large pot, combine water, bones, carrots, celery, leeks, *bouquet garni*, salt and pepper. Let stock come to a boil. Skim off scum from top and simmer for 45 minutes to 1 hour, partially covered. Strain stock; return it to the pot. Add lamb and simmer, partially covered, for 1 to 1½ hours, until meat is tender. Thirty minutes before lamb is done, add onions. In a 10-inch skillet, melt the 2 tablespoons butter. Add mushrooms; season with salt and pepper and sauté for

3 minutes over high heat. Set aside. When meat is done remove meat and onions to a serving platter and keep hot in a 200° oven. Reserve stock. Serve lamb and onions with Sauce and garnish with additional sprigs of fresh dill weed, if desired.

Sauce:

3 tablespoons sweet butter	1 teaspoon sugar
3 tablespoons flour	3 tablespoons minced fresh dill
2 tablespoons lemon juice	weed

Strain reserved lamb stock into a saucepan. Over high heat, reduce it to 2 cups. In a large heat-proof casserole (in which sauce may be served), melt butter; add flour and cook for 2 to 3 minutes; do not brown. All at once, add hot reduced stock and cook sauce, whisking constantly until completely smooth. Add lemon juice, sugar and dill and correct seasonings. Add the sautéed mushrooms; simmer for 5 minutes.

BUTTER-WHEAT BREAD

3 cups whole wheat flour	⅓ cup butter
2 packages active dry yeast	1½ cups old-fashioned rolled oats
2½ cups buttermilk	2 eggs
¼ cup molasses	2½ to 3 cups unsifted all-purpose
¼ cup honey	flour
1 tablespoon salt	2 tablespoons butter, melted

Combine whole wheat flour and yeast and set aside. In a saucepan, heat buttermilk, molasses, honey, salt and the ⅓ cup butter until warm. Pour into a large mixing bowl. Add flour-yeast mixture, rolled oats and eggs; blend with an electric mixer at low speed until dough is moistened. Next, beat for 3 minutes at high speed. Stir in enough all-purpose flour to make a stiff dough. Brush top of dough with melted butter; cover and let rise in a warm place (85°) until doubled, about 1 hour. Punch down, and shape into 2 round loaves. Place loaves in 2 greased, 2½-inch-deep, 1½-quart round casseroles. Cover and let rise in a warm place until doubled, about 45 minutes. Bake in a preheated 375° oven for 25 to 35 minutes, until loaves sound hollow when tapped on bottoms. Remove from casseroles and cool on wire rack. Makes 2 loaves.

SESAME-LETTUCE SALAD

2 heads lettuce, torn into bite-size pieces
½ cup chopped sweet red or green pepper
2 green onions, sliced

1 11-ounce can mandarin orange segments, drained
½ medium cucumber, thinly sliced

Combine lettuce with green pepper and onions. Arrange lettuce mixture in a salad bowl, along with mandarin oranges and cucumbers. When ready to serve, pour Sesame Seed Dressing over salad and toss gently.

SESAME SEED DRESSING

½ cup mayonnaise
½ cup French dressing
2 tablespoons grated Parmesan cheese

1 tablespoon sugar
1 tablespoon vinegar
½ teaspoon salt
2 tablespoons sesame seeds

Combine mayonnaise, French dressing, Parmesan, sugar, vinegar and salt. Toast sesame seeds in a skillet until lightly browned. Add to dressing.

APRICOT CRUMB CAKE

1 12-ounce package dried apricots
1 32-ounce jar apricot preserves
½ pound butter

1 cup sugar
2 teaspoons vanilla
2 eggs
3 cups sifted all-purpose flour
1 teaspoon baking powder

Cut dried apricots into diagonal strips, put into saucepan, cover with water and bring to boil. Pour off water and add apricot preserves. Set this filling aside to cool. Cream butter and sugar, add vanilla. Add eggs, one at a time, beating well after each addition. Add flour and baking powder which were sifted together. Beat just until mixed. Divide dough into 2 balls; wrap and freeze at least 48 hours (can be frozen for a longer period and used whenever needed). Using a coarse grater, grate one frozen ball of dough into a slightly greased 2-quart, oblong casserole. Pour apricot filling over crumbs and then grate second frozen ball of dough over filling. Bake in a preheated 350° oven about 30 to 40 minutes, until golden brown.

Simple Dinner

(SERVES 8)

Cabbage Rolls on Sliced Beef
Old World Bread
Boiled New Potatoes (see Index)
Chilled Fruit Compote
Crunch Cake
Coffee

ADVANCE PREPARATION SCHEDULE

Freezer

Cabbage Rolls on Sliced Beef
Old World Bread
Crunch Cake

Early Morning

Chilled Fruit Compote
Remove Cabbage Rolls on Sliced Beef, Old World Bread and Crunch Cake from freezer

CABBAGE ROLLS ON SLICED BEEF

1 small, very firm head cabbage
¼ cup rice (uncooked)
2 pounds ground beef
1 onion, grated
Salt and pepper to taste

2 eggs, well beaten
2 to 3 marrow bones, with no fat
1 pound sliced uncooked lean beef brisket, cut into thin slices

Trim cabbage; remove core. Place whole cabbage in a pan and add just enough boiling water to cover. Simmer about 10 minutes, until leaves separate easily. Remove from water and cool. Make meat filling by combining rice, ground beef, onion, salt, pepper and eggs. Separate cabbage leaves; place 1 heaping tablespoon of meat mixture on each leaf; tuck ends in and roll up. Place bones and sliced beef in a shallow baking pan, season to taste; place cabbage rolls on top and pour Tomato Sauce over all. Bake, covered, in a preheated 400° oven about 2 hours, until meat is tender and sauce is thick.

TOMATO SAUCE

2 6-ounce cans tomato paste	½ cup honey
Juice of 2 large lemons, strained	½ · cup sugar

Combine tomato paste with lemon juice, honey and sugar.

OLD WORLD BREAD

2 envelopes active dry yeast	1¼ cups water
¼ cup warm water	6 cups sifted all-purpose flour
1½ tablespoons salt	3 egg yolks, beaten
½ cup sugar	1 egg yolk
½ cup vegetable oil	1 tablespoon water

Dissolve yeast in the ¼ cup warm water; set aside. Combine salt, sugar, oil and the 1¼ cup water with 2 cups of the flour, beat well. Add yeast mixture and the 3 beaten egg yolks, mix well. Mix in 4 cups of flour. Remove dough to a lightly floured board and knead about 8 minutes until dough is shiny and elastic. Place dough in greased bowl, turning dough over to grease top. Cover with a towel and let rise in a warm place (85°), until double in size, about 1 to 1½ hours. Punch dough down and let rise again 1 hour. Punch dough down and turn out onto a lightly floured board. Divide dough into 2 equal parts. Divide each part into 3 pieces. Roll each piece into a 16-inch rope. Place 3 ropes on a greased cookie sheet and form into a braided loaf. Repeat with rest of dough. Cover loaves and let rise in a warm place 1 hour. Beat the 1 egg yolk with the 1 tablespoon water; brush loaves with egg mixture. Bake in a preheated 375° oven for 40 minutes. Makes 2 loaves.

CHILLED FRUIT COMPOTE

4 to 6 bananas, peeled and cut into thick slices
1 21-ounce can peach or apricot pie filling
1 20-ounce can pineapple chunks, drained
1 29-ounce can pears, drained and cut into chunks
1 16-ounce can mandarin orange segments, drained

Add bananas to pie filling, carefully stirring to coat bananas well. Add remaining fruits. Cover and refrigerate several hours.

CRUNCH CAKE

½ cup butter, softened
1 cup sifted all-purpose flour
1 cup sifted cake flour
1 cup sugar
1 cup firmly packed brown sugar
½ teaspoon cinnamon
½ teaspoon salt
2 eggs
½ teaspoon baking soda
1 cup sour cream
1 teaspoon vanilla

With a pastry blender or 2 knives, cut butter into the flours, sugars, cinnamon and salt until mixture is crumbly. Set aside ½ cup of the crumb mixture. Combine remaining ingredients; add remaining crumb mixture and beat well. Pour batter into a greased 9-inch spring form pan with tube and top with the ½ cup reserved crumb mixture. Bake in a preheated 350° oven for 50 minutes. Cool and remove from pan.

Family Celebration Dinner

(SERVES 6)

E-Z Pizzas   Shrimp Sauté
Chicken Vesuvio
Calico Vegetable Crunch
Angel Food–Fruit Cake
Coffee

ADVANCE PREPARATION SCHEDULE

Early Morning

Prepare E-Z Pizzas for broiling
Shell and devein shrimp for Shrimp Sauté
Fry chicken and potatoes for Chicken Vesuvio
Prepare vegetables for Calico Vegetable Crunch
Angel Food–Fruit Cake

E-Z PIZZAS

18 slices cocktail rye bread
1 6-ounce can tomato paste
18 slices salami, trimmed to fit bread

18 slices Mozzarella cheese, trimmed to fit bread

Spread each slice of bread lightly with tomato paste. Cover with a slice of salami and top with a slice of cheese. These may be assembled on a cookie sheet, covered and refrigerated 6 hours before serving. To serve, place in a preheated broiler 3 to 4 inches from source of heat and broil 3 to 4 minutes until cheese melts and pizza is heated through.

SHRIMP SAUTE

18 to 24 large raw shrimp, shelled and deveined
Milk
Oil for sautéeing
Flour for dredging shrimp
Salt and pepper

2 cups Sauterne or sweet white wine
1 tablespoon chopped shallots
½ teaspoon minced garlic
½ cup butter, softened
6 lemon wedges

Parsley for garnish

Cover shrimp with milk and soak 10 to 15 minutes. Pour 1½ inches oil into a deep skillet and heat to a temperature of 375° on a deep-fat-frying thermometer. Drain shrimp; dry them well on paper towels. Dredge them in flour, seasoned with salt and pepper. Fry shrimp, a few at a time, in the hot oil for about 2 minutes until lightly browned. Drain on paper towels and keep warm. To make sauce, pour Sauterne into a 12-inch skillet. Add shallots and garlic. Boil until liquid is reduced to 1 cup. Add shrimp and simmer for 1 minute. Add butter and when it has melted, stir until sauce is creamy. Immediately remove from heat and serve with lemon wedges and parsley.

CHICKEN VESUVIO

2 tablespoons grated Parmesan cheese
½ cup all-purpose flour
2 teaspoons paprika
2 teaspoons dried oregano leaves
1½ teaspoon garlic powder

1½ teaspoon salt
3 2½-pound chickens, cut-up, or 6 whole large, boneless chicken breasts, halved
⅓ cup oil
2 pounds potatoes, peeled and cut into quarters

Mix cheese, flour and seasonings in a paper bag. Add chicken pieces and shake to coat pieces evenly. Heat oil in a large skillet and fry, skin side down, in hot oil until brown. Turn and brown other side. Remove pieces as they brown. Dip potatoes in remaining flour mixture and fry in the same skillet until brown. Place chicken and potatoes in a single layer in a large roasting pan and brush with drippings from skillet. Cover and bake in a preheated 350° oven for 1 hour, spooning pan drippings over chicken every 15 minutes. Cannot be frozen, but potatoes and chicken may be browned early in the morning and refrigerated until baking time.

CALICO VEGETABLE CRUNCH

2 cups thinly sliced raw yellow squash
2 cups thinly sliced raw zucchini
1 pint cherry tomatoes, stemmed and halved

2 cups diced green pepper
1 teaspoon salt
½ cup bottled herb-and-garlic French dressing

Combine vegetables in lettuce-lined bowl. Sprinkle with salt; drizzle with dressing and toss lightly.

ANGEL FOOD–FRUIT CAKE

½ cup sour cream
¼ cup sugar
¼ cup crushed strawberries
1 cup heavy cream, whipped
1 cup sliced strawberries

¾ cup sliced bananas
1 8-inch packaged angel food cake, cut into 4 horizontal layers

Combine sour cream, sugar and crushed strawberries. Fold in whipped cream. Then gently stir in sliced strawberries and bananas. Fill layers and top cake with this mixture. Chill several hours, until firm. May be garnished with whole strawberries and additional banana slices, if desired.

Casual Dinner

(SERVES 6)

Overnight Appetizer Salad
Oxtail Stew
Cornmeal Yeast Buns
Deep-Dish Apple Pie
Coffee

ADVANCE PREPARATION SCHEDULE

Freezer	Previous Day	Early Morning
Cornmeal Yeast Buns *Deep-Dish Apple Pie*	*Prepare Overnight Appetizer Salad* *Oxtail Stew*	*Remove Cornmeal Yeast Buns and Deep-Dish Apple Pie from freezer*

OVERNIGHT APPETIZER SALAD

1 head lettuce
½ cup chopped celery
¼ cup chopped red onion
½ cup chopped green pepper
½ cup chopped peeled cucumber
½ cup sour cream

½ cup mayonnaise
Juice of 1 large lemon
2 tablespoons vinegar
1 tablespoon sugar
½ cup grated Parmesan cheese
½ pound bacon, crisply cooked

2 tomatoes, cut into wedges

Break up lettuce into bite-size pieces in a salad bowl. Sprinkle celery, onion, green pepper and cucumber in layers over lettuce. Combine sour cream, mayonnaise, lemon juice, vinegar and sugar; pour over salad, but do not toss. Sprinkle with cheese; cover and refrigerate for at least 3 hours or overnight. Before serving, crumble bacon over salad and decorate with tomato wedges. Serve salad without tossing.

OXTAIL STEW

3 pounds lean oxtails, cut into pieces
¼ cup flour
Salt and pepper
¼ cup butter

1 12-ounce can stewed tomatoes
1 13-ounce can oxtail soup
6 carrots, peeled and thinly sliced
1 10-ounce package frozen peas, defrosted

Lightly dust oxtail pieces with flour and season with salt and pepper. Brown in butter over low heat, turning to brown all sides. Place oxtails, tomatoes, oxtail soup in a 4-quart casserole. Add water to cover, about 1 cup. Cover casserole and bake in a preheated 325° oven about 3½ hours until tender. Remove oxtails. Add carrots and peas to gravy to cook, adding more water, if necessary. When peas and carrots are done, return oxtails to casserole and serve stew. If oxtail stew is made the previous day, remove fat from top and reheat over low heat.

CORNMEAL YEAST BUNS

1 package active dry yeast	1 teaspoon salt
3 cups sifted all-purpose flour	2 eggs
2¼ cups milk	1½ cups yellow cornmeal
½ cup butter	2½ to 3 cups sifted all-purpose
½ cup sugar	flour

In a large mixing bowl, combine yeast and the 3 cups flour. Set aside. In a saucepan, heat milk, butter, sugar and salt, stirring until mixture is warm and butter is melted. Add to flour mixture with the eggs; beat with an electric mixer at low speed until well blended. Then beat at high speed for 3 minutes. At low speed again, beat in cornmeal and 2 cups of the remaining flour. Turn dough out onto a floured board and knead in ½ to 1 cup of the remaining flour, kneading for 6 to 8 minutes until smooth and elastic. Place dough in a greased bowl, turning it over to grease entire surface of dough. Cover, and let rise in a warm place (85°) until doubled, about 1 to 1½ hours. Punch down and shape dough into 72 balls. Place 2 balls in each greased 2½-inch muffin cup in a muffin pan. Cover, and let rise until nearly doubled, about 1 hour. Bake in a preheated 375° oven for 12 to 15 minutes. May be frozen.

DEEP-DISH APPLE PIE

8 large Greening apples	2 tablespoons melted butter
1 cup granulated sugar	1½ tablespoons cornstarch
½ cup firmly packed brown sugar	Few drops lemon juice
½ teaspoon cinnamon	1 frozen pie crust, thawed
¼ teaspoon nutmeg	1 egg, beaten well
¼ cup sugar	

Pare, core and thinly slice apples; combine with the 1 cup sugar, brown sugar, cinnamon, nutmeg, butter, cornstarch and lemon juice. Place mixture in a greased, deep 8-inch round pie plate or 1½-quart round baking dish. Cover apples with crust, brush crust with beaten egg and sprinkle with sugar. Bake in a preheated 350° oven for 1 hour.

Less than 1 C sugar
for 6 lg apples

Suppers

A GOOD FORMULA for a supper menu includes a hearty main dish with well-orchestrated accompaniments. Texture, aroma, color and tastes all blend to provide harmony and balance. A well-planned supper is an easy and relaxed form of entertainment.

New Orleans Supper

(SERVES 6)

Deep-Sea Cocktail
Chicken Clemenceau
Crusty French Bread
Salad-of-the-House
Icy Lemon Cream
Butterscotch Bites
Coffee

ADVANCE PREPARATION SCHEDULE

Freezer

Icy Lemon Cream
Lemon shells and
*   caps*
Butterscotch Bites
French bread (do not
*   bake)*

Previous Day

Cocktail Sauce
*   (without whipped*
*   cream)*
Red Wine Vinai-
*   grette Dressing*

Early Morning

Prepare ingredients for
*   Deep-Sea Cocktail*
Brown chicken

DEEP-SEA COCKTAIL

1 pound fresh crabmeat
4 slices smoked salmon
Freshly ground pepper
1 teaspoon Worcestershire sauce

Cocktail Sauce
½ small head lettuce, shredded
1 hard-cooked egg yolk, sieved
2 tablespoons chopped chives

Place crabmeat in a bowl, separate gently with a fork. Slice salmon into thin strips. Mix together, and season with pepper and Worcestershire. Add Cocktail Sauce and spoon into individual serving dishes or seashells lined with shredded lettuce. Garnish each serving with sieved yolk and chives.

COCKTAIL SAUCE

6 tablespoons mayonnaise
2 heaping tablespoons whipped
   cream
1 tablespoon catsup
2 teaspoons lemon juice
1 teaspoon grapefruit juice

1 teaspoon Dijon mustard
Paprika
1 tablespoon horseradish
   (optional)
1 tablespoon dry sherry
   (optional)

Combine mayonnaise, whipped cream and catsup. Add lemon and grapefruit juices, mustard and a sprinkling of paprika. For stronger flavor, horseradish and sherry may be added. Mix thoroughly and refrigerate until ready to use.

CHICKEN CLEMENCEAU

8 whole chicken breasts, cut into quarters (32 pieces)
½ teaspoon garlic salt
½ teaspoon salt
¼ teaspoon pepper
¼ teaspoon paprika

3 tablespoons vegetable oil
1 24-ounce package frozen shoestring potatoes
2 9-ounce packages frozen peas
½ cup butter
1 large clove garlic, minced

Season chicken with garlic salt, salt, pepper and paprika. Brown in heated oil in a skillet until crisp and cooked through, approximately 12 to 15 minutes. Bake shoestring potatoes on a cookie sheet in a preheated 450° oven about 15 to 18 minutes until golden and crisp. Cook peas for 5 minutes; do not overcook. Melt butter with garlic. Place chicken on a large serving platter. Sprinkle potatoes on and around chicken and spoon peas over all. Pour garlic butter over chicken, potatoes and peas and serve immediately.

CRUSTY FRENCH BREAD

1 loaf unsliced French bread
1 tablespoon coarse salt

½ cup sweet butter, softened

Spread top crust of an unsliced loaf of French bread with soft, sweet butter and sprinkle with coarse salt. Warm bread in preheated 300° oven for 10 minutes and serve.

SALAD-OF-THE-HOUSE

1 large clove garlic, crushed
1 teaspoon salt
2 pounds Bibb lettuce, washed and crisped
1 14-ounce can artichoke hearts, cut in halves or quarters, if large

1 14-ounce can hearts of palm, cut into 2-inch slices
1 pint cherry tomatoes, halved
Red Wine Vinaigrette Dressing

Season a wooden salad bowl by mashing crushed garlic clove and salt into sides and bottom of bowl. Shake out residue. Arrange lettuce, artichoke hearts, hearts of palm and tomatoes in salad bowl, chill. Chill salad plates and forks. Just before serving, add Red Wine Vinaigrette Dressing and toss together.

Red Wine Vinaigrette Dressing:

¾ cup olive oil	½ cup red wine vinegar
¼ teaspoon freshly ground pepper	½ teaspoon Dijon mustard

Combine oil, pepper, vinegar and mustard. Mix well and refrigerate.

ICY LEMON CREAM

6 large lemons	1 cup sugar
1 cup heavy cream	Juice and grated peel of 2 large
1 cup milk	lemons

Place each of the 6 lemons horizontally. Cut a slice from the top of each lemon about ¼ of the way down. Reserve slices. Scoop out pulp from lemons and cut a thin slice off lemon bottoms so that they stand up firmly. Freeze lemon shells and top slices.

Mix cream, milk and sugar, stirring until sugar dissolves. Freeze for 2 hours in freezer or freezer tray of refrigerator. Remove mixture and add juice and grated peel of the 2 lemons. Beat until smooth. Return to freezer for another 2 hours and then beat again until smooth. Refreeze 15 minutes. Spoon ice cream into frozen lemon shells, piling ice cream high above the shell, and top with lemon slices.

BUTTERSCOTCH BITES

1 cup butter	2 cups sifted all-purpose flour
1 cup firmly packed brown sugar	½ teaspoon salt
1 egg	1 12-ounce package semi-sweet
1 teaspoon vanilla	chocolate pieces, melted
½ to ¾ cup chopped nuts	

Mix together butter, brown sugar, egg, vanilla, flour and salt until crumbly. Press mixture into a 10" x 15" pan to form a crust. Bake in a preheated 350° oven for 20 to 25 minutes until golden brown. Remove from oven and while still very hot, pour melted chocolate over crust and spread evenly with spatula or flat knife. Sprinkle any type of chopped nuts over chocolate and mark into squares while still quite warm. Serve cookies when cool.

Texas Supper

(SERVES 6)

Piquant Stuffed Celery   Pickled Peppers

Texas Short Ribs

Cheesy Potato-Bake   Vegetable Pancake

Pumpkin Ice Cream Pie

Coffee

ADVANCE PREPARATION SCHEDULE

Freezer	**Previous Day**	**Early Morning**
Texas Short Ribs	*Pickled Peppers (3*	*Shred cheese for Cheesy*
Pumpkin Ice Cream	*days before)*	*Potato-Bake*
Pie	*Celery stuffing*	*Remove short ribs from*
	Cook vegetables for	*freezer*
	Vegetable Pancake	

PIQUANT STUFFED CELERY

4 ounces Roquefort or blue
cheese
¼ cup mayonnaise
1 3-ounce package cream cheese,
softened
1 teaspoon anchovy paste

1 teaspoon Madeira wine
½ teaspoon dill seed
½ teaspoon dry mustard
½ teaspoon Worcestershire sauce
Small pinch cayenne pepper
4 to 6 celery stalks
Paprika

Thoroughly blend all ingredients, except celery and paprika, to make a smooth paste and refrigerate overnight or longer. Cut chilled celery stalks into 3-inch lengths, and fill with mixture. Dust with paprika and keep chilled until ready to serve. Cheese mixture will stuff 15 to 20 celery pieces.

Variation:

Stuffing may be used as a cheese spread on crackers or rounds of thinly sliced rye bread.

PICKLED PEPPERS

3 large green peppers, seeded
and cut into slices
8 tablespoons vinegar
1 tablespoon lemon juice

1 tablespoon salt
2 teaspoons dill seed
2 teaspoons pickling spice
2 cloves garlic

Fill a 1-quart jar with green peppers. Combine remaining ingredients and pour into jar. Add enough water to fill jar to the top. Cover tightly and let stand for 72 hours at room temperature. Then refrigerate and use as desired. Keeps for weeks in refrigerator.

TEXAS SHORT RIBS

4 pounds beef short ribs
2 cups canned tomatoes
⅓ cup seedless raisins

1 1¼-ounce package chili seasoning mix

Brown ribs slowly on all sides in a large skillet. Cover and cook for 90 minutes over a low heat. Remove meat from skillet and pour off drippings. Combine remaining ingredients in skillet; return meat to pan. Cover and simmer for 20 minutes. May be frozen or prepared 1 day in advance.

CHEESY POTATO-BAKE

4 large baking potatoes, peeled
  and thinly sliced
2 cups shredded Cheddar cheese
1 1¼-ounce package white
  sauce mix

1½ cups milk
1 teaspoon salt
1 teaspoon caraway seed
¼ teaspoon pepper
Paprika

In a buttered, 2-quart, shallow baking dish, alternate layers of potatoes and cheese. Prepare white sauce mix according to package directions, using the 1½ cups of milk. Add seasonings to sauce and pour over potatoes. Sprinkle top with paprika. Bake uncovered in a preheated 350° oven for 1 hour and 10 minutes or until potatoes are tender.

VEGETABLE PANCAKE

¼ teaspoon pickling spice
½ cup cooked carrots
½ cup cooked green beans
½ cup cooked broccoli
½ cup cooked asparagus

½ cup cooked cauliflower
½ cup cooked zucchini
2 eggs, beaten lightly
Salt and pepper to taste
Butter

Add ¼ teaspoon pickling spice to water when cooking vegetables. Refrigerate vegetables overnight. The next day, drain and chop vegetables finely and mix with eggs, salt and pepper. Drop by spoonfuls into a hot buttered skillet and cook slowly, like pancakes, browning them on both sides. Serve at once.

Note: Any leftover vegetables may be used in this recipe.

PUMPKIN ICE CREAM PIE

1 deep 9-inch pastry shell, baked
  and cooled
1 pint vanilla ice cream,
  softened
1 16-ounce can pumpkin
1½ cups sugar
½ teaspoon salt

1 teaspoon cinnamon
½ teaspoon ginger
¼ teaspoon powdered cloves
1 teaspoon vanilla
1 cup heavy cream, stiffly
  whipped
1 cup slivered blanched almonds

¼ cup sugar

Bake pastry shell and cool completely. Spread ice cream over bot-

tom of pastry shell and return to freezer until firm. Combine pumpkin with sugar, seasonings and vanilla; mix well. Fold in whipped
cream and cover solidly frozen ice cream in pastry shell with pumpkin mixture. Return pie to freezer. In a small pan (do not use
Teflon), combine almonds and sugar. Stir continuously over medium heat to caramelize; this will take between 10 and 15 minutes.
Spread almonds out on a buttered plate. When pie is firm, break
up almonds and press over entire top. Wrap in foil or other freezer
wrap and freeze; will keep for months. Remove from freezer 45
minutes before serving. To serve, cut into small wedges.

Sunday Soup Supper

(SERVES 4)

Melted Cheese Hors d'Oeuvres
Sunday Soup with Dumplings
Garden Mushroom Salad
Grandma's Strudel Cookies
Coffee

ADVANCE PREPARATION SCHEDULE

Freezer	Previous Day	Early Morning
Grandma's Strudel Cookies	*Sunday Soup*	*Melted Cheese Hors d'Oeuvres*
		Garden Mushroom Salad

MELTED CHEESE HORS D'OEUVRES

6 hamburger buns or English muffins
1 pound sharp Cheddar cheese, grated
6 hard-cooked eggs, chopped

2 small onions, grated
2 teaspoons mustard
Dash of Worcestershire sauce
Salt and pepper to taste

Split buns and cut each into halves. Combine cheese, eggs, onion, mustard, Worcestershire, salt and pepper; spoon onto bun wedges and refrigerate. Just before serving, place on a cookie sheet in a preheated broiler, about 4 inches from source of heat; broil until cheese mixture is melted.

SUNDAY SOUP WITH DUMPLINGS

1 28-ounce can tomatoes
5 17-ounce cans red kidney beans, drained
4 quarts water

1 pound bacon
1 large onion, diced
1½ pounds ground beef
1 tablespoon salt
¼ teaspoon pepper

Place tomatoes, kidney beans and water in a 6- or 8-quart pot; bring to boil. Cook bacon until crisp; remove bacon and crumble. Pour off all but 2 tablespoons of the bacon fat. Brown onion in the bacon fat. Add ground beef to onion, and brown meat, stirring with a fork to break it up. Add beef, onions and crumbled bacon to soup, along with salt and pepper; cover and cook for 90 minutes.

Dumplings:

1 egg
½ teaspoon salt

1 cup milk
1½ cups sifted all-purpose flour

Beat ingredients with a spoon in a mixing bowl. Mixture should be thick enough to drop off a spoon; if not, add a little more flour. When soup is cooked, drop teaspoons of dumpling batter into hot soup. Place a teaspoon of mixture on spoon; place spoon in soup, and mixture will come off of spoon. Simmer, covered, for 10 minutes. May be prepared 3 days in advance and refrigerated. Do not freeze.

GARDEN MUSHROOM SALAD

1 pound raw mushrooms	1½ teaspoons salt
Juice of 1 lemon	½ teaspoon pepper
½ cup finely chopped onion	¼ cup vegetable oil
½ cup finely chopped celery	Bibb lettuce
Pimiento	

Rinse mushrooms; wipe dry and slice as thinly as possible. Sprinkle immediately with lemon juice. Add onion, celery, salt, pepper and oil; toss well and chill. Serve salad on lettuce and garnish with pimiento.

GRANDMA'S STRUDEL COOKIES

Dough:

1½ cups butter, softened   1 16-ounce container sour cream
4 cups sifted all-purpose flour

Filling:

1 12-ounce jar pineapple jam or preserves	1 15-ounce package seedless raisins
1 12-ounce jar apricot jam or preserves	2 cups chopped nuts
	½ cup graham cracker crumbs

Mix butter and sour cream until well-blended. Add flour and mix well. Divide dough evenly into 6 balls and place in small plastic bags with 1 tablespoon of flour to prevent sticking. Refrigerate overnight or chill in freezer. On a well-floured board, roll each ball of dough into a rectangle ¼ inch thick. Mix jams together and cover dough with a light coating of mixture; sprinkle with raisins, nuts and a small amount of crumbs. Starting from small side of rectangle, roll dough jelly-roll fashion, securing ends to prevent filling from leaking. Place on an ungreased jelly-roll pan, 3 strudels per pan. Bake in a preheated 350° oven for 1 hour until lightly browned. While still hot, slice rolls diagonally. Makes about 60 cookies, which may be frozen. Uncooked dough may also be frozen for weeks.

Supper à la Suisse

(SERVES 6)

Artichoke Hearts and Shrimp
Buttered Toast
Sliced Veal and Crusty Potatoes
Lettuce Flower with Roquefort
Banana-Cream Eclairs
Coffee

ADVANCE PREPARATION SCHEDULE

Freezer	**Previous Day**	**Early Morning**
Banana-Cream Eclairs	*Artichoke Hearts and Shrimp*	*Soften Rouqefort Cheese*
	Boil potatoes	*Wash and chill Bibb lettuce*

ARTICHOKE HEARTS AND SHRIMP

1 9-ounce package frozen artichoke hearts	¼ cup wine vinegar
24 medium raw shrimp, peeled and deveined	2 tablespoons Dijon mustard
1 egg yolk	2 tablespoons minced parsley
½ cup olive oil	2 tablespoons minced chives
½ cup peanut oil	1 tablespoon minced shallots
	Salt to taste
	Lemon juice to taste

Cook artichoke hearts; drain and chill. Cook shrimp in simmering water or beer for 3 to 5 minutes. Put egg yolk in mixing bowl, add oils, vinegar and mustard, beating well. Stir in remaining ingredients; add artichokes and shrimp last. Marinate in refrigerator for at least 2 hours, or overnight, occasionally turning artichokes and shrimp. Serve with buttered toast.

SLICED VEAL AND CRUSTY POTATOES

1½ pounds veal, thinly sliced	½ pound fresh mushrooms, sliced
Salt and pepper to taste	½ cup dry white wine
4 tablespoons vegetable oil	1½ cups heavy cream
4 tablespoons butter	3 teaspoons chopped parsley
6 tablespoons chopped shallots	Juice of 1 lemon

Crusty Potatoes

Sprinkle veal with salt and pepper. Heat oil in a skillet, add butter and quickly sauté veal. Add shallots and mushrooms to veal and sauté 5 minutes longer. Transfer veal, shallots and mushrooms to a serving platter, keeping meat warm while making sauce. For sauce, deglaze pan with wine and cream. Cook sauce over high heat, for 3 to 4 minutes to reduce it. Add lemon juice to sauce and pour over meat. Garnish with chopped parsley. Serve with Crusty Potatoes.

Crusty Potatoes:

6 potatoes, scrubbed ½ cup butter
Salt and pepper to taste

Boil potatoes in their skins until tender; drain and peel immediately. Cool potatoes in refrigerator overnight. Cut potatoes into thin slices. Heat butter in skillet. Season potatoes with salt and pepper and fry over high heat, turning at intervals to brown and crisp on all sides. Lower heat and press potatoes into the skillet firmly. Fry gently for several minutes until a golden crust forms underneath potatoes. Serve at once, crust-side up.

LETTUCE FLOWER WITH ROQUEFORT

6 heads Bibb lettuce	¼ cup butter
6 ounces Roquefort cheese,	½ cup oil
softened at room	¼ cup lemon juice or vinegar
temperature	½ teaspoon salt

Freshly ground pepper

Carefully wash lettuce and separate leaves, dry and chill. Mix cheese and butter together until well blended. Place a rounded scoop on each chilled salad plate. Stick base of each lettuce leaf into cheese-butter mound on plate until lettuce looks like a flower with leaves all secured in cheese center. Chill. Combine oil, lemon juice, salt and pepper; when ready to serve, pour 1 teaspoon dressing over each salad.

BANANA-CREAM ECLAIRS

Cream Puff Paste:

1 cup water	7 tablespoons butter
1 tablespoon sugar	1 cup sifted all-purpose flour
4 eggs, at room temperature	

Make a pâte à choux for cream puff pastry by bringing water, sugar and butter to boil in a saucepan. The moment butter melts and mixture boils, immediately remove pan from heat, and add flour to mixture all at once. Stir vigorously with a wooden spoon until mixture forms a ball and comes away from sides of pan. Add eggs one at a time, beating well after each addition so that next egg is not added until previous one has been thoroughly incorporated into dough. Grease a large heavy cookie sheet. Spoon dough onto cookie sheet in 2 giant narrow fingers, each about 12 inches long and 2 inches wide. Bake pastry in a preheated 400° oven for 20 minutes; then reduce heat to 350° and bake for 20 minutes longer. Finally reduce heat to 300° and bake for 10 minutes longer. Remove from oven and cool. Split cooled pastry in half lengthwise, leaving bottom half larger than top. Remove and discard soft inside of pastry, and fill shell bottoms with the chilled Banana-Cream Filling. Chill filled pastry shell bottoms. Reserve tops.

Banana-Cream Filling:

4 overripe bananas; skins must be at least 50% brown, thin-skinned, soft and aromatic	½ cup boiling water
	3 tablespoons light rum
	1 pint heavy cream, whipped
2 envelopes unflavored gelatine	stiff, with 4 tablespoons sugar
3 tablespoons water	folded in
4 tablespoons sugar	

Mash bananas with fork until puréed, and set aside. Dissolve gelatine in the 3 tablespoons water; add the ½ cup boiling water and stir until gelatine is dissolved. Cool mixture in ice water until mixture begins to thicken (do not take eyes off mixture while waiting for it to thicken; it happens quickly). Gently fold rum into cooled gelatine. Pour gelatine mixture over surface of sweetened whipped cream. Then gently fold gelatine into cream mixture. Stir the remaining 4 tablespoons of sugar into puréed bananas, and fold banana mixture into whipped cream mixture. Chill.

Garnish:

1 6-ounce package semi-sweet chocolate pieces

4 tablespoons toasted sliced almonds

Melt chocolate over hot water, and frost top halves of eclairs with chocolate. While frosting is still warm, sprinkle it with almonds. Let dry. With a sharp knife, cut eclair tops into serving-size pieces. Place pieces on filled bottoms, and finish cutting through the eclairs when ready to serve. May be served when chilled, or frozen and defrosted 30 minutes before serving.

Sophisticated Supper

(SERVES 6)

Shrimp with Caviar Cocktail Sauce
Fillets of Sole Veronique
Straw Potatoes (see Index)
Steamed Artichokes with Melted Butter
Gazpacho Salad Mold
Fiesta Fruit   Chocolate Crinkle Cookies
Coffee

ADVANCE PREPARATION SCHEDULE

Previous Day   Early Morning
Gazpacho Salad Mold   *Cook shrimp*
Chocolate Crinkle Cookies   *Make Caviar Sauce*
                                      Fiesta Fruit

SHRIMP WITH CAVIAR SAUCE

½ head lettuce, shredded   6 lemon wedges
24 large shrimp, cleaned, cooked
   and chilled

Arrange shredded lettuce in 6 cocktail glasses and divide shrimp
among glasses on lettuce beds. Before serving, pour Caviar Cocktail
Sauce over shrimp and serve each cocktail with a lemon wedge.

Caviar Cocktail Sauce:

1 2¼-ounce jar black or red   1 tablespoon lemon juice
  caviar   1 cup sour cream

Combine all ingredients and chill thoroughly.

FILLETS OF SOLE VERONIQUE

1 tablespoon butter   1 tablespoon flour
2 shallots, finely chopped   ¼ cup milk
6 fillets of sole   ¼ cup heavy cream
Salt and pepper   Salt and white pepper
¼ cup dry white wine   1 egg yolk, slightly beaten
¼ cup water   1 8¼-ounce can white seedless
¼ cup butter   grapes
          3 tablespoons whipped cream

In a heat-proof serving dish melt the 1 tablespoon butter and add
shallots. Season fish with salt and pepper and arrange fillets over
shallots in skillet. Add wine and water. Butter a waxed paper circle
and place it, buttered-side down, on top of fish. Bring to a boil and
gently cook for 10 to 12 minutes. Remove from heat. Keep fish
warm while preparing sauce. Drain fish liquid into a skillet and
cook until reduced to ½ cup. In a saucepan, melt 1 tablespoon of
the butter, add flour and stir until blended. Meanwhile, bring milk

and cream to boil and add all at once to butter-flour, stirring vigorously with a whisk until sauce is thick and smooth. Season with salt and white pepper. Slightly beat egg yolk with a small amount of the hot sauce. Add egg yolk, remaining sauce and the remaining 3 tablespoons butter to reduced cooking liquid in skillet. Cook, stirring, until butter melts. Place grapes around fish. Fold whipped cream into sauce and pour over fish. Brown quickly under preheated broiler; serve immediately.

STEAMED ARTICHOKES

Cut off stems from 6 small or 3 large artichokes. Remove bottom row of leaves, nearest stem. Cut sharp tips of all the other leaves, about ½ inch, with a scissors. Dip prepared artichokes into lemon juice to prevent discoloration of cut areas. Place artichokes upright in a pan, one-third filled with boiling water. Artichokes should be tightly packed in pan so that they remain upright. Cook, covered, 30 to 45 minutes or until a leaf is easily pulled off artichoke.

Serve one per person if small, or one-half per person for very large artichokes. Serve with melted butter on the side.

GAZPACHO SALAD MOLD

3 envelopes unflavored gelatine	1 medium green pepper, diced
1 18-ounce can tomato juice	(¾ cup)
⅓ cup red wine vinegar	1 tablespoon chopped chives
1 teaspoon salt	¼ cup finely chopped red onion
2 dashes Tabasco	3 large avocados, sliced and
2 tomatoes, peeled and diced	brushed with lemon juice
(1¼ cups)	⅓ cup bottled vinegar and oil
1 large cucumber, peeled and	dressing
diced (1½ cups)	

Soften gelatine in ¾ cup of the tomato juice. Stir over low heat until dissolved. Add remaining tomato juice, vinegar, salt and

Tabasco. Cool to the consistency of unbeaten egg whites. Fold in all vegetables, except avocados. Pour into oiled 1½-quart mold and refrigerate for at least six hours, until firm. Before serving, unmold and surround with avocado slices; serve with vinegar and oil dressing.

FIESTA FRUIT

1 cup firmly packed light brown
   sugar
½ cup water
Juice of 1 large orange

Juice of 1 large lemon
1 tablespoon vanilla
4 cups fresh fruit (sliced peaches,
   nectarines, pears, berries)

Combine sugar, water and fruit juices. Bring to a boil and simmer 5 minutes. Remove from heat and stir in vanilla. Pour hot syrup over any combination of fresh fruit and chill until serving time.

CHOCOLATE CRINKLE COOKIES

½ cup corn oil
4 1-ounce squares unsweetened
   chocolate, melted
2 cups sugar
4 eggs

2 teaspoons vanilla
½ teaspoon salt
2 cups sifted all-purpose flour
2 teaspoons baking powder
1 cup confectioners' sugar

Combine corn oil, chocolate and sugar; blend in eggs, one at a time, until well blended. Add vanilla and stir in salt, flour and baking powder. Chill dough overnight. Drop teaspoonfuls of chilled dough into confectioners' sugar. With the fingers roll dough in sugar, shaping it into balls. Place balls 2 inches apart on a greased cookie sheet, and bake in preheated 350° oven for 10 to 12 minutes. Makes about 60 cookies.

Post Game Supper

(SERVES 6)

Salad Romaine
Flank Steak with Spaghetti
Zucchini, Mushrooms and Onion Casserole   Italian Bread Chunks
Plum Pie
Coffee

ADVANCE PREPARATION SCHEDULE

Previous Day   **Early Morning**

Plum Pie   *Cut up vegetables and cheese for*
Salad Romaine
Prepare Swiss Vinaigrette Dressing
Cook sauce for steak
Zucchini, Mushrooms and Onion
Casserole (do not bake)
Marinate steak

SALAD ROMAINE

½ pound Gruyere cheese, thinly   3 tablespoons chopped parsley
sliced   1½ pounds Romaine lettuce,
1 cup thinly sliced celery   washed and crisped
¾ pound mushrooms, sliced

Combine cheese, celery, mushrooms and parsley. Before serving,
toss salad with Swiss Vinaigrette Dressing; let stand for 15 minutes
before serving. Serve on a bed of Romaine lettuce.

SWISS VINAIGRETTE DRESSING

2 tablespoons wine vinegar   Freshly ground pepper to taste
5 tablespoons olive oil   ½ teaspoon sugar
1 scant teaspoon salt   1½ teaspoons Dijon mustard

Combine ingredients; blend well.

FLANK STEAK WITH SPAGHETTI

1 1½ to 2-pound flank steak, scored	2 8-ounce cans tomato sauce
⅓ cup bottled Italian dressing	¼ cup hickory-flavored catsup
2 medium onions, sliced	½ teaspoon salt
1 green pepper, sliced	¼ teaspoon pepper
1 clove garlic, crushed	1 bay leaf
3 tablespoons vegetable oil	¼ teaspon dried oregano leaves
	¼ teaspoon dried basil leaves

1 8-ounce package spaghetti

Marinate steak 2 hours in dressing. Cook onions, green pepper and garlic in oil until tender-crisp. Stir in tomato sauce, catsup, salt, pepper and bay leaf. Simmer, covered, for 30 minutes. During last 10 minutes, add oregano and basil. While sauce cooks, cook spaghetti in salted, boiling water. Broil steak in a preheated broiler for 3 to 5 minutes on each side. Slice very thinly on diagonal when done. Heap cooked spaghetti on serving platter; arrange steak slices on top of spaghetti, and garnish with a ribbon of sauce. Serve remaining sauce on side.

ZUCCHINI, MUSHROOMS AND ONION CASSEROLE

6 small or 3 large zucchini, thinly sliced	4 tablespoons butter
1 pound fresh mushrooms, thinly sliced	½ cup freshly grated Parmesan cheese
3 medium yellow onions, thinly sliced	

Separately sauté each vegetable in 1 tablespoon of the butter. Layer vegetables in a 2-quart casserole, sprinkling Parmesan cheese *sparingly* between each layer. Last layer should be zucchini. Top with the remaining 1 tablespoon butter and remaining cheese. Bake in a preheated oven for 45 minutes.

ITALIAN BREAD CHUNKS

3 eggs   1 cup grated Parmesan cheese
6 tablespoons milk   ½ cup instant minced onions
1 loaf Italian bread, cut into
   2-inch chunks

Beat eggs with milk; briefly dip bread chunks in mixture. Dust chunks with grated cheese and instant minced onion and bake as individual rolls on a heavy cookie sheet in a preheated 350° oven until brown. Serve hot.

PLUM PIE

Crust:

1¾ cups sifted all-purpose flour   Salt
 ¼ teaspoon baking powder   6 tablespoons butter
               3 tablespoons cream

Mix flour, baking powder and salt together; using a pastry blender to cut butter into flour mixture. Stir in cream. Pat dough onto bottom and sides of a 10-inch pie plate.

Plum Filling:

24 fresh prune plums   1 tablespoon flour
 1 cup sugar   Butter
          Cinnamon

Cut plums in half, removing pit, and place skin side down on pie dough. Combine sugar and flour and sprinkle mixture on plums; dot with butter and sprinkle with cinnamon. Bake in a preheated 375° oven for 15 minutes, then reduce heat to 325° and bake for 1 hour more.

Glaze:

2 tablespoons cornstarch   6 fresh prune plums, cut and
½ cup sugar   pitted
      ¾ cup water

Combine cornstarch and sugar; slowly stir in water. Add plums. Cook until glaze is clear; place in blender to purée plums. Pour hot glaze over pie as soon as it has been removed from oven.

Special Night Supper

(SERVES 6)

Onion Soup
Chicken Calvados
Straw Potatoes (see Index)   Asparagus with Pecans
Artichoke Hearts and Tomatoes Vinaigrette
Fruited Crêpe Stack
Coffee

ADVANCE PREPARATION SCHEDULE

Freezer	Early Morning
Onion Soup	*Sweet Vinaigrette Dressing*
Croutons	*Make crêpes*
	Remove soup and croutons from freezer

ONION SOUP

6 large white onions, sliced	1 cup Burgundy wine
2 tablespoons butter	2 teaspoons Worcestershire sauce
4 10½-ounce cans condensed beef consommé	Salt and freshly ground pepper to taste
2½ soup cans water	Gruyere cheese, grated

Sauté onions in butter until lightly browned. Add consommé, water, wine, Worcestershire and salt and pepper; simmer 30 minutes. To serve, pour soup into a crock or individual oven-proof bowls. Place Croutons on top. Cover top of soup and Croutons thickly with grated Gruyere cheese. Broil in a preheated broiler for several minutes until cheese is melted and crispy at edges.

Croutons:

6 ½-inch-thick slices French bread	2 tablespoons butter

Sauté bread in butter until lightly browned and crisped on both sides.

Note: Croutons and soup may be made 1 week ahead, and frozen separately. Defrost 12 hours in advance.

CHICKEN CALVADOS

2 3-pound broilers, cut into parts	1 tablespoon chopped parsley
½ cup butter	1 sprig thyme or ¼ teaspoon dried thyme leaves
¼ cup Calvados, apple brandy or applejack	½ cup cider or white wine
4 to 5 shallots, finely chopped	½ cup heavy cream

Brown chicken lightly on all sides in heated butter. Lower heat and cook for 15 minutes, turning parts often. Heat Calvados; pour into skillet and ignite. Shake pan until flames die. Add shallots, parsley, thyme and cider or wine, blending well. Cover and cook until chicken is tender. Arrange chicken on a warm serving platter. Stir cream into liquid in pan; pour over chicken or serve as a sauce on side.

ASPARAGUS WITH PECANS

2 pounds asparagus	2 tablespoons chopped pecans
¼ cup butter	Salt and pepper to taste
1 tablespoon lemon juice	6 slices white bread, toasted

Cook asparagus in a small amount of boiling salted water until crisp but tender. Drain and set aside; keeping it warm. Melt butter with lemon juice in a skillet; add chopped pecans, salt and pepper. Arrange asparagus on slices of toast, cutting stems so asparagus fits toast well. Pour butter-pecan sauce over asparagus and toast. Serve at once.

ARTICHOKE HEARTS AND TOMATOES VINAIGRETTE

3 beefsteak tomatoes   1 14-ounce can artichoke hearts
Sweet Vinaigrette Dressing

Slice tomatoes and halve artichoke hearts. Chill in refrigerator. Pour Sweet Vinaigrette Dressing over tomatoes and artichoke hearts to serve.

SWEET VINAIGRETTE DRESSING

3 tablespoons sweet pickle relish   1 teaspoon salt
2 tablespoons snipped parsley   6 tablespoons vinegar
¾ teaspoon sugar   ¾ cup salad oil

Combine all ingredients, blending with egg beater or electric mixer.

FRUITED CREPE STACK

7 egg yolks   ¼ cup butter, softened
2 whole eggs   ½ teaspoon vanilla
2 cups confectioners' sugar   7 egg whites, stiffly beaten
1½ cups sifted all-purpose flour   Vegetable oil
1 cup heavy cream   Raspberry or strawberry jam
1 cup milk   Kirsch or Grand Marnier

Beat egg yolks with whole eggs and confectioners' sugar until mixture is light and frothy. Mix flour with cream, milk, butter and vanilla; add to sugar-egg mixture and combine thoroughly; finally fold in beaten egg whites. Heat oil in a crêpe pan or small skillet and make pancakes with batter, using about 2 tablespoons batter for each. Cool on flat surface. When ready to assemble stack, spread each crêpe with jam which has been slightly thinned with a small amount of Grand Marnier or Kirsch. Stack jam-spread crêpes as high as possible; use a minimum of 8 crêpes and go as high as 32. Spread Frosting generously over sides and top of stack. Bake in a preheated 450° oven until puffed, golden brown, and gorgeous.

Frosting:

4 egg yolks   ¼ cup confectioners' sugar
4 egg whites, stiffly beaten

Beat egg yolks with confectioners' sugar and add beaten egg whites; fold together.

Note: Crêpes may be made early in the day and assembled and baked just before serving.

Victory Supper

(SERVES 6)

Hot Dogs En Croûte   Sizzling Mushroom Hors d'Oeuvres
Marinated Crusty Ribs
Country Baked Potatoes (see Index)
Cucumber Salad
Peaches-After-Five
Cinnamon-Nut Butter Cookies

ADVANCE PREPARATION SCHEDULE

Freezer	Previous Day	Early Morning

Peaches-After-Five
Cinnamon-Nut Butter
  Cookies
	Prepare bread rounds
	  and make mush-
	  room mixture for
	  Sizzling Mushrooms
	Prepare marinade and
	  topping for ribs
		Prepare Hot Dogs En
		  Croûte (do not bake);
		  Potatoes (do not
		  bake)
		Cucumber Salad

HOT DOGS EN CROUTE

1 loaf thin-sliced bread	2 packages cocktail hot dogs or
¼ cup mustard	smoky links
1 medium onion, finely chopped	½ cup butter, melted
1 cup grated Parmesan cheese	

Remove crusts from bread and roll thin. Spread with a thin layer of mustard and sprinkle with chopped onion. Cut across bread to form 2 triangles. Place a hot dog along wide edge of each bread triangle; roll up bread, with a portion of each hot dog peeking through bread. Brush with melted butter and dip into grated cheese. Bake in a preheated 300° oven for 10 to 15 minutes, until hot and crisp.

SIZZLING MUSHROOM HORS D'OEUVRES

1½ pounds mushroom caps, finely chopped	1 tablespoon heavy cream
1 medium onion, grated	1 tablespoon Madeira wine
Salt and pepper to taste	20 bread rounds
2 tablespoons butter	Melted butter
1 tablespoon flour	1 cup grated, sharp Cheddar cheese

Sauté mushrooms, onion, salt and pepper in butter. Add flour and blend well. Stir in cream and Madeira and cook for 5 minutes more. Toast bread rounds on one side and dip in melted butter. Pat mushroom mixture on untoasted side of bread rounds and sprinkle cheese over tops. Broil in a preheated broiler for several minutes, until cheese is melted. Makes about 20.

MARINATED CRUSTY RIBS

8 pounds spare ribs

Marinade:

2 cups catsup	2 tablespoons vinegar
1 cup water	1 tablespoon sugar
⅔ cup vegetable oil	1 teaspoon paprika
½ cup soy sauce	½ teaspoon Tabasco
2 tablespoons Worcestershire sauce	

Topping:

⅔ cup fine bread crumbs
⅓ cup flour
¼ cup firmly packed brown sugar

1 tablespoon cornstarch
1 tablespoon dry mustard
¼ teaspoon nutmeg
¼ teaspoon ginger

Combine Marinade ingredients. Place ribs in a shallow pan and pour Marinade over meat. Let stand for 1 hour; drain, reserving Marinade. Bake in a preheated 425° oven for 10 to 15 minutes only; reduce heat to 350° and bake for 45 to 50 minutes, basting occasionally with reserved Marinade. Combine Topping ingredients; sprinkle over ribs and return to oven for 10 to 15 minutes longer.

CUCUMBER SALAD

3 medium cucumbers, peeled, seeded and diced
1 tablespoon chopped fresh dill (or 1½ teaspoons dried dill weed)

1 8-ounce container plain yogurt (1 cup)
3 teaspoons white wine vinegar
½ teaspoon salt
Chopped parsley

Mix all ingredients together thoroughly. Chill until serving time. Serve garnished with chopped parsley.

PEACHES-AFTER-FIVE

6 large fresh peaches, peeled, pitted and cut into cubes
1 cup sugar

2 cups orange juice
¼ cup lemon juice
¼ cup apricot brandy

Combine peaches, sugar, orange and lemon juices and brandy. Freeze in 6 individual serving cups. Remove from freezer 20 to 30 minutes before serving. At table, if desired, float 1 teaspoon additional brandy on top of each dessert.

CINNAMON-NUT BUTTER COOKIES

1 cup butter or margarine	1 teaspoon vanilla
½ cup sugar	1 egg white, slightly beaten
1 egg yolk	2 tablespoons sugar
¼ cup firmly packed brown sugar	1 teaspoon cinnamon
2 cups unsifted all-purpose flour	¼ cup ground nuts

Cream butter and sugars; beat in egg yolk. Add flour gradually; stir in vanilla. Work with hands till well mixed. Roll into small balls; place on cookie sheet and crisscross cookies with tines of a fork dipped in egg white. Sprinkle flattened dough with mixture of sugar, cinnamon and ground nuts, if desired. Bake in a preheated 400° oven about 10 minutes, till brown. When cookies are done, they should be approximately the size of a fifty-cent piece.

Summer Supper

(SERVES 8)

Chilled Cucumber Soup

Onion Bread

Crispy Whitefish

Spinach Soufflé   August Baked Tomatoes

Fresh Fruit Salad

Chocolate Crispies   Lemon Slices

ADVANCE PREPARATION SCHEDULE

Freezer	Previous Day	Early Morning
Chocolate Crispies	*Chilled Cucumber*	*Spinach Soufflé (do not*
Lemon Slices	*Soup*	*bake)*
	Onion Bread	*August Baked Tomatoes (do not bake)*
		Prepare Fresh Fruit Salad (omit berries)

CHILLED CUCUMBER SOUP

2 large cucumbers, peeled
  and grated (1½ cups)
1 quart buttermilk
3 scallions, minced
1 teaspoon salt
¼ cup fresh chopped parsley

1 tablespoon lemon juice
1 tablespoon dried dill weed
Freshly ground black pepper
  to taste
Thin cucumber slices
Chopped parsley

Combine grated cucumbers with buttermilk, scallions, salt, parsley, lemon juice and dill; cover and chill for several hours before serving. Soup will keep for several days. Garnish with pepper, cucumber slices, and chopped parsley.

ONION BREAD

1 cup finely chopped onions
2 eggs, beaten
1½ cup milk

4 dashes Tabasco
3 cups prepared biscuit mix
½ cup butter, melted

Caraway seeds

Combine onions, eggs, milk, Tabasco and biscuit mix. Mix well and pour into a greased 9" x 13" baking pan. Pour butter over batter and sprinkle caraway seeds on top. Bake in a preheated 350° oven for 25 minutes.

CRISPY WHITEFISH

4 pounds boned jumbo whitefish,
  cut into 8 individual portions
½ teaspoon salt
¼ teaspoon pepper
½ teaspoon onion salt

½ teaspoon seasoned salt
Dash paprika
4 tablespoons butter
Juice of 2 lemons
2 cups sour cream

2 cups corn flakes, barely crushed

Season fish with salt, pepper, onion salt and paprika; dot with butter and sprinkle with lemon juice on both sides. Place in preheated pan and bake in preheated 350° oven for 30 minutes. Spread each piece of fish with ¼ inch of sour cream and cover completely with corn flakes. Bake for 30 minutes more at 350°; serve immediately.

SPINACH SOUFFLE

1 16-ounce container small-curd
cottage cheese
3 eggs
¼ cup butter, melted
3 tablespoons flour

½ pound Mozzarella cheese,
grated
2 10-ounce packages frozen,
chopped spinach, defrosted
and well drained

Salt and pepper to taste

Beat cottage cheese with eggs. Add butter, flour and cheese. Stir in spinach and seasoning. Pour mixture into a greased 2-quart casserole; bake, uncovered, in a preheated 350° oven for 30 minutes. Serve immediately.

AUGUST BAKED TOMATOES

4 large tomatoes, cut into halves
4 tablespoons chopped parsley
½ cup ground blanched almonds

1 large clove, garlic minced
½ cup butter
¼ teaspoon salt

⅛ teaspoon pepper, or to taste

Arrange tomato halves in a shallow baking pan. Mix together the remaining ingredients and spread on tomato halves. Bake in a preheated 350° oven for 10 to 15 minutes, depending upon size of tomatoes.

FRESH FRUIT SALAD

2 large grapefruit, peeled and
sectioned
3 oranges, peeled and sliced or
sectioned
2 apples, sliced

3 bananas, sliced
3 pears, sliced
1 pint strawberries, washed and
hulled
Juice of 2 large lemons

½ cup sugar

Mix all ingredients well, substituting any fruits in season. May be made several hours in advance and chilled, but do not add berries until serving time.

CHOCOLATE CRISPIES

2 1-ounce squares unsweetened
  chocolate
½ cup butter
1 cup sugar

2 eggs
½ cup sifted all-purpose flour
½ teaspoon vanilla
¼ teaspoon salt

½ cup chopped nuts

Melt chocolate with butter; add sugar, unbeaten eggs, flour, vanilla and salt. Beat well. Spread evenly on an 11″ x 16″ baking sheet and sprinkle with nuts. Bake in a preheated 400° oven for 15 minutes. Immediately after removing from oven, cut into 2-inch squares. Break apart when cool.

LEMON SLICES

1 cup sifted all-purpose flour
¼ cup confectioners' sugar
½ cup butter, softened
2 eggs

1 cup sugar
2 tablespoons fresh lemon juice
Grated peel of 1 lemon
2 tablespoons flour

Confectioners' sugar

Combine the 1 cup flour with the ¼ cup confectioners' sugar. Cut butter into mixture with a pastry blender or 2 knives until fine crumbs form; pat dough into a greased 8-inch square pan and bake in a preheated 350° oven for 20 minutes, until slightly browned. Beat eggs; add remaining ingredients and stir well. Pour mixture over partially baked crust and bake for 20 minutes more at 350°. Remove from oven and immediately sprinkle with additional confectioners' sugar. When cool, cut into 16 2-inch squares.

Adriatic Supper

(SERVES 6)

Red Caviar Dip

Unsalted Crackers   Zucchini Appetizer-Pancakes

Chicken Paprikash

Rice

Green and Red Salad

Icebox Apple Strudel

Coffee

ADVANCE PREPARATION SCHEDULE

Freezer	Previous Day	Early Morning
Icebox Apple Strudel	*Prepare Chef's Salad Dressing*	*Prepare Red Caviar Dip Zucchini Appetizer-Pancakes Chicken Paprikash (up to point of adding sour cream) Prepare greens and radishes for salad*

RED CAVIAR DIP

8 ounces red caviar
Juice of 2 lemons
4 ounces cream cheese, softened
2 cups sour cream

Dash of Tabasco
Dash of Worcestershire sauce
5 to 6 scallions, diced
Dash of white pepper

Drain caviar in strainer; squeeze lemon juice over it until well soaked, and let it sit in strainer for several minutes while preparing remainder of recipe. Combine all remaining ingredients. When well blended, carefully fold caviar into cheese mixture. Serve with unsalted crackers and Zucchini Appetizer-Pancakes.

ZUCCHINI APPETIZER-PANCAKES

3 large zucchini, grated and
    drained well
2 eggs
3 tablespoons flour
2 tablespoons grated Parmesan
    cheese

1 teaspoon chopped chives
½ teaspoon chopped parsley
Pinch of garlic powder
Salt and pepper to taste
Oil for frying

Mix zucchini with eggs, flour, cheese and seasonings. Heat about 2 tablespoons oil in a large skillet and drop "batter" in skillet by tablespoonfuls, forming small pancakes. Brown lightly on each side. Pancakes may be prepared several hours in advance, and reheated in a 350° oven for serving. Pancakes may be served hot or cold.

Variation:

Make pancakes in larger sizes, and serve with main course as a vegetable.

CHICKEN PAPRIKASH

2 to 3 2½-pound frying chickens,
    cut up, or chicken parts
Salt and pepper
Flour
2 large onions, sliced

Butter
2 large green peppers, quartered
2 large tomatoes, quartered
1 tablespoon paprika
1 cup sour cream

Season chicken well with salt and pepper and lightly dust with flour. Brown onions in butter until soft and golden. Add chicken to onions and brown chicken pieces on all sides, while onions continue to brown. Add green peppers, tomatoes and paprika and transfer contents to a large stew pot or Dutch oven. Pour a small amount of hot water into skillet and scrape up any remaining particles of onion or chicken. Pour water and particles over chicken and add enough additional water to just cover ingredients. Cover and cook over medium heat for 1 hour. Just before serving, bring mixture to a boil; remove 2 cups of liquid from pot and very gradually add sour cream to liquid. When well blended, return gravy to pot and mix well; do not allow mixture to boil. Serve chicken and gravy with rice.

GREEN AND RED SALAD

2 cups thinly sliced radishes   2 quarts torn mixed salad greens

Combine radishes with salad greens in a bowl and coat with Chef's Salad Dressing.

CHEF'S SALAD DRESSING

2 cups olive or salad oil
1 cup tarragon vinegar
2 teaspoons salt

1 teaspoon freshly ground pepper
2 scant teaspoons Dijon mustard
2 teaspoons dry mustard

Mix all ingredients together in a jar and chill. Shake well before serving. Makes 1 quart of dressing.

ICEBOX APPLE STRUDEL

2 cups sifted all-purpose flour
1 cup sour cream
1 cup butter, softened

¾ teaspoon salt
Apple Filling
Confectioners' sugar

Combine flour, sour cream, butter and salt to make a dough. Shape into a ball, wrap in waxed paper, refrigerate overnight. Divide dough into 4 pieces; roll out each piece as thin as possible on a sheet of floured waxed paper. In center of each piece of dough, place one fourth of the Apple Filling. Fold sides of dough over each other, and pinch ends to seal in filling. Repeat process with all 4 pieces of dough and remaining Filling. Place on greased cookie sheets. Bake strudel in a preheated 450° oven for 10 minutes; reduce heat to 350° and bake for another 30 minutes. When cool, slice and sprinkle with confectioners' sugar.

Apple Filling:

2 21-ounce cans apple pie filling   1 cup chopped nuts
Cinnamon and nutmeg to taste

Combine all ingredients in a bowl.

Variation:

Combine 1 jar apricot preserves, 1 cup chopped pecans and 1 package coconut and use in place of Apple Filling.

Late Night Suppers

WHETHER after the theater or a sporting event, a concert or a quiet evening at home, the late night supper remains an intimate and friendly way to culminate an evening's entertainment. Assemble your warming plates, chafing dishes and casseroles, and have fun.

Midnight Special Supper

(SERVES 8)

Bull Shot Soup
Rolled Cheese Crisps
Beef Casserole
French Bread
Green Salad with Spiced French Dressing
Key Lime Pie
Coffee

175

ADVANCE PREPARATION SCHEDULE

Freezer	Previous Day	Early Morning
Rolled Cheese Crisps (unbaked)	*Spiced French Dressing*	*Prepare salad greens Key Lime Pie*
Beef Casserole	*Crust for Key Lime Pie*	*Remove Cheese Crisps and Beef Casserole from freezer*

BULL SHOT SOUP

3 10½-ounce cans consommé   Vodka to taste
16 lemon slices

Serve hot consommé in mugs. Pass vodka and lemon slices and permit each guest to "season to taste."

ROLLED CHEESE CRISPS

⅓ cup grated Gruyere cheese   Freshly ground black pepper
1 teaspoon heavy cream   16 slices very thin white bread,
1 egg, slightly beaten   crusts removed
¼ cup butter, softened

Blend together cheese, cream, egg, butter and pepper. Remove crusts and flatten bread with a rolling pin. Spread each slice of bread with the cheese mixture and roll up, securing with a toothpick. Place prepared ones, seam side down, on a cookie sheet, cover with a damp towel while you are rolling up rest. (May be frozen at this point). Bake in a preheated 350° oven for 15 minutes or until golden. Remove toothpicks and serve on napkins.

BEEF CASSEROLE

3 pounds beef top round steak
½ cup flour
½ teaspoon salt
½ teaspoon pepper
½ teaspoon paprika
½ teaspoon seasoned salt
Cayenne pepper to taste
Vegetable oil
2 cloves garlic, minced
1 medium onion, finely chopped
2 cups Burgundy wine

24 small potatoes, cooked and peeled
2 cups diced cooked carrots
2 cups cooked peas
2 bunches scallions, cut into 2-inch pieces
2 4½-ounce cans button mushrooms
1 cup chili sauce
Salt and pepper to taste
Pinch of dried marjoram leaves

Cut meat into small chunks. Season flour with salt, pepper, paprika, seasoned salt and Cayenne pepper. Roll meat in seasoned flour and brown in a skillet with a small amount of hot oil, garlic and onions. Put meat and onions into a Dutch oven or deep casserole. Put enough hot water into skillet to loosen browned onions and meat drippings, add wine; add to casserole. Add enough water to casserole to barely cover meat. Bake, covered, in a preheated 325° oven for 1½ hours, or until meat is almost tender. Add remaining ingredients and cook just until vegetables are tender and heated through. Left-over vegetables may be used in this dish.

SPICED FRENCH DRESSING

⅓ cup sugar
1 teaspoon salt
½ teaspoon paprika
¼ teaspoon cinnamon
¼ teaspoon ground cloves
¼ cup vinegar

1 tablespoon steak sauce or Worcestershire sauce
½ cup vegetable or olive oil
⅔ cup catsup
Juice of 1 lemon

Beat all ingredients with an egg beater until thick. Serve over mixed salad greens.

KEY LIME PIE

Pie Crust Dough
1 cup sugar
¼ cup flour
3 tablespoons cornstarch
¼ teaspoon salt
2 cups water
3 egg yolks, beaten well

1 tablespoon butter
¼ cup lime juice
Grated peel of 1 lemon or 1 lime
3 drops green food coloring
3 egg whites, at room
    temperature
¼ teaspoon cream of tartar

6 tablespoons sugar

Using a half recipe of the Pie Crust Dough, prepare and bake a 9-inch pastry shell. Cool. Combine the 1 cup sugar, flour, cornstarch and salt in a saucepan, and gradually stir in water. Cook mixture over low heat until thickened, stirring constantly. Slowly stir mixture into beaten egg yolks; return to saucepan and cook over low heat for 2 minutes, stirring constantly. Stir in butter, lime juice, peel and food coloring; cool slightly; pour into baked pastry shell and cool completely. Make meringue topping by beating egg whites with cream of tartar until soft peaks form. Gradually beat in the 6 table-spoons sugar; beat until meringue is stiff and glossy. Pile meringue topping on cooled pie filling, spreading meringue to sides of pastry. Bake in a preheated 425° oven until meringue browns, about 5 min-utes. Chill pie several hours before serving.

Pie Crust Dough:

¼ cup soft butter
4 teaspoons granulated sugar
⅓ cup soft shortening

1½ cups plus 3 tablespoons sifted
    all-purpose flour
½ teaspoon salt

3 tablespoons water

Beat butter and sugar with fork until creamy; then blend in short-ening. Combine flour and salt, and blend into butter mixture with fork. Gradually stir in water with fork until mixture cleans side of bowl. If needed, add extra water, one-half teaspoon at a time. Di-vide dough in half and roll to ⅛-inch thickness. Bake at 450° for 15 to 20 minutes or until golden brown. Makes enough dough for two 9-inch pastry shells or one 9-inch double crust.

Soup and Sandwich Supper

(SERVES 12)

Minestrone
Italian Beef Sandwiches
Green Peppers
Tomato and Onion Salad
Apricot Pastries
Beer   Chianti
Coffee

ADVANCE PREPARATION SCHEDULE

Freezer	Previous Day	Early Morning
Minestrone	*Prepare beef for Italian Beef Sandwiches*	*Tomato and Onion Salad*
	Red Wine Vinaigrette Dressing	*Remove Minestrone from freezer*
	Apricot Pastries	

MINESTRONE

½ cup dried kidney beans, soaked
overnight in cold water
2 slices bacon, diced
¼ pound ham, diced
½ pound Italian sausage (hot or
mild) diced
1 large onion, chopped
3 cloves garlic, minced
3 large stalks celery, chopped
1 large leek, chopped

2 small zucchini, chopped
2 quarts beef stock
½ large cabbage, shredded
1 cup Italian red wine
1 18½-ounce can Italian tomatoes
½ cup elbow macaroni
Salt and pepper to taste
¼ cup chopped fresh basil or 2
teaspoons dried basil leaves

Grated Parmesan cheese

In a heavy skillet, fry bacon, ham and sausage until brown. Add
onions, garlic, celery, leek and zucchini; cook until well-blended,

about 10 minutes. Heat beef stock in a large soup kettle. Add contents of skillet, plus drained kidney beans, cabbage and wine to stock. Simmer, partially covered, for 90 minutes. Add tomatoes, macaroni, salt, pepper and basil (if using dried basil); cook for 15 minutes. If using fresh basil, add to soup now. Simmer for 5 minutes. Serve with freshly grated Parmesan cheese.

ITALIAN BEEF SANDWICHES

1 5-pound beef rump roast, slashed on all sides, with 2 slivered garlic cloves stuck into slashes
1 tablespoon fennel seed
6 beef bouillon cubes
3 cups boiling water
½ cup chopped green pepper

1 clove garlic, minced
2 tablespoons Worcestershire sauce
1 teaspoon each dried marjoram, oregano and thyme leaves
Salt and pepper to taste
Few drops Tabasco
Italian bread

Place prepared meat on a wire rack in an open roasting pan; sprinkle with fennel seed. Dissolve bouillon cubes in water and pour into pan underneath rack. Roast in a preheated 325° oven, allowing 20 minutes per pound. Roast should be rare. When done, cool and slice meat paper thin. Add all the remaining ingredients, except bread, to the gravy in pan. Simmer for 15 minutes and add sliced beef to gravy. Cover and let beef marinate in gravy for 4 to 5 hours or overnight, refrigerated. Before serving, simmer beef and gravy over low heat. When heated through, serve meat and gravy on slices of Italian bread.

Variation:

Cut 6 large green peppers in half. Remove seeds and white membrane, and cut each into 8 sections, lengthwise. Place peppers in a skillet with 3 tablespoons of oil and sauté over low heat until soft and beginning to lose shape; cook for at least 30 minutes. Salt to taste and serve on top of Italian Beef Sandwiches.

TOMATO AND ONION SALAD

6 large tomatoes, cut into wedges
6 red onions, cut into wedges
1 teaspoon each dried oregano
  leaves, salt and pepper

Red Wine Vinaigrette Dressing
  (see Index)
2 ounces Roquefort cheese
  (optional)

Combine tomato and onion wedges with seasonings and chill. Make dressing and, if desired, mash cheese into it. Before serving, toss vegetables with dressing.

APRICOT PASTRIES

2 cups butter
1 cup sugar
1 large or 2 small eggs, well
  beaten

1 teaspoon vanilla
5 cups sifted all-purpose flour
2 16-ounce jars apricot jam

Cream butter and sugar; add eggs and vanilla. Slowly add all the flour, using hands to combine well. Chill dough for several hours, until easy to handle. Pat two-thirds of the dough into bottom and on sides of an ungreased 10½ x 15½ x 1-inch jelly-roll pan. Keep remaining dough refrigerated. Spread jam over dough with a spatula. Roll out remaining dough and cut into thin strips; place strips over jam in a lattice pattern, 1-inch apart. Bake in a preheated 350° oven for 40 minutes. Cut into bars while still warm. Makes about 60 bars.

Day-Before Supper

(SERVES 8)

Cheese Snacks   Cold Spinach Soup
Veal Curry
Condiments: coconut, raisins, mandarin oranges,
cashews, chutney, sunflower seeds
Rice   Lemonade-Ring Mold
World's Best Chocolate Cake
Coffee

ADVANCE PREPARATION SCHEDULE

Previous Day

Cheese Snacks
Cold Spinach Soup
Veal Curry
Lemonade-Ring Mold
World's Best Chocolate Cake

CHEESE SNACKS

8 ounces Cheddar cheese, grated   ½ teaspoon salt
1 cup butter, softened   2 cups sifted all-purpose flour
⅛ teaspoon cayenne pepper   2 cups crisp rice cereal

Blend together cheese and butter; add Cayenne, salt and flour, blend
well. Mix cereal in last. Form mixture into 60 to 70 small balls,
about ¾ inch in diameter. Place on an ungreased cookie sheet,
about 20 balls per sheet. Flatten with a fork when ready to bake.
Bake in a preheated 400° oven for 10 minutes. May be served cold
or warm.

COLD SPINACH SOUP

2 10-ounce packages frozen spinach, defrosted and drained
3 10½-ounce cans condensed cream of chicken soup, undiluted

Juice of 2 lemons
1 medium cucumber, peeled and cut up
6 tablespoons sour cream

Place all ingredients in the container of an electric blender; blend completely. Refrigerate until ready to serve. Serve with a dollop of additional sour cream on top of each serving.

VEAL CURRY

2 cloves garlic
4 tablespoons shortening
3 pounds lean boneless veal, cut into bite-size pieces
2 cans condensed cream of mushroom soup, undiluted
1½ soup cans of milk
1½ teaspoons salt

¼ teaspoon pepper
2 tablespoons curry powder
10 scallions, thinly sliced
2 cups drained pineapple chunks
2 cups green pepper chunks
2½ cups rice, cooked as directed on package

Brown garlic in shortening, and remove. Add veal to shortening and brown it well. Stir in soup, milk, seasonings and scallions. Simmer, covered, for 30 minutes. Refrigerate. (Can be made to this point the previous day). To serve, gradually reheat curry, stir in pineapple and green pepper and serve over hot cooked rice. If desired, curry may be served with a selection of condiments.

LEMONADE-RING MOLD

3 3-ounce packages lemon-flavored gelatin
4 cups boiling water

1 12-ounce can frozen lemonade concentrate
1 9-ounce container Whipped Topping

Dissolve gelatin in boiling water, add lemonade concentrate and cool in refrigerator. When cool, whip with an electric mixer and add whipped topping mixing until smooth. Pour into a 7- to 8-cup mold and refrigerate overnight. Serve surrounded by condiments for Veal Curry.

WORLD'S BEST CHOCOLATE CAKE

½ cup butter, softened
2 cups sugar
2 eggs
½ cup sour cream
2 cups sifted cake flour
3 1-ounce squares unsweetened
chocolate, melted

1 teaspoon baking soda
1 cup strong coffee
1 to 2 16-ounce cans chocolate
fudge topping

Cream butter and sugar, blend in eggs and sour cream. Add flour gradually, mixing thoroughly. Blend in melted chocolate. Dissolve baking soda in coffee and add to batter. Blend well and pour into two buttered and floured round 9-inch cake pans. Bake in a pre-heated 350° oven for 30 minutes, or until toothpick inserted in center of cake comes out clean. Set aside until cool enough to handle. Remove from pans. Cool completely. Thickly frost with chocolate fudge topping between layers, on sides and top. Chill for several hours or overnight.

October Supper

(SERVES 6)

Chicken and Bacon Hors d'Oeuvres
Beef Stew Goulash
Vegetable Salad
Hot Herb Bread
Apricot Icebox Cake
Coffee

Freezer	Previous Day	Early Morning
Chicken and Bacon Hors d'Oeuvres	*Honey Vinaigrette Dressing*	*Marinate salad ingredients in dressing*
Beef Stew Goulash (omit sour cream and potatoes)	*Apricot Icebox Cake*	*Remove Herb Bread, Beef Stew Goulash and Hors d'Oeuvres from freezer*
Herb Bread (do not bake)		

CHICKEN AND BACON HORS D'OEUVRES

2 large whole chicken breasts, skinned, boned and cut into small pieces
¾ pound thin-sliced bacon, each slice cut into 3 pieces
1 tablespoon cornstarch
1 cup all-purpose flour
1½ teaspoons baking powder
2 teaspoons salt
1 tablespoon sugar
1 egg, beaten
½ cup milk
½ cup water
Oil for frying
Sweet and Sour Sauce

Wrap each piece of chicken in ⅓ slice of bacon, and secure with toothpicks. Add dry ingredients, one at a time, to beaten egg, stirring until smooth. Add milk and water to mixture and mix well. Heat oil to a depth of about 2 inches in a deep saucepan to a temperature of 375° on a deep-fat-frying thermometer. Dip bacon rolls into batter and fry a few at a time in the hot oil until brown. Drain on paper towels. Serve hot with Sweet and Sour Sauce. Makes about 30 hors d'oeuvres, which may be frozen and reheated in a 425° oven.

Sweet and Sour Sauce:

Mix 1 cup apricot preserves with 2 tablespoons white vinegar. More vinegar may be added if desired.

BEEF STEW GOULASH

3 pounds boneless beef chuck, cut
into ½-inch cubes
2 tablespoons butter
2 tablespoons Hungarian paprika
Dash of salt
2 tablespoons flour

½ medium onion, chopped
⅛ teaspoon dried marjoram
leaves
1 cup beef stock or water
¼ cup sherry or dry white wine
1 cup sour cream

6 to 10 boiled peeled potatoes

Sauté beef chunks in butter until browned. Sprinkle paprika, salt
and flour over meat in skillet; stir to blend. Add onion, marjoram,
beef stock or water and wine. Cover and simmer until meat is
tender, about 2 to 3 hours. Add sour cream slowly to 1 cup of the
gravy and then add combined sour cream and gravy to stew. Do
not boil after sour cream is added. Heat carefully and garnish
with hot boiled potatoes.

VEGETABLE SALAD

1 16-ounce can whole dill string
beans, drained
1 2-ounce jar pimento, drained
and cut in strips
1 17-ounce can black olives,
drained and sliced
1 stalk celery, cut up
6 raw mushrooms, sliced

1 bunch scallions, sliced thin
1 small cauliflower, separated into
flowerettes
1 16-ounce can artichoke hearts,
drained
2 zucchini, sliced
1 4-ounce bottle stuffed green
olives, drained

1 large green pepper, sliced

Combine salad ingredients and mix with Honey Vinaigrette Dressing: marinate for 6 hours in the refrigerator, stirring frequently.
Before serving salad, drain well.

HONEY VINAIGRETTE DRESSING

1 cup salad oil
⅓ cup red wine vinegar
1 heaping tablespoon honey

1 clove garlic, mashed
1 tablespoon pickle relish
Salt and pepper to taste

Mix dressing ingredients well and refrigerate. Make the day before
using. Stir or shake dressing occasionally.

HOT HERB BREAD

1 large loaf French bread	8 to 10 scallions, finely chopped
½ cup butter, softened	1 small bunch chives, finely chopped
1 small bunch parsley, finely chopped	1 sprig fresh dill, finely chopped
	½ teaspoon salt

Split bread in half lengthwise. Combine butter with remaining ingredients and cream well. Spread butter mixture on each half of loaf and press loaf together again. Heat bread in a preheated 350° oven for 20 minutes. Cut into 1-inch slices and serve hot.

APRICOT ICEBOX CAKE

1 pound dried apricots	4 packages ladyfingers
½ cup sugar	1 cup heavy cream, whipped
2 3-ounce packages lemon-flavored gelatin	Shaved chocolate or grated lemon peel

Soak apricots in cold water for several hours. Drain and measure liquid from apricots, adding enough water to make 4 cups. Add apricots and sugar; cook until soft. Cool and drain apricots, reserving liquid; if necessary add water to make 4 cups. Heat liquid to boiling; add to gelatin and stir until dissolved. Strain apricots through a sieve and add to gelatin mixture. Refrigerate until jelly-like consistency. Arrange some of the ladyfingers on sides and bottom of a lightly greased 9-inch spring form pan. Alternate layers of apricot-gelatin mixture and the remaining ladyfingers in lined pan. Top cake with whipped cream, chocolate or lemon peel and refrigerate until serving time.

Winner's Supper

(SERVES 4)

Appetizer Salad
Veal Jackpot
Eggplant-Rice Casserole
Strawberry Bonanza
Champagne

ADVANCE PREPARATION SCHEDULE

Freezer

*Vanilla ice cream for Strawberry
Bonanza*

Early Morning

*Appetizer Salad
Veal Jackpot (except sour cream)
Prepare Eggplant-Rice Casserole
(do not bake)*

APPETIZER SALAD

Dressing:

6 tablespoons olive oil
1 large clove garlic, crushed

3 tablespoons wine vinegar
1 teaspoon chopped fresh basil

Salad:

½ pound fresh white mush-
rooms, thinly sliced
¼ pound boiled ham, thinly
sliced
2 ounces white truffles,
thinly sliced (optional)

Salt and freshly ground pepper
1 small head iceberg lettuce,
shredded

Combine dressing ingredients; set aside. Combine all salad ingredients; toss well and chill. Thirty minutes before serving, toss salad
with dressing. Return to refrigerator and chill until serving time.

VEAL JACKPOT

1½ pounds veal steak, cut into thin strips
2 tablespoons butter
½ cup water
1 teaspoon dried basil leaves
1 medium green pepper, diced
1 cup thinly sliced onions
2 tablespoons butter
1 6-ounce can broiled sliced mushrooms, drained
1 15-ounce can tomato sauce
½ cup canned, halved water chestnuts
Few drops Tabasco
1 teaspoon Worcestershire sauce
Salt and pepper to taste
½ cup dry sherry
1 cup sour cream

Slowly brown veal in the 2 tablespoons butter, stirring often; add water and basil. Cover and simmer for 20 minutes. Meanwhile, cook green pepper and onions in the remaining 2 tablespoons butter, cooking until soft. Combine veal with green pepper, onions, mushrooms, tomato sauce and water chestnuts. Mix well; cover and simmer for 15 minutes. Stir in all the remaining ingredients except sour cream. Simmer for 5 minutes; lower heat and slowly stir in sour cream. Heat but do not boil.

EGGPLANT-RICE CASSEROLE

1 young eggplant, unpeeled and sliced into 8 ½-inch thick slices
2 tablespoons butter
½ small yellow onion, diced
2 large tomatoes, peeled and cut into 12 slices
4 fresh basil leaves
Salt
1 cup raw rice, cooked in chicken broth
Butter
Grated Parmesan cheese

Brown eggplant slices lightly on both sides in butter. Arrange half the eggplant slices and half of the diced onion on bottom of a buttered 1½-quart casserole. Put 6 tomato slices and 2 basil leaves on top; sprinkle with salt. Spread with half of rice and repeat layers. Dot top with butter and sprinkle with Parmesan cheese. Bake in a preheated 350° oven for 30 minutes.

STRAWBERRY BONANZA

1 pint strawberries, sliced	¼ cup butter, melted
2 large bananas, sliced	2 tablespoons Cointreau
1 tablespoon sugar	1 tablespoon brandy
Juice of 1 large lemon	Vanilla ice cream
⅓ cup firmly packed brown sugar	

Sprinkle sliced strawberries and bananas with sugar; squeeze lemon juice over fruit; toss together gently, and set aside. Heat brown sugar with melted butter; when hot, add Cointreau and brandy. Heat until syrupy and hot; add strawberries and bananas, and serve warm over vanilla ice cream.

Champagne Supper

(SERVES 6)

Shrimp and Cantaloupe Cocktail
Pepper Steak with Rissolé Potatoes
Garlic Bread
Green Salad with Anchovy Dressing (see Index)
Tarte à l'Orange
Champagne

ADVANCE PREPARATION SCHEDULE

Freezer	Previous Day	Early Morning
Garlic Bread (do not broil)	*Anchovy Dressing*	*Shrimp and Cantaloupe Cocktail* *Pepper Steak* *Prepare greens for salad* *Tarte à l'Orange*

SHRIMP AND CANTALOUPE COCKTAIL

2 cups mayonnaise
1½ cups half-and-half
5 tablespoons medium dry
   sherry

2 large cantaloupes
2 pounds shrimp (cooked, shelled
   and deveined)

Combine mayonnaise, half-and-half and sherry. Chill. Cut melon in half and form balls with melon ball scoop. Lightly toss melon balls, shrimp and sauce; serve cold.

PEPPER STEAK WITH RISSOLE POTATOES

2 pounds beef tenderloin or
   sirloin steak
¼ cup butter
1 large sweet onion, diced
1 large green pepper, diced
½ pound fresh mushrooms, diced

2 cloves garlic, minced
1 teaspoon salt
¾ tablespoon ground peppercorns
2 tablespoons Maggi seasoning
2 tablespoons dry sherry
Rissolé Potatoes

Slice beef into strips ¼ inch thick. Sauté in 2 tablespoons of the butter just until meat changes color. Sauté onions, green pepper, mushrooms and garlic in the remaining butter until tender. Add meat to vegetables in skillet and add remaining ingredients and set aside. May be prepared ahead up to this point. When ready to serve, heat meat and vegetables through, about 5 to 10 minutes. Place in chafing dish or on platter and top with hot Rissolé Potatoes.

Rissolé Potatoes:

18 small potatoes, peeled
¼ teaspoon salt

⅛ teaspoon pepper
⅛ teaspoon paprika

½ cup butter

Drop potatoes into boiling water and parboil for 5 minutes. Remove to a baking pan; sprinkle with salt, pepper and paprika; dot with butter. Bake potatoes in a preheated 350° oven for 30 minutes, until brown and crispy.

GARLIC BREAD

1 loaf Italian bread, cut into 1
    inch slices
½ cup butter

1 cup grated Parmesan cheese
1 tablespoon garlic powder

Place the bread slices on a cookie sheet. Melt butter and blend in cheese and garlic powder. Spoon some of the mixture over each slice of bread, covering it well. Place in a preheated broiler and broil until cheese melts and bread is golden. Serve hot.

TARTE A L'ORANGE

1 12-ounce package frozen patty
    shells, thawed
2 tablespoons sugar
4 egg yolks
⅓ cup sugar
¼ cup flour
1½ cups orange juice
Grated peel of 1 small lemon

Grated peel of 1 small navel orange
6 ladyfingers, split
½ cup apricot preserves
1 tablespoon sugar
6 tablespoons Grand Marnier
2 large navel oranges, sliced
    paper-thin and seeds removed
    (notch peel if desired)

Roll patty shells into one large shell to fit a 9-inch tart pan with removable bottom. Fit waxed paper or foil into pastry shell and fill with raw rice to keep shell from puffing up in center. Bake in a preheated 400° oven for 15 minutes. Remove rice and paper; sprinkle shell with the 2 tablespoons sugar. Prick with fork and return to oven. Bake 20 minutes longer or until shell is golden and sugar is carmelized. Cool on rack. In a saucepan beat egg yolks until pale yellow and thick. Beat in the ⅓ cup sugar, flour and orange juice. Cook until custard is thickened, stirring constantly, about 5 minutes. Cool. Add lemon and orange peels. Cut split ladyfingers lengthwise in halves. Make a glaze by combining apricot preserves, sugar and 2 tablespoons of the Grand Marnier. Cook several minutes until well blended. Strain and set aside.

Place orange slices on flat plate and sprinkle with the remaining

4 tablespoons Grand Marnier. Set aside for 15 minutes. Fill tart shell with the orange custard. Cover completely with ladyfingers, filling in open spaces with additional pieces. Drain juice from orange slices and spoon juice over ladyfingers. Arrange orange slices decoratively over ladyfingers. Brush top with the apricot glaze and chill. Serve same day.

Foreign Menus

THE CONTRIBUTIONS of the various cultures found in our country offer an opportunity for many taste delights. A sampling is offered here. The Continental Menus embody exciting recipes and a departure from ordinary dining. The Italian, Greek, Mexican and Indonesian menus represent some national favorites, and a few American standards which work well.

When serving Oriental food, it is well worth the time spent chopping and dicing, and cooking the food at the last minute, so it can be brought to the table hot and delicious. A traditional Chinese menu offers the same number of courses as there are guests. An interesting and useful addition for an Oriental dinner is a wok. A wok is a cooking pan (in the shape of the old coolie's hat that has been inverted), which is placed upon a metal collar over the heat.

Wherever possible, we have added interesting coffee recipes to be used as you choose and which are often served in demitasse cups. An espresso maker (Macchinetta) is nice to have. However, Instant Espresso is now available and creates an outstanding finish to any meal.

★

CONTINENTAL

Five Star Dinner

(SERVES 8)

Seviche
Poularde en Papillote
Cheese Soufflé with Broccoli Sauce
Green Salad with Tomato French Dressing
Crème Brûlée
Café Diable

ADVANCE PREPARATION SCHEDULE

Freezer	Previous Day	Early Morning
Cheese Soufflé (ready to bake)	*Seviche*	*Cook broccoli for Broccoli Sauce*
	Tomato French Dressing	*Prepare salad greens*
	Crème Brûlée	

Note: Because of the different baking temperatures of Poularde en Papillote and Cheese Soufflé, this menu requires two ovens.

SEVICHE

2 pounds halibut fillets, cut into cubes
2 cups lemon juice
2 cups chopped onion
½ cup tomato purée
½ cup tomato juice
1 tablespoon salt
16 green pimiento-stuffed olives, chopped

2 tablespoons Worcestershire sauce
1 teaspoon Tabasco
2 small green chilies, chopped
3 firm tomatoes, peeled and chopped
2 tablespoons chopped fresh parsley
1 green pepper, diced

Marinate raw halibut in lemon juice for 6 hours in refrigerator. Remove fish from refrigerator. Pour off and discard 1 cup of the lemon juice. Combine the remaining ingredients and add to fish. Mix well, cover and refrigerate overnight.

POULARDE EN PAPILLOTE
(CHICKEN IN THE BAG)

8 whole chicken breasts, cut in half
Salt and pepper
1 cup butter
1 tablespoon chopped shallots
¾ cup chopped mushrooms
1½ cups dry white wine
¾ cup dry vermouth

1½ cups beef stock or rich bouillon
⅓ cup slivered cooked ham
3 tablespoons chopped fresh tarragon
3 tablespoons flour
3 tablespoons soft butter

Season chicken pieces with salt and pepper. In a large skillet, sauté chicken in the 1 cup butter over low heat until lightly browned on both sides. Remove chicken and keep warm. Add shallots to skillet and cook for 1 minute. Then add mushrooms and cook shallots and mushrooms for 5 minutes. Pour wine and vermouth into skillet; cook until liquid is reduced by half. Add beef stock; replace chicken in skillet. Cover and cook for 20 minutes. Remove chicken and keep warm. To make sauce, add ham and tarragon to juices in the skillet. Mix flour and the 3 tablespoons of butter to a smooth paste; add to juices. Cook, stirring constantly, until sauce is thickened and smooth. To serve chicken, rub insides and outsides of 8 brown, unglazed sandwich bags with soft butter. Place 2 pieces of chicken inside each bag and cover with 3 or 4 tablespoons of sauce. Fold over bag edges; twist and seal tightly. Place in a large shallow baking pan. Bake in a preheated 400° oven for 10 minutes; serve chicken inside paper bags.

CHEESE SOUFFLE WITH BROCCOLI SAUCE

6 tablespoons butter or margarine
⅓ cup all-purpose flour
2 cups milk
12 ounces sharp American processed cheese, shredded (3 cups)

6 egg yolks, beaten until thick and lemon-colored
6 egg whites
½ teaspoon cream of tartar
Broccoli Sauce

Melt butter and blend in flour. Add milk; cook and stir until thick and bubbly. Add cheese, stirring until melted. Remove from heat. Gradually stir hot sauce into beaten egg yolks; cool. Beat egg whites with cream of tartar until stiff. Fold egg yolk mixture into whites. Pour into 8 ungreased 1-cup soufflé dishes. Cover with foil and freeze. To serve, remove foil from dishes and place frozen soufflés in shallow pan with ½ inch hot water in the bottom. Bake in a preheated 300° oven until a knife inserted off-center comes out clean, about 1¼ hours. While soufflés cook, prepare Broccoli Sauce. When soufflés are done, serve immediately with sauce.

Broccoli Sauce:

¼ cup chopped onion
2 tablespoons butter
2 tablespoons flour
1 chicken bouillon cube, dissolved in ½ cup boiling water

1 cup milk
1 10-ounce package frozen chopped broccoli, cooked and drained

In a saucepan, cook onion in butter until tender. Blend in flour. Gradually add bouillon and milk. Cook, stirring, until thick and bubbly. Add broccoli to sauce and heat through.

TOMATO FRENCH DRESSING

2 cups salad oil
1 cup vinegar
½ cup sugar
2 tablespoons Worcestershire
  sauce

1 tablespoon dry mustard
Salt, pepper and paprika to taste
1 10¾-ounce can condensed
  tomato soup
1 clove garlic

Shake all ingredients well in large jar and store in refrigerator.
Makes about 1½ quarts.

CREME BRULEE

3 cups heavy cream
6 egg yolks
6 tablespoons sugar

1 teaspoon vanilla
¾ cup firmly packed light brown
  sugar

Scald cream by bringing it just to the boiling point and removing
from heat. In a double boiler, over hot water, beat egg yolks, and
sugar with rotary beater, slowly add scalded cream. Stir mixture
constantly until the consistency of thin mayonnaise. Add vanilla,
mix well and pour into a shallow 1½-quart baking dish. Refrigerate
several hours or overnight. Sift brown sugar evenly over custard
to a depth of ¼ inch. Place in a preheated broiler 3 inches from
heat and broil about 2 minutes, until sugar melts and makes a shiny
caramel glaze. Watch carefully to avoid burning. Chill and serve.
May be served with fresh fruits.

CAFE DIABLE

½ cinnamon stick
6 whole cloves
1 curl orange peel

8 lumps sugar
8 ounces brandy
4 cups strong hot coffee

Mix all ingredients, except coffee, in chafing dish. Heat and flame
with lighted match, slowly add coffee and ladle into demitasse cups.

Riviera Dinner

(SERVES 8)

Artichoke Hors d'Oeuvres   Egg Salad de la Mer
Rosettes de Boeuf
Garden Fresh Tomatoes   Pommes Suisse
Mixed Green Salad with Vegetable Dressing
Marron Mousse
Coffee

ADVANCE PREPARATION SCHEDULE

Freezer

*Marron Mousse (must defrost for 8
hours: note well!)*

Early Morning

*Artichoke Hors d'Oeuvres (do not
broil)
Egg Salad and Crabmeat Sauce
Vegetable Dressing
Prepare salad greens*

ARTICHOKE HORS D'OEUVRES

2 cups mayonnaise
1¼ cups grated Parmesan cheese
1 teaspoon Dijon mustard
½ teaspoon grated onion
Dash Worcestershire sauce
1 loaf sliced white bread, cut
into 3-inch rounds and
toasted on one side under
broiler
2 14-ounce cans artichoke hearts,
quartered

Mix mayonnaise with cheese, mustard, onion and Worcestershire.
On untoasted sides of bread rounds, spread a thin layer of mayonnaise mixture. Center one-quarter artichoke heart on each round
and spread the artichoke with a generous layer of mayonnaise mixture. Place hors d'oeuvres on a cookie sheet and broil in a preheated
broiler until slightly puffed and golden brown. Can be prepared
without broiling up to six hours in advance. Makes 40 to 44 hors
d'oeuvres.

EGG SALAD DE LA MER

12 hard-cooked eggs, chopped fine
Mayonnaise
  3 tablespoons chopped green
    pepper

2 tablespoons chopped scallion
  tops
Salt and pepper to taste

Mix eggs with just enough mayonnaise to moisten. Add green pepper, scallions and seasoning, and press mixture into a greased 6-cup ring mold. Refrigerate. To serve, unmold onto a serving plate and serve with Crabmeat Sauce.

CRABMEAT SAUCE

1 cup mayonnaise
1 package frozen crabmeat,
  drained, flaked and
  sprinkled with lemon juice
⅓ cup chili sauce

⅓ cup sour cream
2 tablespoons drained, chopped
  pimiento
1 tablespoon chopped scallion
  bottoms

Juice of ½ lemon

Combine all ingredients and chill. Serve Crabmeat Sauce in a dish accompanying Egg Salad.

ROSETTES DE BOEUF

8 filet steaks, seasoned with salt,
  pepper, and garlic salt
Butter to sauté steaks, about ¼
  cup
½ cup port wine
½ cup beef stock or beef bouillon
Salt and pepper

1 pound mushrooms, sliced or
  quartered
Butter to sauté mushrooms, about
  2 tablespoons
3 tablespoons heavy cream
Juice of ½ lemon
Pimientos to garnish

In preheated heavy skillet, sauté seasoned steaks in butter. Cook according to taste, remove from pan and keep steaks warm. Make sauce by adding port, stock, salt and pepper to pan juices. In another pan, sauté mushrooms in butter. Add cream and cook for several minutes; add lemon juice. Transfer filets to a warmed serving dish and top with mushrooms. Heat sauce and pour it over filets. Decorate with fine slices of pimiento criss-crossed over filets.

GARDEN FRESH TOMATOES

4 tablespoons butter	2 pounds firm tomatoes, peeled
Salt and pepper to taste	and quartered

In a saucepan melt butter. Add salt, pepper and tomatoes. Heat and stir gently about 4 minutes, just until tomatoes are heated. Serve at once.

POMMES SUISSE

2 16-ounce packages frozen hash browned potatoes	Salt and pepper to taste
½ cup butter	1 cup coarsely grated Swiss cheese
½ cup chopped onion	

One hour before preparing them, remove potatoes from freezer. Separate potato pieces with a fork. Melt butter in a 10-inch skillet. Combine onions and potatoes and add to butter in skillet. Season with salt and pepper, and stir to coat potatoes evenly with melted butter. Sprinkle with cheese, and with a broad spatula press mixture into firm layer in the skillet. Cook, without stirring at all, over medium-high heat for 20 to 25 minutes. When crusty and browned on the bottom, loosen potatoes with spatula and invert on a platter.

VEGETABLE DRESSING

1 cup sour cream	¼ cup finely chopped radishes
½ cup mayonnaise	¼ cup finely chopped cucumbers, drained
1½ to 2 tablespoons vinegar	
1 tablespoon sugar	1 clove garlic, finely chopped
1 teaspoon salt	¼ cup finely chopped green peppers
Dash pepper	
¼ cup finely chopped green onions	

Blend sour cream, mayonnaise, vinegar, sugar and seasonings. Stir in chopped vegetables. Chill. Serve over mixed green salad.

MARRON MOUSSE

2 egg yolks, beaten well
¾ cup confectioners' sugar
1 teaspoon vanilla
9 stale macaroons, cut into small
   bits
1½ cup miniature marshmallows

1 10-ounce jar marron pieces,
   in brandy or vanilla syrup
3 cups heavy cream
Maraschino cherries or whole
   marrons for garnish

Blend first 3 ingredients thoroughly. Add macaroon bits, marshmallows and marrons and mix well. Whip cream until stiff, and
fold into marron mixture. Pour into 8-inch spring form pan. Cover
and freeze mousse. To serve, defrost mousse for 8 hours in refrigerator. Remove rim of pan and garnish with maraschino cherries or
whole marrons.

Classic Dinner

(SERVES 6)

Cream of Watercress Soup
Sole en Papillote
Rissolé Potatoes (see Index)
Mushrooms Stuffed with Spinach
Cucumber Mold
Orange Compote à la Française
Pecan Cookies
Coffee

ADVANCE PREPARATION SCHEDULE

Freezer	Previous Day	Early Morning
Pecan Cookies	*Cucumber Mold*	*Soup (up to point of adding cream)*
	Orange Compote	*Sole en Papillote (up to point of baking)*
		Stuff mushrooms with spinach (ready to bake)
		Remove Pecan Cookies from freezer

CREAM OF WATERCRESS SOUP

1 pound firm, tender watercress, chopped
¼ cup butter, melted
Béchamel Sauce
1 cup chicken consommé

Salt and white pepper to taste
1 cup heavy cream
1 tablespoon chopped fresh chervil or 1 teaspoon dried chervil leaves

Combine watercress with butter in a large skillet. Add the Béchamel Sauce. Simmer gently uncovered for 15 minutes. Rub mixture through a fine sieve or food mill. Add consommé and heat soup to boiling point. Add salt and pepper to taste. At last minute, add cream and chervil.

BECHAMEL SAUCE

4 cups milk
6 tablespoons flour

6 tablespoons butter, melted

Heat milk just to boiling. Combine flour and butter in a saucepan. Gradually stir in milk. Simmer over low heat for 5 minutes stirring constantly. Strain through a fine sieve. Makes 4 cups.

SOLE EN PAPILLOTE

6 filets of sole, ½-pound each
1 cup chopped scallions
2 tablespoons butter
2 tablespoons flour

4 tomatoes, peeled and chopped
2 teaspoons red wine vinegar
1 teaspoon dried thyme leaves
1 teaspoon salt

6 aluminum foil squares

Wash filets and dry on paper towels. Sauté scallions in butter for several minutes; blend in flour, stirring until smooth. Add tomatoes, vinegar and seasonings and cook for several minutes longer. Remove from heat; cool slightly. Cut foil into squares large enough to hold filets. Place one filet on each square and turn up edges; spoon sauce over each. Wrap tightly and place in a shallow baking pan. Bake in a preheated 350° oven for 30 to 40 minutes. Serve filets in foil with Rissolé Potatoes on the side.

MUSHROOMS STUFFED WITH SPINACH

12 large mushrooms, with stems removed
¼ cup butter
1 10-ounce package frozen

spinach soufflé (or 2 packages, if mushrooms are unusually large), defrosted

Sauté mushroom caps in butter until lightly browned. Arrange in a shallow baking pan or casserole. Fill cavities with spinach soufflé mixture. Bake in a preheated 350° oven for 15 minutes or until browned.

CUCUMBER MOLD

2½ cups boiling water
3 3-ounce packages lime-flavored gelatin
2 teaspoons unflavored gelatine
¼ cup cold water
1 cup heavy cream, whipped

3 large cucumbers, unpeeled and grated
3 tablespoons grated onion
⅓ cup prepared horseradish
1½ teaspoons salt
⅓ cup vinegar or lemon juice
Radish roses

Pour boiling water over lime-flavored gelatin. Dissolve unflavored gelatine in cold water. Add to lime gelatin and stir until completely dissolved. Place in refrigerator until mixture is the consistency of unbeaten egg white. Beat with a rotary beater until frothy; fold in whipped cream and add all the remaining ingredients. Pour into an oiled 7-cup mold and chill. To serve, unmold and garnish with radish roses.

ORANGE COMPOTE A LA FRANÇAISE

6 large oranges	Juice of 2 lemons
¾ cup water	1 teaspoon vanilla
1 cup sugar	¼ to ½ cup Grand Marnier

Carefully remove outer layer of peel from oranges in wide strips. Do not include any of the inner white membrane. Cut strips into a fine julienne, half the thickness of a matchstick. Plunge these into a pan of boiling water for 8 minutes. Strain; cover with cold water for several minutes. Strain again and set aside. Remove outer white membrane from oranges with a sharp knife and discard. Slice oranges, and lay slices in a serving dish. Meanwhile, boil the ¾ cup water with sugar for 10 minutes; then add lemon juice and vanilla. Add strips of orange peel to this syrup; bring it to a boil again and add Grand Marnier. While very hot, pour over sliced oranges; cool. Refrigerate for at least 1 hour before serving.

Variation:

Compote may also be spooned over vanilla ice cream.

PECAN COOKIES

1 cup butter, softened	2 cups chopped pecans
¼ cup sugar	2 cups sifted all-purpose flour
2 tablespoons vanilla	Confectioners' sugar

Cream butter; blend with sugar and vanilla. Stir in nuts. Add flour and combine all ingredients well. Roll into small balls and place balls on a greased cookie sheet. Bake in a preheated 300° oven for 45 minutes. While cookies are still hot, roll in confectioners' sugar. When cool, roll cookies in confectioners' sugar once more.

Continental Dinner

(SERVES 6)

French Cheese Wafers   Caviar Pie

Escallopes of Veal with Lemon

Tomato Pudding Française

Spinach Salad

Chocolate Covered Pears

Coffee

ADVANCE PREPARATION SCHEDULE

Previous Day
French Cheese Wafers
Caviar Pie
(without sour cream or caviar)
Poach pears

Early Morning
Wash and chill spinach for salad
Lemon Dressing

FRENCH CHEESE WAFERS

½ cup butter, softened
½ pound Brie cheese, softened
1 cup sifted all-purpose flour

½ teaspoon cayenne pepper
¼ teaspoon seasoned salt
Sesame seeds

Combine butter and cheese in medium-sized bowl. Add flour, cayenne pepper and salt. Beat well, and shape into 2 8-inch-long rolls. Wrap in wax paper and refrigerate overnight. Preheat oven to 400°. Slice cheese rolls into thin wafers and place on cookie sheets; sprinkle with sesame seeds. Bake in preheated oven for about 8 minutes. Cool and store in tin box. Will keep a week or longer. Makes 60 wafers.

Note: To serve after storing, put wafers in a flat pan in preheated 400° oven and immediately turn oven off. Leave wafers in oven for 15 minutes and serve. They will be even crisper than when fresh.

CAVIAR PIE

8 to 10 warm hard-cooked eggs
½ cup sweet butter, melted
Celery salt
Dry mustard
Snipped chives
Salt
Pepper
1 to 1½ cups sour cream
1 8-ounce jar black or red caviar

Chop warm eggs finely or mash through a strainer. Mix with butter and add seasonings to taste. Press into a 9-inch glass pie plate, rinsed in cold water, and cover eggs with a thick layer of sour cream. Freeze 1 hour; remove from freezer and spread top with caviar. Refrigerate until serving time. Should be cold, not frozen, when served. Cut and serve in wedges like a pie.

Variation:

Substitute sliced Scotch or Nova Scotia salmon for caviar.

ESCALLOPES OF VEAL WITH LEMON

1½ pounds very thinly sliced veal
Salt
Pepper
Flour
6 tablespoons butter
2 tablespoons olive oil
Grated peel of 1 lemon
1 large lemon, thinly sliced
2 tablespoons lemon juice
Dash white wine or vermouth
Chopped parsley

Sprinkle veal with salt and pepper, and dust with flour. Sauté quickly on each side in heated butter and oil. Add lemon peel, slices and juice and simmer 3 to 4 minutes; add wine. Remove to hot platter; sprinkle with parsley and serve immediately.

TOMATO PUDDING FRANÇAISE

6 slices bread, crusts removed
  and cubed
¾ cup butter, melted
1⅓ cups firmly packed brown
  sugar
½ teaspoon salt
½ cup boiling water
2 10-ounce cans tomato purée

Place bread cubes in a 1½-quart buttered casserole dish and pour melted butter over. Let stand 15 to 20 minutes until butter is well absorbed. Meanwhile, add sugar, salt and water to tomato purée and boil for 5 minutes. Add tomato mixture to bread. Bake covered in a preheated 325° oven for 30 minutes, stirring occasionally.

SPINACH SALAD

1 pound fresh young spinach	6 strips bacon, cooked, drained
¼ pound fresh mushrooms, sliced	and crumbled
2 whole scallions, thinly sliced	

Discard stems from spinach leaves; tear leaves into bite size pieces, wash, dry and chill. When ready to serve, add mushrooms, bacon and scallions to spinach leaves. Pour Lemon Dressing over salad, toss and serve.

LEMON DRESSING

6 tablespoons salad oil	¾ teaspoon salt
2 tablespoons lemon juice	¼ teaspoon pepper
1 egg yolk	¼ teaspoon sugar
1 clove garlic, mashed	⅛ teaspoon dry mustard

Combine dressing ingredients in a blender; blend for several seconds. Chill.

CHOCOLATE COVERED PEARS

1 cup sugar	2 1-ounce squares unsweetened
4 cups water	chocolate
Juice of 1 lemon	4 1-ounce squares semisweet
2 cinnamon sticks	chocolate
4 whole cloves	¼ cup unsalted butter, softened
6 firm pears, preferably Anjou,	Fresh or crystallized mint
with stems intact	

Dissolve sugar in water. Add lemon juice and spices and simmer, tightly covered, for 10 to 15 minutes. Peel pears carefully, leaving stems intact and cut a slice off bottoms so pears will stand upright. Poach pears in gently boiling syrup until tender, about 30 to 40 minutes. Cool pears in syrup and chill overnight. Melt chocolate

in a pan over warm water. Add butter and stir until melted and
mixture is smooth. Remove pears from syrup and dry gently with
paper towel. Dip pears in the melted chocolate to coat evenly.
Lift pears with a slotted spoon to drain off excess chocolate. Arrange in a serving dish. Decorate the top of each pear with a sprig
of fresh or crystallized mint.

★

ITALIAN

Florentine Dinner

(SERVES 6)

Anchovy Eggs   Carpaccio
Hot Buttered Thin-Sliced Toast
Veal Marsala
Mostaccioli with Broccoli
Tomato and Mozzarella Salad
Strawberry Meringue Torte
Coffee

ADVANCE PREPARATION SCHEDULE

Previous Day

Cook eggs for Anchovy Eggs
Dressing for salad
Meringue Layers for Torte

Early Morning

Slice tomatoes and Mozzarella
for salad, prepare lettuce
Assemble Strawberry Meringue
Torte

ANCHOVY EGGS

2 tablespoons butter	Dash of lemon juice
1 small sweet onion, finely chopped	6 hard-cooked eggs, chopped
4 anchovy fillets, finely chopped	12 to 16 small toast rounds, lightly sautéed in butter
	Fresh chopped parsley

Melt butter in a skillet; add onions and sauté over low heat until golden brown. Add anchovies, lemon juice and chopped eggs. Heat thoroughly and serve immediately on toast rounds. Garnish plate with parsley.

CARPACCIO

1 cup mayonnaise	English mustard to taste
Dash of Tabasco	1½ pounds raw strip steak, chilled
Worcestershire sauce to taste	
Juice of 1 lemon	

Season mayonnaise according to taste, and refrigerate. Slice steak, across the grain, into 18 paper-thin slices. Slices should be see-through. To serve, arrange raw slices of steak on serving platter and sprinkle well with lemon juice. Serve mayonnaise sauce on the side. Must be eaten immediately. Serve with hot buttered toast.

VEAL MARSALA

2 pounds boneless veal, thinly sliced	Salt and pepper
Flour	½ cup butter
	1½ cups Marsala wine

Flatten veal slices with cleaver or broad side of French knife. Lightly flour slices and sprinkle with salt and pepper. Brown meat quickly on both sides in heated butter; add wine and heat through, cooking for about 2 minutes. Serve at once.

MOSTACCIOLI WITH BROCCOLI

1 large bunch broccoli, chopped
  into large pieces
½ pound mostaccioli or ziti
1 tablespoon vegetable oil
2 large cloves garlic, minced

½ cup chopped parsley
½ teaspoon black pepper
¼ cup vegetable oil
2 tablespoons butter
¼ cup grated Parmesan cheese

Cook broccoli in salted boiling water until crisply tender; drain. Cook mostaccioli in salted boiling water with 1 tablespoon oil until just tender (do not overcook). Drain. While broccoli and mostaccioli are cooking, prepare sauce: Blend together garlic, parsley, pepper, oil and butter; heat thoroughly. In a heated serving bowl, combine broccoli, mostaccioli and sauce. Sprinkle with grated Parmesan and serve immediately.

TOMATO AND MOZZARELLA SALAD

3 large beefsteak tomatoes,
  chilled and sliced ½-inch thick
½ pound Mozzarella cheese,
  sliced ¼-inch thick
1 large bunch leaf lettuce
½ cup finely chopped fresh basil
  or 1 tablespoon dried basil
  leaves

1 tablespoon chopped parsley
1 teaspoon salt
1 teaspoon freshly ground black
  pepper
6 tablespoons olive oil
1 tablespoon lemon juice
1 small red onion, chopped
  (optional)

Arrange tomatoes and cheese in overlapping slices on a bed of lettuce. Combine remaining ingredients, pour over salad and serve immediately.

STRAWBERRY MERINGUE TORTE

Meringue Layers:

4 egg whites, at room
  temperature
Pinch of salt

1 cup sugar
½ teaspoon cream of tartar
1 teaspoon vanilla
Cornstarch

Place egg whites in a mixing bowl with salt, cream of tartar and vanilla. With an electric mixer, beat at high speed for *exactly* 3 minutes; with a hand beater, beat for *exactly* 5 minutes. Add sugar,

1 tablespoon at a time, beating only until blended. Sugar should be added and blended in within 90 seconds. Watch timing! Lightly grease 3 cookie sheets and sprinkle with cornstarch, shake off excess when cookie sheet is covered with a thin layer of cornstarch. Place an 8-inch round cake pan upside down on center of cookie sheet; with your finger, make an outline of pan shape on cookie sheet. Remove pan and fill in circle with ⅓ of the meringue mixture. Repeat for three meringue layers. Bake in a preheated 250° oven for 20 to 25 minutes, until pale gold but still pliable. Let cool for 10 minutes only; slip a long-bladed knife under meringue to loosen from cookie sheet. Set aside. Meringues may be made a day in advance.

Filling:

12 ounces semi-sweet chocolate pieces	1½ pints heavy cream
6 tablespoons water or 3 tablespoons water and 3 tablespoons Grand Marnier	⅓ cup sugar
	3 pints strawberries

Melt chocolate pieces and the 6 tablespoons water (or 3 tablespoons Grand Marnier and 3 tablespoons water) over hot water. Set aside. Whip cream until stiff; gradually add sugar and beat until very stiff. Wash strawberries, slice 2 pints of the berries. Leave rest whole for garnish.

To Assemble Torte:

Place 1 layer of meringue on a serving platter; spread with a thin layer of melted chocolate. Top chocolate with a layer of whipped cream, ¾-inch thick and arrange 1 pint sliced strawberries over whipped cream. Add second meringue layer; repeat process of layering chocolate, whipped cream and 1 pint sliced strawberries and top with last meringue layer. Frost torte with remaining whipped cream, covering top (and sides, if desired) smoothly. Drizzle remaining melted chocolate over whipped cream in a random pattern. Decorate with 1 pint whole strawberries, placing any remaining strawberries around base. Refrigerate for at least 2 hours before serving.

Note: If cake is prepared early in the day, the whipped cream may be stabilized as follows: soak 1 tablespoon (1 envelope) of un-flavored gelatine in 3 tablespoons of water for 5 minutes. Heat over very low heat until gelatine is dissolved. Whip cream until it begins to thicken, beat in gelatine slowly and whip until cream is stiff.

Italian Dinner

(SERVES 6)

Pimientos, Artichokes and Anchovies

Beef Filets Italiano   Linguine with Clam Sauce

Belgian Endive and Radish Salad

Basket of Fruit: Apples, Grapes and Pears

Assorted Cheeses: Bel Paese, Gorgonzola, Fontina and Fontinella

Florentine Pound Cake

Cappuccino

ADVANCE PREPARATION SCHEDULE

Freezer
Florentine Pound Cake

Early Morning
Pimientos, Artichokes and Anchovies
Fry bread for filets
Prepare endive and radishes for salad
Cream Vinaigrette Dressing
Fruits and Cheeses
Remove Florentine Pound Cake from freezer

PIMIENTOS, ARTICHOKES AND ANCHOVIES

2 4-ounce jars whole pimientos
1 14-ounce can artichoke
  hearts, drained

1 2-ounce can flat anchovy filets
Red wine vinegar
Olive oil

Freshly ground black pepper

Cut pimientos in half diagonally; lay slices on a serving platter and top each with half an artichoke heart. Criss-cross 2 anchovy filets over the artichoke hearts and sprinkle with vinegar, oil and pepper. Serve with toasted garlic bread or bread sticks.

BEEF FILETS ITALIANO

3 tablespoons butter
1 large clove garlic, minced
6 slices day-old French bread
6 beef filets
Flour
Salt
Pepper
¼ cup olive oil
1 tablespoon butter
6 large mushroom caps

6 thick tomato slices
3 tablespoons fine dry bread
  crumbs
Garlic salt
2 tablespoons butter
½ cup Madeira wine
3 scallions, finely chopped
1 tablespoon finely chopped
  parsley

Melt the 2 tablespoons butter and add garlic. Fry bread in garlic butter on both sides; set aside. Reserve garlic butter. Dust filets lightly with flour, and season with salt and pepper. Heat olive oil with the 1 tablespoon butter. Sauté filets to taste; place each on a slice of the fried French bread and keep in a warm oven. Reserve drippings from cooking filets. Quickly sauté mushrooms in garlic butter and reserved drippings. Combine drippings from filets and mushrooms, add the 2 tablespoons butter, wine, scallions and parsley; boil over high heat for several minutes until sauce is slightly reduced. Place tomato slices on a cookie sheet and sprinkle with bread crumbs, salt, pepper and garlic salt. Broil in a preheated broiler until just brown. Place 1 tomato slice and 1 mushroom cap on each filet, spoon hot sauce over all and serve.

LINGUINE WITH CLAM SAUCE

1 8-ounce package linguine Italian noodles	2 tablespoons butter Clam Sauce

Just before serving cook noodles according to package directions. Drain; add Clam Sauce and toss to coat noodles with sauce. Serve immediately.

Clam Sauce:

2 cloves garlic, crushed	Dash of white pepper
⅓ cup olive oil	1½ teaspoons flour
⅓ cup dry white vermouth	2 8-ounce cans minced clams,
1½ teaspoons crushed basil	drained with liquid reserved
¼ teaspoon onion salt	½ cup chopped fresh parsley

Sauté garlic in oil. Add vermouth, basil, onion salt and white pepper. Stir in flour and continue stirring until sauce thickens. Add clam liquid to sauce. Five minutes before serving, add minced clams and parsley to sauce.

BELGIAN ENDIVE AND RADISH SALAD

6 heads Belgian endive	Cream Vinaigrette Dressing
18 radishes, thinly sliced	

Wash endive and separate leaves; wrap in a towel and chill in refrigerator. Just before serving, toss endive with radishes. Add Cream Vinaigrette Dressing to salad and toss well.

CREAM VINAIGRETTE DRESSING

6 tablespoons olive oil	Juice of 1 large lemon
3 hard-cooked egg yolks, mashed to a paste	1 large clove garlic, mashed
	⅓ teaspoon freshly ground pepper
3 tablespoons tarragon vinegar	⅓ teaspoon salt
2 tablespoons heavy cream	

Slowly add oil to mashed yokes, whipping constantly with a fork. When all oil is incorporated add remaining ingredients. Blend well.

FLORENTINE POUND CAKE

2 cups butter, softened
1 pound confectioners' sugar
6 large eggs (or 8 medium sized
   eggs)

4 cups sifted cake flour
1 teaspoon vanilla or lemon
   extract (optional)
Confectioners' sugar

Cream butter and sugar together, using a wooden spoon or electric mixer. Alternately add eggs and flour, beating well after each addition. Add extract, if desired, and mix all ingredients together thoroughly. Pour into a well-greased Bundt cake pan. Preheat oven to 350°. Put cake in oven and reduce temperature to 325°. Bake for 20 minutes; raise temperature back to 350°. Bake 20 minutes longer and reduce temperature to 325°. Bake for 30 minutes. Cool cake and sift confectioners' sugar over top.

CAPPUCCINO

1 tablespoon quick chocolate-
   flavored milk mix

1 cup milk
3 cups hot double-strength coffee

¼ cup brandy

Heat milk, stir in chocolate-flavored milk mix. Add coffee and brandy, serve at once.

Informal Italian Dinner

(SERVES 8)

Spinach Soup
Veal and Eggplant Casserole
Spaghetti Verde
Cucumber-Tomato Salad
Italian Ice Cream Torte
Coffee

Freezer	Previous Day	Early Morning
Italian Ice Cream Torte	*Marinade for salad*	*Spinach Soup*
		Prepare Veal and Eggplant Casserole (do not bake)
		Marinate cucumber slices for salad
		Wash and chill Bibb lettuce

SPINACH SOUP

2 pounds spinach, or 2 10-ounce packages frozen spinach, cooked and drained	¼ teaspoon white pepper
	⅛ teaspoon nutmeg
¼ cup butter	4 egg yolks
1¼ teaspoons salt	¼ cup grated Parmesan cheese
	6 cups chicken broth, boiling

Croutons (optional) (see Index)

Purée cooked spinach in the container of an electric blender or force it through a sieve. Melt butter in a saucepan; add spinach and seasonings. Cook over low heat for two minutes, stirring constantly. Beat egg yolks with cheese and add to spinach mixture. Gradually add boiling chicken broth to spinach mixture, stirring constantly. Bring soup to a boil (do not panic, the egg yolks will curdle); serve with croutons, if desired. May be prepared early in the day and reheated to serve.

VEAL AND EGGPLANT CASSEROLE

1 large eggplant, peeled	⅓ cup olive oil
Flour	½ cup butter, cut into bits
6 eggs	2 cups dry white wine
½ cup olive oil	2 cups tomato sauce
16 thin veal scallops	16 thin slices prosciutto ham
Salt and pepper	16 thin slices Mozzarella cheese

⅔ cup grated Parmesan cheese

Cut eggplant into 16 slices about ¼ inch thick. Dust with flour. Slightly beat 3 of the eggs. Dip eggplant slices in egg. Brown eggplant slices on both sides in the ½ cup olive oil, over medium-high heat. Drain on paper towels and set aside. With a cleaver flatten veal slightly between sheets of waxed paper. Slightly beat remaining 3 eggs. Season veal with salt and pepper; dust with flour and coat with egg. Brown veal scallops over high heat in the ⅓ cup olive oil, turning to brown on both sides. Transfer veal to a heated dish and pour off oil in skillet. Add butter and wine to skillet; cook over medium heat, stirring in brown bits clinging to bottom and sides of pan. Return veal to pan and cook for 3 minutes over low heat. Arrange veal pieces in a buttered baking dish just large enough to hold them, so that slices overlap slightly. Mix pan juices and tomato sauce and pour over meat. Arrange one eggplant slice on top of each veal scallop; top with one slice each of prosciutto and Mozzarella and sprinkle Parmesan cheese over all. Bake casserole uncovered in preheated 375° oven for 10 minutes, or until cheese is melted and golden.

SPAGHETTI VERDE

1 cup butter	1½ cups finely chopped fresh
1 clove garlic, minced	parsley
1 pound spaghetti	4 ounces grated Parmesan
	cheese

Additional grated Parmesan cheese

Melt butter; add garlic. Simmer until butter is very lightly browned. Strain butter to remove all garlic particles; set aside. Cook spaghetti in salted, boiling water for *exactly* 12 minutes. Immediately drain cooked spaghetti in a colander and run cold water over it. Return spaghetti to pan. Scatter parsley and Parmesan cheese over spaghetti; pour butter over all and toss thoroughly. Quickly heat again. Serve hot and pass extra cheese on the side.

CUCUMBER-TOMATO SALAD

⅔ cup salad oil	1 teaspoon dill weed
6 tablespoons white vinegar	2 large cucumbers, sliced paper
Dash pepper	thin with a vegetable parer
½ teaspoon sugar	Bibb lettuce, washed and chilled
½ teaspoon salt	4 large tomatoes, thinly sliced

Combine oil, vinegar, pepper, sugar, salt and dill weed; beat with wire whisk until well blended. Set aside. Place cucumber slices in a shallow dish. Cover with marinade and chill for 6 hours. Drain and reserve marinade. To serve salad, line a serving platter with Bibb lettuce leaves. Arrange tomato slices on lettuce; top with cucumber slices and pour marinade over all.

ITALIAN ICE CREAM TORTE

28 macaroons or Italian Amaretti, crushed
1 quart chocolate ice cream, slightly softened
¼ cup canned chocolate sauce

1 quart coffee ice cream, slightly softened
14 pieces English toffee, crushed
Chocolate Fudge Sauce (optional) (see Index)

Spread half of the crushed macaroons on the bottom of an oiled 8-inch spring form pan. Spread softened chocolate ice cream on top of macaroons; dribble half of chocolate sauce over ice cream. Top with remaining macaroons. Spread softened coffee ice cream over macaroon layer; dribble remaining chocolate sauce over coffee ice cream. Spread crushed English toffee over top of torte. Freeze for 4 to 5 hours, until hard. Thirty minutes before serving, remove torte from spring form and place on a round platter. Leave at room temperature for 30 minutes. May be served with additional Chocolate Fudge Sauce, if desired.

Neapolitan Dinner

(SERVES 4)

Tarragon-Garlic Shrimp
Chicken Cacciatore   Vermicelli Parmesano
Italian Fennel Salad
Biscuit Tortoni
Espresso

ADVANCE PREPARATION SCHEDULE

Freezer
Biscuit Tortoni

Early Morning
Prepare shrimp (ready to broil)
Chicken Cacciatore (up to final
15 minutes baking)
Vermicelli Parmesano
Prepare ingredients for Italian
Fennel Salad

TARRAGON-GARLIC SHRIMP

2 pounds uncooked, shelled
  shrimp
½ cup butter
½ cup olive oil
2 teaspoons lemon juice
¼ cup finely chopped shallots
1 tablespoon finely minced garlic
1 tablespoon finely chopped fresh

tarragon or 1 teaspoon dried
  tarragon leaves
Freshly ground black pepper
Coarse salt
1 tablespoon finely chopped fresh
  parsley
1 tablespoon finely chopped fresh
  tarragon

Place shrimp in a single layer in a large shallow baking dish. Melt butter; cool. Stir in olive oil, lemon juice, shallots, garlic, the 1 tablespoon tarragon and pepper. Pour over shrimp in baking dish; sprinkle with a small amount of coarse salt. Place in a preheated broiler, 3 inches from heat and broil for 5 minutes, basting every 3 minutes with butter mixture in bottom of dish. When lightly browned, turn shrimp over one by one; sprinkle a bit more coarse salt over shrimp and broil for 5 minutes longer. Baste every 3 minutes; do not overcook. Combine parsley and the 1 tablespoon tarragon; sprinkle over shrimp and serve.

CHICKEN CACCIATORE

2 2-pound broilers, cut into serving pieces
¼ cup olive oil
2 medium onions, chopped
1 clove garlic, crushed
Pinch of dried oregano leaves
1 cup sliced green pepper

2 cups canned tomatoes, mashed
  with a fork
¼ cup white wine or sherry
1 tablespoon minced parsley
1 cup sliced mushrooms
Salt and pepper to taste
½ 6-ounce can tomato paste

Wash and dry chicken. In a large skillet brown chicken in hot oil for about 10 minutes over high heat, cooking on all sides. Add onion, garlic, oregano, green pepper and tomatoes. Cover skillet tightly and simmer for 30 minutes. Add remaining ingredients; continue to cook covered for 15 minutes longer, until chicken is tender.

VERMICELLI PARMESANO

¾ pound vermicelli
½ cup butter
2 tablespoons grated Parmesan cheese
1 heaping teaspoon seasoned salt
1 teaspoon garlic powder
1 teaspoon dried oregano leaves

1 teaspoon dried savory leaves
1 teaspoon dried chervil leaves
½ teaspoon pepper
2 tablespoons heavy cream
1 tablespoon grated Parmesan cheese

Boil vermicelli until *almost* tender; drain. In the same pan, melt butter over low heat with the 1 tablespoon cheese. Add all seasonings, then add cream and mix well. Pour noodles back into pan on top of cream mixture. Gently toss noodles with 2 forks, to coat well. Add the remaining 1 tablespoon cheese and keep warm over low heat until ready to serve. May be prepared in advance and reheated.

ITALIAN FENNEL SALAD

1 clove garlic, cut in half
1 large head fennel, thinly sliced
1 small head chicory, torn into bite-size pieces
2 large tomatoes, peeled and cut in wedges

Salt and freshly ground black pepper to taste
6 tablespoons olive oil
3 tablespoons wine vinegar

Rub inside of salad bowl with garlic; discard. Add fennel, chickory, tomatoes, salt and pepper to bowl. Blend oil and vinegar; pour over salad, toss and serve.

BISCUIT TORTONI

2 egg whites
¼ cup sugar
2 tablespoons instant coffee powder or 1 tablespoon light rum
2 egg yolks, slightly beaten
2 teaspoons vanilla

¼ cup sugar
2 cups heavy cream, whipped
½ cup semi-sweet chocolate pieces, melted and cooled
½ cup chopped toasted blanched almonds
Whole cherries with stems

Beat egg whites until soft peaks form; slowly add the ¼ cup sugar. Beat until stiff and set aside. Fold coffee powder, egg yolks, vanilla and the ¼ cup sugar into the whipped cream. Fold into egg whites. Quickly fold in chocolate and almonds. Pour mixture into four small cups or wine glasses; top each with a cherry and freeze. May be made several days in advance.

Italian Supper

(SERVES 6)

Triscuitinis   Sardine Pâté in Lemon Shells
Veal Parmesan
Spaghetti al Pesto   Artichoke Hearts
Green Salad with Italian Dressing (see Index)
Sicilian Cream Cake
Coffee

ADVANCE PREPARATION SCHEDULE

Previous Day

Sicilian Cream Cake

Early Morning

Sardine Pâté in Lemon Shells
Veal Parmesan (do not bake)
Make Pesto sauce
Prepare greens for salad
Italian Dressing (see Index)

TRISCUITINIS

½ pound beef round steak, freshly
    ground twice
Salt
Pepper

Triscuits
Catsup
Raw onion, finely chopped

Season ground beef steak well with salt and pepper to taste. Spread meat on Triscuits and broil in preheated broiler until meat is browned. Top with a dollop of catsup and chopped onion. Serve hot.

SARDINE PATE IN LEMON SHELLS

Juice of 1 large lemon
2 thick onion slices
4 sprigs parsley
1 8-ounce package cream cheese, cubed
2 4-ounce cans sardines in oil, drained

Dash Tabasco sauce
3 large lemons, halved, with pulp scooped out
Chopped parsley
Hot toast

Place all ingredients except lemon shells, chopped parsley and toast, in the container of an electric blender in the order they are listed. Blend at high speed until smooth. Fill lemon shells with pâté and sprinkle with chopped parsley. Serve with hot toast.

VEAL PARMESAN

6 veal cutlets, pounded thin
½ cup flour, mixed with seasoned salt and pepper
2 eggs beaten with 2 tablespoons water
¾ cup fine dry bread crumbs

¼ cup grated Parmesan cheese
Olive or salad oil
1 cup tomato sauce
6 thin slices Mozzarella cheese
Grated Parmesan cheese

Dip cutlets in seasoned flour, then in diluted egg. Combine bread crumbs and the ¼ cup Parmesan and coat cutlets with mixture. Brown cutlets in small amount of oil until golden brown on both sides and meat is tender. Transfer cutlets to a shallow baking dish. Pour tomato sauce over meat; top with slices of Mozzarella, and sprinkle generously with grated Parmesan. Bake in preheated 350°

oven for about 15 to 20 minutes, until heated through and cheese is slightly browned and melted. Can be made ahead and baked just before serving.

SPAGHETTI AL PESTO

18 large fresh sweet basil leaves or 1 tablespoon dried basil
½ cup olive oil
½ cup freshly grated Parmesan cheese
½ teaspoon salt
⅓ cup pine nuts (optional)

5 cloves garlic, peeled
1 pound thin spaghetti, cooked 10 minutes until "al dente" (*Reserve 3 tablespoons cooking water*)
2 tablespoons butter
Grated Parmesan cheese

Place basil, oil, Parmesan, salt, pine nuts and garlic in the container of an electric blender and blend at high speed for 30 seconds, until thick and smooth. Place hot cooked spaghetti in a large mixing bowl and add butter, Pesto sauce and 3 tablespoons hot spaghetti water. Toss until butter is melted. Serve with additional grated Parmesan.

ARTICHOKE HEARTS

1 10½-ounce can condensed chicken broth
3 tablespoons butter
2 tablespoons minced scallions

¼ teaspoon salt
2 10-ounce packages frozen artichoke hearts
Chopped parsley

Combine chicken broth, 1 tablespoon of the butter, scallions and salt. Bring to boil; add artichoke hearts and boil again. Cover and cook slowly for 7 to 10 minutes, or until hearts are tender. Drain and arrange in heated serving dish. Melt the remaining 2 tablespoons butter and pour over artichokes. Sprinkle with parsley and serve.

SICILIAN CREAM CAKE

1 11¼-ounce frozen pound cake, thawed
1 pound ricotta cheese
¼ cup sugar
¼ cup crème de cacao
¾ cup miniature semi-sweet chocolate pieces

1 cup ready-to-spread canned chocolate frosting
Shaved chocolate or chocolate sprinkles to decorate

Cut cake horizontally to make 3 layers. Combine cheese, sugar and 3 tablespoons of the crème de cacao in a small mixing bowl. Beat with electric mixer until smooth. Fold in chocolate pieces. Spread bottom layer of cake with one-half of the ricotta mixture. Top with second layer of cake and spread with remaining ricotta mixture. Place third layer of cake on top. Combine frosting with the remaining 1 tablespoon of crème de cacao and spread on cake. Sprinkle with shaved chocolate or chocolate sprinkles; chill for at least 30 minutes and serve in thin slices.

ORIENTAL

Oriental Dinner

(SERVES 6)

Tipsy Shrimp
Stir-Fried Beef and Watercress   Chicken-in-the-Garden
Rice With Toasted Almonds   Chinese Fried Noodles (Packaged)
Harvey Wallbanger Oranges
Butter Cookies
Tea

Freezer	Previous Day	Early Morning
Harvey Wallbanger Oranges	*Butter Cookies*	*For Tipsy Shrimp: Make sauce. Prepare shrimp for cooking. For Stir-Fried Beef: Slice beef. Wash watercress and separate stems from leaves. For Chicken-in-the-Garden: Prepare chicken for cooking. Prepare vegetables. Make sauce.*

TIPSY SHRIMP

2 thin slices fresh ginger root, finely diced
2 tablespoons diced scallions
¼ cup Chablis (dry white wine)
3 tablespoons light soy sauce

3 tablespoons peanut oil
¼ teaspoon salt
2 pounds large raw shrimp, butterflied, washed and patted dry

To prepare sauce: Combine ginger root, scallions, Chablis and light soy sauce. Set aside. Heat peanut oil and add salt. Sauté shrimp in oil, stirring rapidly. When shrimp are nearly done, pour sauce into pan. Stir for several seconds and serve instantly.

STIR-FRIED BEEF AND WATERCRESS

1 tablespoon peanut oil
1 pound lean steak, chilled and cut in strips
1 tablespoon crushed ginger root
1 clove garlic, crushed
1 teaspoon salt
½ teaspoon pepper

2 teaspoons cornstarch
1½ teaspoons sugar
2 teaspoons soy sauce
½ cup beef broth
1 bunch watercress, stems and leaves separated

Heat oil in a large skillet. Add beef, ginger and garlic, and brown meat quickly, stirring constantly. Sprinkle meat with salt and pepper. Mix cornstarch, sugar, soy sauce and broth until smooth.

Add to beef and heat, stirring, until mixture boils. Toss in water-cress stems; mix well and add leaves. Stir through and serve.

CHICKEN-IN-THE-GARDEN

¾ teaspoon cornstarch
2 small cloves garlic, mashed
2 thin slices fresh ginger root, diced
3 whole chicken breasts, boned, skinned and cut into bite-size pieces
4 tablespoons peanut oil

1 teaspoon salt
1 cup finely sliced celery
1 medium onion, diced
6 water chestnuts, sliced
¼ cup bamboo shoots
1 cup fresh Chinese snow peas
½ cup fresh sliced mushrooms
Sauce

Combine cornstarch, garlic and ginger with chicken pieces: mix well. Set aside. Place oil and salt in heavy cast-iron skillet or wok. Heat thoroughly. Add chicken mixture to skillet, stir-frying until chicken is almost cooked. Add celery, onions, water chestnuts, bamboo shoots, and stir-fry 2 minutes. Next add snow peas and mushrooms. After about 90 seconds, when pods turn bright green, add Sauce. When mixture comes to a boil, approximately 1 minute longer, stir rapidly and serve.

Sauce:

¾ cup water or chicken broth
1 tablespoon dry white wine
1 teaspoon cornstarch
1 teaspoon light soy sauce
3 to 4 drops sesame oil

Combine all ingredients in a small bowl. Set aside.

Note: If fresh snow peas are not available, eliminate them from recipe.

RICE WITH TOASTED ALMONDS

2 cups long grain rice
3 cups cold water
1¾ ounces sliced blanched almonds
½ cup butter

Place rice in saucepan, add cold water and bring to a boil. Lower heat, cover and cook for 20 minutes. Sauté almonds in melted butter for 3 to 5 minutes, until they are golden brown. Watch closely. Pour over cooked rice before serving.

HARVEY WALLBANGER ORANGES

6 large oranges	¼ cup Galliano or Grand
1 quart orange ice or sherbet	Marnier
1 2-ounce package slivered	¼ cup vodka
almonds	

Cut a thick slice off tops of oranges and scoop out insides with sharp spoon or grapefruit knife. Let orange ice soften slightly and mix with nuts, Galliano and vodka. Fill oranges with mixture and freeze until firm.

BUTTER COOKIES

1 cup soft butter	1 teaspoon vanilla
1 cup confectioners' sugar	2 cups sifted all-purpose flour

Cream butter thoroughly; add sugar, vanilla and flour. Beat ingredients well, and drop from a teaspoon onto cookie sheets. Bake in a preheated 350° oven for 15 minutes. When done, remove cookies to a paper towel to cool.

Oriental Banquet

(SERVES 8)

Shrimp Canton   Chinese Spareribs

Cantonese Chicken   Sesame Beef

Stir-Fried Snow Peas   Fried Rice Peking

Strawberry-Orange Ice   Ginger Cookies

Tea

SHRIMP CANTON

24 raw shrimp, cleaned and deveined (with or without shells
removed)
2 slices fresh ginger root, diced,
or 1 teaspoon powdered ginger

¼ cup chopped scallions
2 tablespoons dry white wine
2 tablespoon soy sauce
½ teaspoon salt
2 tablespoons sugar

Prepare shrimp. Place in a shallow baking pan. Combine remaining ingredients and pour over shrimp; marinate shrimp for several hours in the refrigerator. Drain shrimp and reserve marinade. Bake shrimp in a preheated 325° oven for 10 minutes; baste with reserved marinade. Bake for an additional 5 minutes, or until pink and cooked through.

CHINESE SPARERIBS

2½ to 3 pounds young spareribs,
cracked in half lengthwise
1 clove garlic, crushed
½ cup soy sauce

⅓ cup sugar
1 teaspoon salt
¼ teaspoon pepper
1 tablespoon grated orange peel

Place spareribs in a shallow pan. Combine the remaining ingredients and pour marinade over ribs and refrigerate for 30 minutes to 1 hour, turning ribs several times and basting with marinade. To cook, drain ribs and place curved-side down on a rack in a shallow baking pan. Preheat broiler; place pan 8 inches from heat and broil for 15 minutes. Turn ribs over and broil other side for 20 minutes, watching carefully. May be frozen or prepared early in the day and reheated in 325° oven for 15 minutes. If frozen, defrost before heating. Before serving cut ribs into hors d'oeuvres–size pieces.

CANTONESE CHICKEN

2 1½-to 2½-pound frying chickens, cut into serving-size
   portions
¼ cup honey

¼ cup soy sauce
½ cup catsup
¼ cup lemon juice

Place chicken in a large baking pan. Combine remaining ingredients and mix for marinade; pour marinade over chicken and refrigerate for several hours or overnight. To cook, pour off and reserve marinade. Cover pan with foil and bake in a preheated 325° oven for 1 hour. Remove foil and bake until tender, about 15 minutes longer, basting often with marinade.

SESAME BEEF

1 tablespoon sesame seeds
2 pounds lean beef (sirloin, beef
   tenderloin), chilled
3 minced garlic cloves
3 scallions, finely chopped

2 tablespoons oil
2 tablespoons sugar
2 tablespoons dry sherry
⅛ teaspoon black pepper
5 tablespoons soy sauce

Over low heat, lightly brown sesame seeds in a skillet. Set aside. Slice beef on the diagonal in very thin slices. Score each slice with an XX. Combine the remaining ingredients and pour over steak slices. Let stand for 30 minutes. Drain meat; strain and reserve marinade. Broil steak in a preheated broiler as close to source of

heat as possible for 30 seconds to 1 minute. Turn; sprinkle with sesame seeds and broil 30 seconds longer. Marinade may be re-heated and served with beef as a sauce.

STIR-FRIED SNOW PEAS

6 dried Chinese mushrooms
2 tablespoons oil
½ cup canned bamboo shoots, sliced

1 pound fresh snow peas, tips snapped off and strings removed
1½ teaspoons salt
½ teaspoon sugar

Soak mushrooms in ½ cup warm water for 30 minutes. Remove from water with a slotted spoon; strain water, and reserve 2 table-spoons. Discard tough stems of mushrooms and cut each cap into quarters. Set aside. Heat wok or heavy skillet; pour in oil and heat. Drop mushrooms and bamboo shoots into pan and stir-fry for 2 min-utes. Add snow peas, salt, sugar and reserved liquid from mush-rooms. Cook over high heat for about 2 minutes, stirring constantly, until water evaporates. Serve at once on a heated platter.

FRIED RICE PEKING

2 cups uncooked rice
3 cups boiling water or chicken stock
½ cup oil
2 eggs, slightly beaten
½ cup chopped scallions (includ-ing tops)

½ cup ground beef or chopped shrimp
2 teaspoons salt
½ teaspoon pepper
6 tablespoons soy sauce

Add rice to boiling water or stock. Cover and bring to boil. Lower heat; simmer 15 minutes, until done but not soft. Turn off heat; let rice sit on burner, covered, for 15 minutes. Pour oil into a large skil-let. When very hot, add eggs and cook for 3 minutes, shredding with a fork. Add remaining ingredients, blending well; cook over moderate heat for 8 minutes. May be prepared in advance and re-heated in a double boiler over boiling water for about 10 minutes. May be served molded in separate custard cups or in a large bowl.

STRAWBERRY-ORANGE ICE

2 quarts strawberries, washed and hulled	¾ cup Curaçao
¾ cup sugar	1½ quarts orange sherbet
	2 tablespoons brown sugar

Shredded coconut to taste

Place strawberries in a bowl; add sugar and Curaçao and mix well. Chill for 1 hour. Drain berries, reserving liquid. Fold liquid into slightly softened orange sherbet; pour sherbet-liqueur mixture into a large serving bowl or 8 individual dishes. Place in freezer. Combine brown sugar with shredded coconut. When ready to serve, spoon drained berries over sherbet and sprinkle with brown sugar-coconut mixture, or serve sugar-coconut on the side.

GINGER COOKIES

¾ cup shortening	2 cups sifted all-purpose flour
1 cup sugar	2 teaspoons baking soda
1 egg	1 teaspoon cinnamon
¼ cup molasses	1 teaspoon ground cloves

1 teaspoon ginger

Combine shortening with sugar; beat in remaining ingredients, combining well. Chill mixture for at least 1 hour. Remove and form into approximately 24 small balls. Sprinkle hands with flour and flatten each ball. Place on greased cookie sheet and bake in a preheated 350° oven for 10 to 12 minutes. Makes about 2 dozen cookies.

Oriental Luncheon

(SERVES 6)

Chicken and Vegetables Far East   Noodle-Rice Casserole
Mandarin Salad
Kahlua Snowballs with Fudge Sauce
Green Tea

Freezer	Previous Day	Early Morning
Kahlua Snowballs	*Cook chicken*	*Slice vegetables and*
	Prepare coconut shells	*chicken for Chicken*
	Fudge Sauce	*and Vegetables*
		Far East
		Mandarin Salad

CHICKEN AND VEGETABLES FAR EAST

1 cup thinly sliced onion	3 tablespoons cornstarch
¼ cup vegetable oil	½ teaspoon salt
3 cups diagonally cut celery	1 tablespoon soy sauce
2 cups peas, uncooked	2⅓ cups chicken broth
4 3-ounce cans mushrooms in	1 teaspoon ground ginger
butter sauce	2 pounds sliced cooked chicken

Cook onion in oil until transparent. Stir in celery and sauté for 1 minute. Add peas; cover and cook for about 4 minutes until peas are tender-crisp. Drain broth from 1 can of the mushrooms and combine with cornstarch, salt, soy sauce, chicken broth and ginger; add liquid to skillet and cook, stirring until it thickens. Stir in all of the mushrooms with their broth and arrange chicken over vegetables. Cover and cook until heated through.

NOODLE-RICE CASSEROLE

½ cup butter	1 13¾-ounce can chicken broth
8 ounces very fine noodles,	½ teaspoon soy sauce
uncooked	½ cup water
1 cup uncooked rice	½ 6-ounce can water chestnuts,
1 10½-ounce can condensed	sliced
onion soup	

Melt butter; add noodles and cook until brown and crisp. Place in buttered 2-quart casserole and stir in remaining ingredients. Bake in a preheated 325° oven for 45 minutes.

MANDARIN SALAD

1 8-ounce can pineapple tidbits
1 8-ounce can mandarin orange
   segments, drained
1 8-ounce carton large-curd cottage cheese

1 4½-ounce container frozen
   whipped topping
1 3-ounce package orange-
   flavored gelatin

Combine pineapple, with juice, oranges, cottage cheese and topping. Mix well. Sprinkle dry gelatin over all; mix well and chill.

KAHLUA SNOWBALLS WITH FUDGE SAUCE

3 coconuts
6 large scoops vanilla ice cream

2 cups shredded coconut
Kahlua or crème de cacao
Fudge Sauce

To make bowls from coconuts, have butcher saw them in half and
then saw a small slice off each end so halves will stand upright.
Roll each scoop of ice cream in shredded coconut, shaping it into
a ball. Wrap each in waxed paper and freeze. Just before serving,
pour Kahlua or crème de cacao in bottom of each coconut shell.
Place ice cream snowball on top and pour hot Fudge Sauce over
all. Serve at once with additional sauce on the side.

Fudge Sauce:

½ cup butter
2 cups superfine sugar
1 13-ounce can evaporated milk,
   undiluted

4 1-ounce squares unsweetened
   chocolate
16 marshmallows

Melt butter, sugar, milk and chocolate in the top of a double boiler
over hot water, stirring well. When melted, add marshmallows.
Cover until marshmallows melt and stir mixture well.

Chinese Dinner

(SERVES 8)

Roast Pork Canton

Instant Rumaki

Barbecued Duckling   Flank Steak-Asparagus

Chinese Vermicelli

Oranges Kowloon

Tea

ADVANCE PREPARATION SCHEDULE

Freezer	Previous Day	Early Morning
Oranges Kowloon	*Marinate pork*	*Slice steak and*
	Wrap Rumaki (do not	*asparagus*
	cook)	*Prepare ingredients for*
	Marinate duckling	*Chinese Vermicelli*

ROAST PORK CANTON

1 5-pound Boston pork butt or boneless smoked pork shoulder	(available in Oriental food shops)
2 tablespoons sugar	¼ cup light soy sauce
1½ tablespoons salt	¼ cup red wine
2 tablespoons Hoi sin sauce	2 tablespoons catsup
	½ teaspoon five-spice powder

Cut meat into 3 long strips. Make a marinade by combining the remaining ingredients. Place meat strips in a pan and pour marinade over pork. Marinate for several hours or overnight in the refrigerator. Drain; place meat on a wire rack in a disposable baking pan. Bake in a preheated 450° oven for 30 minutes on each side until crusty on outside but just done on inside; be careful not to let meat dry out. Slice and serve.

INSTANT RUMAKI

1 10-ounce jar pickled watermelon rind

½ pound bacon, each strip cut in half

Place a piece of watermelon rind on each half piece of bacon; roll up and secure with toothpicks. Place on a wire rack in a pan and either bake in a preheated 400° oven for 15 minutes, or broil in preheated broiler for 5 minutes, until bacon is crisp.

BARBECUED DUCKLING

1 cup sherry
⅓ cup honey or firmly packed brown sugar
1 tablespoon soy sauce
1 teaspoon grated fresh ginger root, (or 1 teaspoon powdered ginger)

1 teaspoon dry mustard
2 to 3 young ducklings, quartered and trimmed of excess fat (choose lean, meaty ducks)
Sesame seeds for garnish (optional)

To make marinade, combine sherry, honey, soy sauce, ginger and mustard. Pour marinade over ducklings and let stand for several hours or overnight, refrigerated. Before cooking, let ducklings return to room temperature. Place duckling quarters on grill over hot coals and barbecue for 10 to 15 minutes on each side, until done. While cooking, baste with marinade. Sprinkle with sesame seeds before serving.

FLANK STEAK-ASPARAGUS

1½ tablespoons soy sauce
½ teaspoon sugar
1 teaspoon dry sherry
1½ teaspoons cornstarch
1 tablespoon chopped scallions
½ teaspoon salt or to taste

1 pound flank steak, chilled and sliced against the grain, ½-inch thick
1 bunch asparagus
3 tablespoons oil

Combine soy sauce, sugar, sherry and cornstarch; pour over scallions and beef and marinate for 15 minutes. Thinly slice asparagus on the diagonal; discard tough ends. Drop asparagus in boiling water for 2 minutes; drain; run under cold water and drain again.

Heat oil in wok or iron skillet and sauté scallions and beef, stirring, for 1 minute. Add asparagus and seasonings and cook, stirring, for 2 minutes more.

CHINESE VERMICELLI

8 ounces cellophane noodles	⅓ cup chicken fat
1 quart chicken broth	½ cup raw, diced shrimp
¼ cup dark soy sauce	2 eggs, well-beaten
6 dried mushrooms, soaked and chopped	Vegetable oil
	2 tablespoons chopped scallions

Soak noodles in cold water for 1 hour. Drain and cut in thirds. Place noodles in skillet; add broth, soy sauce, mushrooms and chicken fat. Stir and bring to a boil; lower heat and simmer for 10 to 15 minutes, or until noodles are cooked. Add shrimp; cook 3 minutes more. Fry eggs in a little oil in the form of a thin pancake. When well cooked, remove and cut into thin strips. Garnish noodles with scallions and egg-strips.

ORANGES KOWLOON

6 egg yolks	8 cleaned orange shells
¾ cup sugar	Sifted cocoa
2 cups heavy cream, whipped	
¼ cup Grand Marnier (or to taste)	

Combine egg yolks and sugar, beating well. Fold in whipped cream; then fold in liqueur. Fill orange shells with mixture. Freeze for at least 2 hours. Before serving, dust lightly with sifted cocoa.

★

GREEK

Greek Dinner

(SERVES 8)

Spinach Strudel   Egg and Lemon Soup
Roast Rack of Lamb
Rice Pilaf
Aegean Peas
Classic Greek Salad
Mocha Parfait
Walnut Horns   Poppy Seed Cookies
Greek Coffee

ADVANCE PREPARATION SCHEDULE

Freezer

Spinach Strudel (do not bake)
Mocha Parfait
Poppy Seed Cookies
Walnut Horns

Early Morning

Prepare lamb for roasting
Classic Greek Salad (without
  dressing)
Greek Salad Dressing

SPINACH STRUDEL

2 10-ounce packages chopped
frozen spinach, defrosted
and well drained
6 ounces Mozzarella cheese,
shredded
½ cup chopped scallions
3 dashes cinnamon
Salt and pepper to taste

1 cup fresh grated Parmesan
cheese
¼ cup cold sweet butter, cut into
small pieces
9 to 12 frozen phylo (strudel)
leaves
¾ cup sweet butter, melted
⅔ cup fine dry bread crumbs

Combine spinach, Mozzarella, scallions, cinnamon, salt, pepper, Parmesan and the cold butter. Use 3 or 4 strudel leaves for each strudel. Spread each strudel leaf with melted sweet butter and sprinkle with bread crumbs, repeating with each strudel leaf. Fill with spinach and cheese mixture and roll as directed on phylo package. Brush top with butter. Cut strudel diagonally, almost, but not quite through to bottom. May be frozen and baked before serving. To serve, bake in a preheated 350° oven for 45 minutes (longer, if baked frozen). Makes 3 strudels.

EGG AND LEMON SOUP

2 quarts chicken stock,
strained
¼ cup raw rice

Salt to taste
4 eggs, separated
Juice of 1 large lemon

Bring stock to boil. Add rice and salt and cook until rice is tender. Beat egg whites until stiff; then slowly add yolks, and then lemon juice. Very gradually, pour about 2 cups of the hot chicken stock into egg mixture. Pour stock-egg mixture back into pot with remaining stock. Stir well. Simmer until soup is heated through; cover, let stand away from heat for several minutes and serve.

ROAST RACK OF LAMB

1 rack of lamb (16 to 18 chops)
Prepared mustard
Salt
Pepper

Crushed dried mint leaves
Garlic powder
Flour

Spread lamb with a thin layer of prepared mustard; sprinkle with salt, pepper, mint and garlic powder. Sprinkle all over with flour and pat coating firmly down onto meat. Place on a rack, bone side down, in a shallow roasting pan. Roast in a preheated 500° oven for 15 minutes. Then reduce heat to 300° and roast for approximately 30 to 45 minutes, until meat is tender. Lamb should be crusty and brown on the outside and juicy and slightly pink inside.

RICE PILAF

¼ cup butter	2 cups unwashed long grain rice
¼ cup finely chopped onion	4 cups hot strong chicken stock
½ teaspoon minced garlic	1 teaspoon salt (or to taste)

Melt butter in a heavy 4-quart Dutch oven. Add onion and garlic; cook over low heat, without browning, for 5 minutes. When onions are soft and translucent, stir in rice, mixing well until each grain of rice glistens with melted butter. Sauté rice over medium heat for 3 minutes; do not let it brown. Pour in chicken stock and bring to a boil, stirring to keep rice from sticking to bottom of pan. Add salt to taste and cover. Simmer over very low heat for about 20 minutes, without lifting cover. Cook until all liquid is absorbed, 20 to 30 minutes. Toss rice with a fork and serve.

AEGEAN PEAS

6 tablespoons butter	½ teaspoon salt
3 10-ounce packages frozen peas	⅛ teaspoon dried thyme leaves
1 small onion, peeled and thinly sliced	⅛ teaspoon white pepper
1 teaspoon sugar	1 tablespoon flour
	¾ cup Madeira wine

Melt butter in a saucepan. Add all the remaining ingredients, except flour and wine, mix well. Cover and cook over medium heat 10 minutes. Sprinkle with the 1 tablespoon flour. Gradually add the ¾ cup Madeira wine. Cook slowly, stirring constantly until sauce thickens.

CLASSIC GREEK SALAD

½ head iceberg lettuce, washed
  and chilled
½ head romaine lettuce, washed
  and chilled
18 medium radishes, sliced
¼ pound feta cheese, grated or
  crumbled
1 2-ounce can anchovy filets,
  minced

¼ teaspoon dried oregano leaves
2 medium tomatoes, cut into
  small pieces
1 tablespoon chopped fresh
  parsley
Freshly ground pepper to taste
2 bunches scallions, washed and
  trimmed, for garnish

Two hours before serving salad, tear lettuce and romaine into salad bowl. Add remaining salad ingredients, except scallions. Toss gently, covering with a damp towel and refrigerate. To serve, pour Greek Salad Dressing over salad, and stand scallions straight up in center.

GREEK SALAD DRESSING

½ cup olive oil
2 tablespoons tarragon vinegar
½ teaspoon salt
¼ teaspoon freshly ground pepper

2 tablespoons mixed dried herbs:
  parsley, savory, chives, chervil,
  marjoram, rosemary, tarragon

Shake all ingredients together in a 1-pint bottle with tight-fitting lid.

MOCHA PARFAIT

1 quart coffee ice cream, slightly
  softened
½ pound chocolate-flavored
  coffee-bean candies or minia-

ture semi-sweet chocolate
  pieces
8 teaspoons crème de cacao
Whipped cream for garnish

Combine ice cream and candies. Divide evenly among 8 parfait glasses. Pour 1 teaspoon crème de cacao over each glass and top with whipped cream. May be stored in freezer until serving time.

WALNUT HORNS

1 cup butter, slightly softened	1 cup chopped walnuts
1 cup large curd, creamed cottage cheese	1 cup sugar
	1 teaspoon cinnamon
2¼ cups sifted all-purpose flour	Milk

Cream butter; add cheese and flour. Mix well and refrigerate for at least 4 hours. Roll out chilled dough about ¼ inch thick and cut into 3-inch squares. To make filling, combine nuts, sugar and cinnamon. Spread some of the filling on each square. Roll into horns; brush with milk and place on cookie sheet. Bake in a preheated 350° oven for 12 to 15 minutes. Makes 3 to 4 dozen.

POPPY SEED COOKIES

1 cup butter, slightly softened	2 eggs, slightly beaten
2 teaspoons vanilla	2½ cups sifted all-purpose flour
1½ cups confectioners' sugar	3 tablespoons poppy seeds
½ cup ground nuts	

Cream butter with vanilla and sugar; add remaining ingredients. Form into 2 rolls, 2 inches in diameter. Refrigerate or freeze. To bake, slice dough thinly; place rounds on a greased cookie sheet. Bake in a preheated 350° oven for 15 minutes or until lightly browned.

GREEK COFFEE

Make double strength coffee, but before brewing add 1 1-inch piece vanilla bean or 1 stick cinnamon, broken up to the ground coffee. Serve with thin lemon slices and sugar.

Greek Buffet

(SERVES 8)

Bloody Mary Soup

Marinated Olives   Ambrosia Cheese Spread

Moussaka   Lemon Baked Chicken

Athenian Salad

Poppy Seed Cake

Coffee

ADVANCE PREPARATION SCHEDULE

Previous Day	Early Morning
Marinated Olives (1 week in advance)	*Soup (combine all ingredients)*
Ambrosia Cheese Spread	*Prepare vegetables for salad*
Poppy Seed Cake	
Moussaka	

BLOODY MARY SOUP

8 cups canned spicy bloody Mary mix	Lemon juice
Celery salt	Vodka
Seasoned pepper	8 thin lemon slices

Combine bloody Mary mix with seasonings and lemon juice. Heat; spike with vodka and serve in mugs with a thin slice of lemon.

MARINATED OLIVES

1 9-ounce jar large green olives	¼ teaspoon crushed red pepper
¼ cup red wine vinegar	1 clove garlic, minced
¼ cup salad oil	¼ cup chopped onion
1 teaspoon dried oregano leaves	

Put olives, vinegar and salad oil into a 1-quart jar with tight-fitting lid. Add remaining ingredients to jar and shake vigorously. Refrigerate marinated olives for several days, at least, before serving. From time to time, shake jar well.

AMBROSIA CHEESE SPREAD

4 8-ounce packages cream cheese, softened
½ cup butter
6 teaspoons drained capers, finely chopped

3 teaspoons paprika
12 flat anchovies, finely chopped
1 tablespoon chopped onions
1 teaspoon salt
2 teaspoons caraway seeds

Blend cream cheese and butter together until smooth. Add remaining ingredients and work into a paste. Place in airtight jar or crock and refrigerate, at least one day before serving. Will keep well in refrigerator. Serve with crackers.

MOUSSAKA

3 medium eggplants, peeled and cut into ½-inch slices
Salt
1 cup olive or vegetable oil
3 large onions, finely chopped
2 pounds ground lamb
¼ cup tomato paste
½ cup red wine
½ cup chopped parsley

Salt and pepper to taste
½ cup butter
6 tablespoons flour
4 cups milk, heated
4 eggs, slightly beaten
2 cups ricotta cheese
¼ teaspoon nutmeg
¼ teaspoon cinnamon
1 cup fine dry bread crumbs

1 cup grated Parmesan cheese

Sprinkle eggplant slices with salt; lay on paper towels and weigh down with a heavy plate for about 30 minutes. Dry well. Heat ½ cup of the oil; brown eggplant slices and set aside. Add more oil if necessary, then cook onions until soft. Stir in lamb and cook for 10 minutes. Combine tomato paste, wine, parsley, salt and pepper to taste, and stir into meat mixture. Simmer until all liquid is absorbed. Meanwhile, make a white sauce by heating butter with flour in a saucepan. Gradually add heated milk to roux, whipping with a wire whisk. When thick and smooth, remove from heat. Cool slightly, add eggs, ricotta, nutmeg and cinnamon.

Grease an 11″ x 16″ pan and sprinkle bottom and sides with a generous layer of bread crumbs, about ½ cup. Alternately fill pan with layers of eggplant, meat mixture and white sauce, in that order. Top each layer of white sauce with Parmesan cheese and bread crumbs. Pour remaining white sauce over top of moussaka and bake in a preheated 350° oven. Cool 20 minutes before serving. Dish may be reheated.

LEMON BAKED CHICKEN

3 1½- to 2½-pound whole fryers
Garlic salt
Salt
Pepper
Poultry seasoning
3 whole lemons, halved

Season chickens inside and out with garlic salt, salt, pepper and poultry seasoning and squeeze fresh lemon over entire surface of chickens. Stuff cavities of birds with the lemon halves after squeezing. Place on a rack in a shallow baking pan. Bake in a preheated 325° oven for 2 hours or until very crisp and tender, adding a little water to baking pan if necessary to prevent burning.

ATHENIAN SALAD

2 heads iceberg lettuce, shredded
3 tomatoes, quartered
1 large cucumber, sliced
6 scallions, sliced
¼ pound feta cheese, cut in small
   pieces
1 2-ounce can anchovies, diced
Salt
Freshly ground pepper
½ cup olive oil
¼ cup cider vinegar
Pitted black olives

Pile lettuce on bottom of wooden bowl or platter. Layer vegetables attractively on top of lettuce and scatter cheese and anchovies over vegetables. Sprinkle salad with seasonings, oil and vinegar. Arrange olives decoratively on salad. Toss at table before serving.

POPPY SEED CAKE

1 18½-ounce package yellow cake
   mix
1 3¾-ounce package instant vanilla pudding
4 eggs
1 cup sour cream
½ cup oil
½ cup cream sherry
⅓ cup poppy seeds
Powdered sugar

Combine all ingredients except powdered sugar, stirring to blend

well. Beat on medium speed of electric mixer for 5 minutes or beat
700 strokes by hand, scraping side of bowl frequently. Pour into
greased 10-inch Bundt pan and bake in a preheated 350° oven for
1 hour. Cool in pan for 15 minutes; turn out cake on wire rack, and
cool completely. Sprinkle with powdered sugar.

★

MEXICAN

Mexico City Supper

(SERVES 6)

Guacamole
Taco Shells
Enchiladas Verdes
Steak Barbacola   Mexican Salad
Flan Español
Sangria

ADVANCE PREPARATION SCHEDULE

Early Morning

Guacamole
Enchiladas (do not bake)
Prepare ingredients for Mexican Salad
Flan
Slice fruit for Sangria

GUACAMOLE

2 large ripe avocados, peeled and pitted
1 medium-ripe tomato, peeled and diced
2 teaspoons minced onion
1 small chili pepper, deseeded and finely chopped

1 teaspoon salt
¼ teaspoon chili powder
1 teaspoon lemon juice
1 clove garlic, minced
Mayonnaise
Taco shells

Mash avocados, add tomato, onion and chili pepper. This may be done in a blender, but do not blend smooth. Add salt, chili powder, lemon juice and garlic. Place in a serving bowl, spread top with a thin layer of mayonnaise. Stir well just before serving. Serve with heated, lightly salted, thin taco shells broken as chips. Makes 1 cup.

ENCHILADAS VERDES

2 whole chicken breasts, split
1 cup chicken broth
6 ounces cream cheese
1 cup heavy cream
¾ cup finely chopped onions
6 fresh poblano chilies, 5″ long, or 6 fresh green peppers, about 3½ inches in diameter
5 medium tomatoes, peeled and chopped

2 canned serrano chilies, rinsed, seeded, chopped
1 egg
1½ teaspoons salt
¼ teaspoon black pepper
3 tablespoons oil
12 tortillas
⅓ cup freshly grated Parmesan cheese

Simmer chicken breasts in broth until tender. Remove chicken and reserve stock. Remove chicken from bones and shred chicken. Beat cream cheese with ½ cup of the cream; stir in onion and chicken, mix well and set aside. Roast fresh chilies under broiler until brown; turn and brown other side, about 5 minutes. Wrap in a damp towel and let rest a few minutes; gently rub with towel until skin slips off. Seed and remove stem. Place roasted chilies in the container of an electric blender with tomatoes, canned chilies, ¼ cup of the reserved chicken stock. Blend until smooth; pour in the remaining ½ cup cream, egg, salt and pepper, blending quickly. Pour into a large bowl. In a heavy skillet, heat oil. Dip tortillas in the chili-tomato sauce and drop into the hot oil, frying 1 minute on each side, until limp. Remove to a plate. Place ¼ cup of the chicken filling in center of tortilla, fold one end up and then roll over to close; place in an 8″ x 12″ baking dish, seam side down. Continue until all tortillas are filled. Tortillas should be in a single layer. Pour rest of chili-tomato sauce and grated cheese over tortillas. Bake in a preheated 350° oven for 15 minutes.

STEAK BARBACOLA

1 3-pound sirloin steak cut 1½- to 2-inches thick
1 cup red wine
2 cloves garlic, minced

1 tablespoon Worcestershire sauce
2 teaspoons dry mustard
1 tablespoon prepared mustard
1 teaspoon dried rosemary leaves

3 tablespoons chili sauce

Place steak in a shallow pan. Combine the remaining ingredients and pour over steak. Marinate for 1 hour. Drain steak and grill over hot coals to desired degree of doneness.

MEXICAN SALAD

1 large head iceberg lettuce
¼ pound bacon
1 small diced onion
¼ can refried beans (optional)
½ cup sour cream
½ cup mayonnaise

Juice of 1 lemon
2 tomatoes, diced
¼ pound Cheddar cheese, diced
1 avocado, diced (optional)
Corn chips or taco-flavored corn chips

Wash lettuce, dry and tear into serving sized pieces; crisp in refrigerator. Cook bacon until crisp, drain, crumble and set aside. Reserve bacon fat. Sauté diced onion in bacon fat until soft; add refried beans. When heated through, mash to a pulp and set aside to cool. Mix sour cream, mayonnaise and lemon juice and set aside. When ready to serve, place lettuce in salad bowl; sprinkle with diced tomatoes, cheese and avocado; spread refried bean mixture over all. Toss well with mayonnaise-sour cream mixture and top with corn chips and crumbled bacon.

FLAN ESPANOL

1 cup firmly packed brown sugar
1 9-inch unbaked pastry shell

4 egg yolks, well beaten
1 cup heavy cream

Sprinkle brown sugar over bottom of shell to cover evenly. Mix egg yolks and cream; pour over sugar. Bake in a preheated 425° oven for 10 minutes. Reduce temperature to 350° and bake until custard is set, about 35 minutes. Cool and serve.

SANGRIA

¼ to ½ cup sugar
2 cinnamon sticks
Fresh fruits (4 oranges, 3 lemons, 2 limes) thinly sliced
Brandy
1 ⅘ bottle red wine (dry Spanish)

1 ounce Cointreau or Triple Sec
1 ounce brandy
Carbonated citrus drink to taste
Strawberries, slices of peaches, apples, pears (optional)

Put sugar in a small saucepan and add enough water to just cover. Add cinnamon sticks and heat until sugar is dissolved. Let cool. Sprinkle fruit with brandy and allow to stand for 1 hour. Remove cinnamon sticks from sugar syrup; pour into a tall pitcher. Add brandied fruits and wine. Add Cointreau or Triple Sec and brandy. Chill. Just before serving, add carbonated drink and additional fruits (optional).

INDONESIAN

Indonesian Dinner I

(SERVES 8)

Eggs Indian
Chutney Spread
Sesame Crackers
Nasi Goreng
Indonesian Pancakes
Green Salad with French Vinaigrette Dressing (see Index)
Pita Bread
Glazed Poached Pears

ADVANCE PREPARATION SCHEDULE

Previous Day

*Hard cook eggs for Eggs
  Indian
Chutney Spread
Marinate beef and chicken
  for Nasi Goreng
Indonesian Pancakes
Poach Pears*

Early Morning

*Eggs Indian (do not bake)
Cook rice and shrimp for Nasi
  Goreng
French Vinaigrette Dressing (see
  Index)
Glaze Pears*

EGGS INDIAN

2 small onions, finely chopped
1 clove garlic, minced
¼ cup butter
½ teaspoon curry powder
2 teaspoons tomato paste

½ cup heavy cream
⅛ teaspoon pepper to taste
8 eggs, hard-cooked and sliced
   lengthwise
Paprika for color

Sauté onions and garlic in butter until tender, but not brown. Add curry powder. Stir in tomato paste, heavy cream, and pepper. Cook until sauce coats spoon. Pour over eggs in a shallow baking dish, sprinkle with paprika. Bake in a preheated 300° oven until hot and bubbly.

CHUTNEY SPREAD

2 8-ounce packages cream cheese
1 teaspoon lemon juice
Garlic salt and pepper to taste

3 tablespoons chutney, chopped
Sliced blanched almonds
Sesame crackers

Soften cream cheese to room temperature. Mix with lemon juice, garlic salt and pepper. Add chutney and blend well. Form into a ball. Coat with almonds and chill until firm. Serve at room temperature with sesame crackers.

NASI GORENG

½ cup vegetable oil
4 cloves garlic, crushed
3 large onions, chopped
2 teaspoons ground coriander
4 teaspoons curry powder
Salt and pepper
2 pounds porterhouse steak,
   sliced into thin strips
4 chicken breasts, boned and
   sliced into thin strips

¼ cup vegetable oil
6 tablespoons butter
5 cups cooked and cooled rice
1 tablespoon curry powder
⅛ teaspoon crushed red pepper
2 pounds shrimp, cooked,
   shelled and deveined
1 cup chopped scallions
Chopped parsley
Condiments

In a bowl combine the ½ cup oil, garlic, onions, coriander, the 4 teaspoons curry, salt and pepper and divide mixture in half. Marinate beef in half of the marinade and chicken in the other half, refrigerate for 6 hours or overnight. Drain meats. In a skillet, sauté beef until brown, adding a little oil if necessary. Remove beef from pan and sauté chicken until lightly browned. In another large pan, heat the ¼ cup oil and butter; add rice and sprinkle with the 1 tablespoon curry and red pepper. Cook for several minutes. Add beef and chicken, cook mixture for 15 minutes, stirring occasionally. Blend in shrimp and scallions; heat through and turn out on a serving platter. Garnish with parsley and Indonesian Pancakes and serve Condiments in small bowls on the side.

Condiments:

Spanish peanuts, chopped   Shredded coconut
Cucumber slices   Banana slices sprinkled with
Raisins   lemon juice

INDONESIAN PANCAKES

6 eggs   1 tablespoon soy sauce
1 teaspoon sugar   1½ tablespoons flour
Salt and pepper   Butter for frying pancakes

Beat all ingredients together, except butter. Drop batter by tablespoonfuls in buttered frying pan, cooking mixture like pancakes. Cook and set aside. Continue until all batter is used. When pancakes have cooled completely, slice them into thin strips. Use as a garnish for Nasi Goreng.

GLAZED POACHED PEARS

8 firm pears, peeled with stems   1 8-ounce jar apricot jelly
   left intact   2 teaspoons Grand Marnier
1 cup sugar   Sweetened whipped cream
1 teaspoon lemon juice   (optional)
⅛ teaspoon salt

Stand pears upright in a large saucepan. Add water to cover, then add sugar, lemon juice and salt. Cover and poach until pears are just tender. Allow pears to cool in their own syrup. Melt apricot jelly and add Grand Marnier. Cook until thick. Cool. When pears are cool, drain and reserve 1 cup of the syrup. Arrange pears in a serving dish, cover pears with apricot glaze and add the 1 cup syrup.

May be topped with whipped cream sweetened with a little powdered sugar, if desired.

Indonesian Dinner II

(SERVES 6)

Bean Sprout Salad with Chicken
Bali Beef
Shrimp with Cashew Nuts
Rice Bangkok   Oriental Asparagus
Blueberries Over-and-Under
Fortune Cookies
Jasmine Tea

ADVANCE PREPARATION SCHEDULE

Previous Day

*Cook chicken for Bean
Sprout Salad*

Early Morning

*Marinate bean sprouts
Cut up beef for Bali Beef
Butterfly shrimp for Shrimp with
Cashew Nuts
Cut up asparagus
Blueberries Over-and-Under*

BEAN SPROUT SALAD WITH CHICKEN

½ teaspoon salt
1 garlic clove, crushed
¼ cup cider vinegar
¼ cup salad oil
1 pound fresh bean sprouts

3 scallions, chopped
2 whole chicken breasts, broiled in
Teriyaki Sauce, cut in thin
strips
Lettuce cups

Combine salt, garlic, vinegar and oil, add to bean sprouts and scallions and marinate for one hour. Broil chicken breasts, basting fre-

quently with marinade. Cut chicken in strips. At serving time, drain bean sprouts and scallions and add to chicken. Serve in lettuce cups.

BALI BEEF

1 pound flank steak, semi-frozen and cut into *very* thin slices
1 tablespoon cornstarch
1 egg, well beaten
2 ounces rice stick (optional) (available at Chinese grocery)

2 cups vegetable oil
1 tablespoon vegetable oil
6 scallions, cut diagonally
1 teaspoon salt
½ teaspoon sugar
2 tablespoons light soy sauce
1 teaspoon sesame oil

Marinate beef slices in cornstarch and egg for 15 to 30 minutes. Loosen rice stick; heat the 2 cups oil in a deep saucepan and deep-fry rice sticks in *very* hot oil for 1 second; then turn and cook on other side for 1 second. Remove from oil and drain on paper towel. Reheat oil and fry beef for 1 minute; remove from oil and drain on paper towel. In a hot wok or skillet, heat the 1 tablespoon oil; add scallions, stir and add salt, sugar, soy sauce and the 1 teaspoon sesame oil. Add beef and mix well. Place beef on top of fried rice sticks and serve at once.

SHRIMP WITH CASHEW NUTS

1 pound raw shrimp, shelled, deveined and butterflied
1 egg white, slightly beaten
1 tablespoon cornstarch
1 teaspoon salt
½ teaspoon black pepper
3 cups vegetable or peanut oil
4 ounces raw cashew nuts (available at health food store)

2 tablespoons vegetable or peanut oil
1 large green pepper, cubed
10 slices fresh ginger root
10 scallions, cut in 1-inch pieces
½ cup peas
2 tablespoons dry white wine
¼ teaspoon salt
1 teaspoon sesame or salad oil

Mix shrimp with egg white, cornstarch, salt and pepper; marinate for 15 to 30 minutes. Heat the 3 cups vegetable oil in a wok or large skillet. Deep-fry nuts until brown, about 1 minute; remove from pan with a slotted spoon. Heat oil again and fry shrimp in oil for several minutes; remove and set aside. In another skillet or wok, heat the 2 tablespoons oil; fry green pepper, ginger, scallions and peas. Combine wine with salt and sesame oil; pour over vegetables in wok, add shrimp and stir well. Turn off heat, add cashew nuts and serve at once.

RICE BANGKOK

1 cup long grain rice 1¾ cups cold chicken stock

Place rice in a saucepan with chicken stock. Bring to boil and cook, covered, for 10 to 15 minutes over low heat. Remove from heat and let stand 10 to 15 minutes longer. Remove cover, stir and fluff.

ORIENTAL ASPARAGUS

¼ cup peanut oil
½ teaspoon salt
1½ pounds asparagus, sliced diagonally from base to tip,
leaving tip intact
2 tablespoons white wine
1 tablespoon light soy sauce

Heat oil and salt in a large skillet until hot; add asparagus and stir-fry until it just begins to feel tender when pierced with a fork, about 5 minutes. Combine wine with light soy sauce; pour over asparagus and continue to cook and stir until asparagus is done, but still crisp.

BLUEBERRIES OVER-AND-UNDER

1 quart blueberries	Juice of 2 large lemons
¼ cup sugar	5 egg whites
5 egg yolks	1 cup heavy cream, whipped
¾ cup sugar	2 teaspoons grated lemon peel

Wash blueberries and sprinkle with the ¼ cup sugar. Beat egg yolks with the ¾ cup sugar until thick and lemon-colored. Add lemon juice and stir constantly over low heat until thick enough to coat spoon. Remove from heat; cool. Beat egg whites until stiff and fold into lemon custard; fold in whipped cream and lemon peel, blending well. This mixture is now a lemon mousse. Place a layer of blueberries in bottom of a glass compote or individual serving dishes. Cover with a thick layer of lemon mousse. Chill thoroughly. When ready to serve, top with remaining fresh blueberries.

Buffets and Barbecues

APARTMENT DWELLER or suburbanite, teen-ager or octogenarian, Buffets and Barbecues offer something for everyone. Perhaps you will furnish wicker baskets for an "indoor barbecue," or artfully designed instructions for the "Informal Fun Party"—the possibilities and ideas can be limitless.

Buffet à la Russe

(SERVES 6)

Smoked Sturgeon   Caviar Dip Bowl
Fresh Melba Toast
Beef Stroganoff
Buttered Noodles
Limestone Lettuce Salad with Special Vinaigrette Dressing
Nut Torte
Coffee

257

ADVANCE PREPARATION SCHEDULE

Previous Day	Early Morning
Fresh Melba Toast	*Caviar Dip Bowl*
Beef Stroganoff	*Special Vinaigrette Dressing*
(omit sour cream)	*Prepare lettuce for salad*
Nut Torte	

SMOKED STURGEON

12 slices smoked sturgeon	Few drops olive oil
Capers	Freshly ground black pepper
Parsley	Dark bread
6 lemon wedges	Sweet butter

Serve 2 slices sturgeon on each plate, garnished with capers, parsley and lemon wedges. Sprinkle with oil and black pepper. Accompany with finger sandwiches of dark bread and sweet butter.

Variation:

Substitute smoked Nova Scotia salmon for sturgeon and serve in the same manner.

CAVIAR DIP BOWL

6 ounces red caviar, drained and sprinkled with lemon juice	2 cups sour cream
1 tablespoon grated onion	Fresh Melba Toast

Combine caviar, onion and sour cream. Serve in bowl surrounded by Fresh Melba Toast or water biscuits.

FRESH MELBA TOAST

1 loaf very thinly sliced white bread, each slice cut in half

Arrange bread slices on a cookie sheet. Bake in a preheated 350° oven for 7 minutes on one side; turn slices over and bake 5 minutes on the other side. Store in plastic bag or tin.

BEEF STROGANOFF

2 pounds beef tenderloin, chilled	1 tablespoon catsup
¼ cup butter	½ teaspoon salt
1 cup chopped onion	⅛ teaspoon pepper
1 pound fresh mushrooms, sliced	1 10½-ounce can beef bouillon
¼-inch thick	¼ cup dry vermouth
3 tablespoons flour	½ teaspoon dried dill weed
2 teaspoons beef extract	1½ cups sour cream

6 cups hot buttered noodles

Slice meat into thin strips. Quickly sauté in 1 tablespoon of the butter until brown on outside, but rare inside. Set aside. Add the remaining butter to pan and sauté onions and mushrooms about 5 minutes. Remove from heat and add flour, beef extract, catsup, salt and pepper. Stir until smooth and add bouillon; continue stirring with a whisk until smooth. Simmer 5 minutes. Add wine and dill. Add meat and heat. Add sour cream, if serving immediately. Heat but do not boil. If preparing ahead, add sour cream just before serving. Serve over noodles.

Note: This recipe is better made a day or two in advance.

SPECIAL VINAIGRETTE DRESSING

6 tablespoons salad oil	1 teaspoon Worcestershire sauce
2 tablespoons spiced tarragon vinegar	1 hard-cooked egg, finely chopped
2 teaspoons prepared mustard	2 stalks celery, finely chopped
	2 cloves garlic, mashed (optional)

Salt and pepper

Combine ingredients and chill. Pour over limestone lettuce.

NUT TORTE

7 egg yolks	1 teaspoon vanilla
1¾ cups sugar	1 teaspoon baking powder
14 unsalted soda crackers, crushed	7 egg whites, stiffly beaten
1 cup finely crushed or ground pecans	Mocha Frosting

Beat egg yolks with sugar until thick and lemon-colored; add crackers, nuts, vanilla and baking powder, mix well. Fold in egg whites. Pour into an ungreased 8-inch spring form pan and bake in a preheated 350° oven for 1 hour or less. Cool; split cake into 2 layers. Frost between layers and on top and sides with Mocha Frosting.

MOCHA FROSTING

2 cups heavy cream   ⅓ cup sifted confectioners' sugar
2 tablespoons sifted cocoa   1 teaspoon instant coffee powder
1 teaspoon vanilla

Whip cream, fold in remaining ingredients and frost cake. Chill overnight.

Luncheon Buffet

(SERVES 10)

Consommé with Sherry
Sesame Toast
Egg Salad Mold   Tuna Salad   Chicken Salad Supreme
Triple Bean Salad
Lemonade-Ring Mold (see Index)
Jam Cakes
Devil's Food Cake
Coffee

ADVANCE PREPARATION SCHEDULE

Freezer	Previous Day	Early Morning
Devil's Food Cake	*Sesame Toast*	*Tuna Salad*
	Egg Salad Mold	*Chicken Salad Supreme*
	Triple Bean Salad	*(omit dressing)*
	Lemonade-Ring Mold	*Remove Devil's Food*
	Jam Cakes	*Cake from freezer*

CONSOMME WITH SHERRY

4 10½-ounce cans beef consommé
2 soup cans water
¼ cup dry sherry

8 thin slices lemon
3 tablespoons chopped chives or parsley

Heat consommé with water and sherry. Serve topped with a lemon slice and a sprinkling of parsley or chives.

SESAME TOAST

1 package frozen Middle East bread (also called pita, Syrian, Sahara or Lebanese bread)

1 teaspoon garlic powder
½ cup butter, melted
Sesame seeds

Split each piece of bread cross-wise through center. Add garlic powder to butter and brush over each half of bread. Sprinkle bread with sesame seeds. Cut into 4 pie-shaped wedges and toast in a preheated 425° oven for 8 to 10 minutes. Makes 40 medium-sized wedges.

Variation:

Substitute dried dill weed, oregano or celery seed for sesame seed.

EGG SALAD MOLD

1 envelope unflavored gelatine
¼ cup cold water
1 cup chicken broth, boiling
1 cup mayonnaise
1 tablespoon lemon juice
1 tablespoon grated onion

1 tablespoon chopped parsley
½ green pepper, chopped (optional)
Salt and white pepper to taste
12 hard-cooked eggs, put through a food mill

Dissolve gelatine in cold water, and add to chicken broth. Mix in all remaining ingredients, adding eggs last. Pour into a greased 6-cup mold immediately, and refrigerate overnight. Unmold to serve.

TUNA SALAD

2 7-ounce cans white tuna, drained
3 celery stalks, diced
1 8-ounce jar green olives with pimiento, sliced
1 8-ounce can black olives, sliced

1 8-ounce can water chestnuts, diced
1 cup mayonnaise
2 heaping teaspoons drained capers

Juice of 1 lemon

Mix all ingredients thoroughly. May be made in early morning for lunch.

CHICKEN SALAD SUPREME

4 cups diced cooked breast of chicken
2 cups diced celery
1 4½-ounce jar whole button mushrooms, drained
½ cup pecan halves, toasted
6 slices bacon, crisply cooked and crumbled

1 cup mayonnaise
1 cup sour cream
1½ teaspoons salt
2 tablespoons lemon juice
¼ teaspoon pepper
¼ teaspoon celery seed
2 tablespoons chopped parsley
½ teaspoon sugar

¼ teaspoon paprika

Combine chicken, celery, mushrooms, pecans and bacon. Blend mayonnaise with remaining ingredients and add to chicken mixture, tossing to coat. Chill thoroughly. Dressing should be added no more than 1 hour before serving. May be served in lettuce cups, garnished with pimiento strips, ripe olives, and avocado slices dipped in lemon juice, if desired.

TRIPLE BEAN SALAD

1 16-ounce can cut green beans, drained
1 16-ounce can cut wax beans, drained
1 15-ounce can dark red kidney beans, drained

½ cup chopped green pepper
½ cup minced onion
½ cup sugar
⅔ cup wine vinegar
⅓ cup salad oil
1 teaspoon salt

¼ teaspoon pepper

Combine green, wax and kidney beans. Add green pepper and onions. Combine sugar with vinegar and oil and pour over vegetables. Add salt and pepper and toss. Chill overnight. Before serving, toss again to coat beans; drain and serve.

JAM CAKES

2 egg yolks
1 cup butter, softened
2 cups sifted all-purpose flour
½ teaspoon vanilla
¼ cup sugar
1 16-ounce jar blackberry or raspberry jam

4 whole eggs
2 egg whites
1 cup sugar
Grated peel of ¼ lemon
½ pound walnuts, chopped

Combine egg yolks, butter, flour, vanilla and sugar. Mix well and pat into a 10½″ x 15½″ x 1″ jelly-roll pan. Spread jam over dough. Beat whole eggs and egg whites well and add remaining ingredients. Spread over jam. Bake in a preheated 375° oven for 30 to 35 minutes. Cool in pan and set aside. Cut into diamonds, oblongs or squares on day they are being served.

DEVIL'S FOOD CAKE

½ cup butter, slightly softened
1½ cups sugar
3 egg yolks
½ cup unsweetened cocoa
1½ cups cake flour, sifted 4 times before measuring

1½ teaspoons baking powder
1 teaspoon vanilla
1 cup strong cold coffee
3 egg whites, well beaten

Cream butter with sugar; add egg yolks, beat well. Mix cocoa and flour and add to butter-sugar mixture. Stir in baking powder, vanilla and coffee and mix well. Add egg whites. Pour into 2 greased and floured 8-inch round cake pans. Bake in a preheated 350° oven for 30 minutes. Remove cake from pans and cool. Frost between layers, sides and top of cake with Chocolate Icing.

CHOCOLATE ICING

¼ cup butter, creamed
1 cup confectioners' sugar
1 1-ounce square unsweetened chocolate, melted

1 egg yolk
1 egg white, well beaten

Combine ingredients in order listed, and beat until smooth and creamy.

Far East Buffet

(SERVES 6)

Cantonese Ribs
Sweet and Sour Chicken
Flank Steak with Caper Sauce
Soft Pan Rolls
Oriental Rice Casserole
Lemon-Rum Sherbet   Almond Cookies
Tea and Coffee

ADVANCE PREPARATION SCHEDULE

Freezer	Previous Day	Early Morning
Lemon Rum Sherbet *Almond Cookies*	*Marinate ribs for* *Cantonese Ribs*	*Cut Chicken for Sweet* *and Sour Chicken* *Caper Sauce for Steak* *Cook rice for Oriental* *Rice Casserole* *Remove Almond* *Cookies from freezer*

CANTONESE RIBS

2 pounds spareribs, cut into small
    pieces
1 cup honey

½ cup soy sauce
2 tablespoons gin
Dash of garlic powder (optional)

Place spareribs in a pan. Make marinade by combining remaining ingredients. Pour marinade over ribs and marinate 2 hours or longer. Preheat oven to 350°, place spareribs on a rack in shallow baking pan and bake 1 to 1½ hours, basting often with marinade.

SWEET AND SOUR CHICKEN

6 boned chicken breasts
½ teaspoon salt
1 teaspoon cornstarch
⅓ cup vegetable oil
2 cloves garlic, crushed
1 8-ounce can pineapple chunks
    in heavy syrup

1 4-ounce jar sweet mixed pickles
2 teaspoons soy sauce
1 cup green pepper strips
2 teaspoons cornstarch dissolved
    in 1 tablespoon water
2 medium tomatoes

Cut chicken meat into thin strips and mix with salt and the 1 teaspoon cornstarch. Heat oil in skillet, add garlic and sauté 1 minute in the hot oil. Remove garlic, add seasoned chicken and stir continuously about 2 minutes over high heat. Add juice from pineapple chunks, liquid from pickles and add soy sauce. Bring to a boil. Add pickles, pineapple and green pepper. Bring to a boil. Dissolve the 2 teaspoons cornstarch in 1 tablespoon water and blend into mixture. Add tomatoes cut into wedges and serve as soon as tomatoes are heated through.

FLANK STEAK WITH CAPER SAUCE

1 1- to 2-pound flank
    steak

½ cup soy sauce
Caper Sauce

Prepare flank steak by marinating for 2 hours in soy sauce. Broil flank steak turning once, until brown on both sides and cooked to the desired doneness. Slice steak by starting at the thick end and slicing across the grain in very thin diagonal slices. Pour Caper Sauce over sliced steak.

Caper Sauce:

1 bouillon cube in ½ cup hot water
½ cup catsup
2 tablespoons soy sauce
⅛ teaspoon pepper

1 sliced onion
1 green pepper cut into chunks
2 teaspoons capers
¼ pound mushrooms, sliced and sauteed in butter or margarine

To make sauce, blend together the dissolved bouillon cube, catsup, soy sauce and pepper, add the onion, green pepper, capers and mushrooms and cook until onions and peppers are tender.

ORIENTAL RICE CASSEROLE

6 cups hot cooked rice
2 tablespoons butter or margarine
1 8-ounce can water chestnuts, sliced

1 package frozen pea pods, thawed
1 tablespoon diced pimiento

Toss rice with butter. Add water chestnuts, pea pods and pimiento, put into a buttered 2-quart casserole and bake in a preheated 350° oven until heated through.

LEMON-RUM SHERBET

1 quart lemon sherbet
1 cup light rum

1 16-ounce can sliced peaches, drained

Soften lemon sherbet slightly, beat together with rum and refreeze. To serve, put in sherbet glasses and decorate with peach slices.

ALMOND COOKIES

2 cups sugar
1 cup butter, softened
1 cup vegetable shortening

1 teaspoon baking soda
3 cups sifted all-purpose flour
1 cup shredded coconut

1 teaspoon almond extract

Cream sugar, butter and shortening. Sift baking soda into flour and add gradually to sugar mixture. Add coconut and almond extract. Form small rolls from the dough, 1½ inches in diameter, wrap each in foil or wax paper. Put in refrigerator until firm. When ready to bake, slice rolls thin and place on ungreased cookie sheets at least one inch apart. Bake in a preheated 350° oven about 10 minutes. *Do not overbake.* Take out of oven when very light in color. This is important, since the flavor changes when they are overbaked.

Pizza Party

(SERVES 6)

Assorted Dips
Chips
Do-It-Yourself Pizza
Salad Bar
Banana Split Mold
Assorted Cold Beverages

ADVANCE PREPARATION SCHEDULE

Freezer	**Previous Day**	**Early Morning**
Banana Split Mold	*Prepare your choice of dips*	*Prepare pizza topping ingredients* *Prepare ingredients for Salad Bar*

DO-IT-YOURSELF PIZZA

2 loaves frozen, unbaked bread
   dough, defrosted and allowed
   to rise according to directions
   on package
Olive oil
1 16-ounce can tomato sauce
½ pound Mozzarella cheese,
   sliced
⅓ pound Parmesan cheese,
   freshly grated

1 pound sweet Italian sausage,
   sliced
1 large sweet onion, coarsely
   chopped
1 teaspoon dried oregano leaves
1 large green pepper, sliced
1 cup fresh mushrooms, sliced
1 4-ounce can anchovy filets
1 tablespoon olive oil

When dough has risen, work loaves together with floured hands to form one large ball. Grease a large pan with olive oil (bottom of broiler pan is perfect). Roll or pat dough to cover pan bottom. Spread tomato sauce over dough and cover sauce well with the cheeses. Arrange all other ingredients in bowls surrounding pizza dough. Let every guest choose a corner of the pizza to trim as he likes. When pizza is assembled by all guests, drizzle the 1 tablespoon oil over top. Bake in a preheated 425° oven for 30 minutes.

SALAD BAR

Romaine
Iceberg lettuce
Escarole
Bibb lettuce
Leaf lettuce
Chick peas
Cherry tomatoes
Sliced cucumbers

Green or black, pitted, chopped
   olives
Croutons
Sliced radishes
Thinly sliced raw zucchini
Crumbled crisp bacon
Garbanzo beans
Assorted dressings (see Index)

Arrange assorted chilled salad greens, vegetables and dressings in separate dishes and let each guest prepare his own salad.

BANANA SPLIT MOLD

1½ quarts ice cream, any
   desired flavor

2 cups commercial fudge sauce,
   not syrup

6 large bananas

In a lightly greased 3-quart mold or bowl, spread a thick layer of ice cream. Cover with a thick layer of fudge sauce and top with a generous layer of banana chunks. Repeat 2 or 3 times, changing flavor of ice cream, if desired. Freeze until ready to serve. Unmold before serving.

Country Buffet

(SERVES 12)

Spanish Shrimp
Oven-Fried Chicken with Lemon Sauce
Parmesan Potatoes   Ham and Apricots
Crunchy Salad
Raspberry Meringue Parfaits
Coffee

ADVANCE PREPARATION SCHEDULE

Freezer	Previous Day	Early Morning
Ice cream balls for Raspberry Meringue Parfaits	*Lemon Sauce for Chicken*	*Prepare ingredients for Spanish Shrimp*
	Salad dressing	*Bake chicken (without sauce)*
	Meringue Shells	
	Chocolate–Sour Cream Sauce for Raspberry Meringue Parfaits	*Prepare crumb mixture for Parmesan Potatoes*
		Prepare ham, ready for baking
		Prepare vegetables for salad

SPANISH SHRIMP

3 tablespoons minced parsley
3 tablespoons red wine vinegar
2 large cloves garlic, minced
6 anchovy filets, drained and minced
¼ cup olive oil
1 onion, minced
2 small hot chili peppers, crushed
½ cup dry white wine
6 ripe tomatoes, peeled, seeded and chopped
Salt and freshly ground pepper to taste
2 pounds raw shrimp, shelled and deveined
1 tablespoon drained capers
Fresh grated lemon peel

In a mixing bowl, combine parsley, vinegar, garlic and anchovies and set aside. Heat oil in a large heavy skillet. Add onions and chili peppers and cook until onion is soft and golden. Add wine and bring to boil. Cook until sauce thickens and add tomatoes, salt and pepper. Cook until most of juice from tomatoes has evaporated. Add shrimp and cook for 5 to 7 minutes, until they turn a bright pink. Stir in capers and parsley-vinegar mixture; heat through, correct seasoning and serve garnished with grated lemon peel.

OVEN-FRIED CHICKEN WITH LEMON SAUCE

1 cup unsifted flour
2 teaspoons salt
½ teaspoon pepper
4 teaspoons paprika
3 2½- to 3-pound fryers, cut-up
1 cup butter, melted
Lemon Sauce

Preheat oven to 400°. Combine flour and seasoning; coat chicken pieces evenly. Arrange chicken, skin side down, in single layer in a shallow baking pan. Drizzle chicken liberally with butter; bake uncovered 30 minutes. (May be made earlier up to this point and set aside.) Turn chicken, pour Lemon Sauce over; bake in a preheated 350° oven 30 minutes longer or until chicken is golden brown and tender.

Lemon Sauce:

3 tablespoons soy sauce
1 teaspoon salt
1 teaspoon pepper
¾ cup salad oil
1½ cups lemon juice
⅓ cup grated lemon peel
3 cloves garlic, minced

Combine all ingredients. Refrigerate for at least one hour before using.

PARMESAN POTATOES

1 cup butter
1 cup dry seasoned bread crumbs
½ cup grated Parmesan cheese
2 eggs, slightly beaten

12 medium red-skinned potatoes,
   peeled and cut into ½-inch
   slices
Salt and pepper to taste
Paprika

Melt ½ cup of the butter in a 10½" x 15½" x 1" jelly-roll pan. Combine bread crumbs and Parmesan cheese. Dip potato slices in beaten egg, then in crumb mixture. Sprinkle with salt and pepper and place in pan with melted butter. Melt remaining butter; drizzle over potatoes and bake in a preheated 350° oven for 40 minutes, until tender. Before serving, sprinkle with paprika.

HAM AND APRICOTS

1 5-pound canned ham
Whole cloves

1 29-ounce can apricots
½ pound brown sugar

Remove ham from can and score fat of ham in a diamond pattern; place 1 clove in center of each diamond. Set ham on a rack in a large roasting pan. Drain apricots, and pour juice over ham; pat brown sugar firmly over ham. Bake ham in a preheated 500° oven for 20 minutes. Remove ham from oven, and reduce oven temperature to 350°. Decorate ham with apricots, held in place with half toothpicks. Return ham to oven and bake for 1 hour, basting every 10 minutes with the syrup in the pan.

CRUNCHY SALAD

2 heads lettuce, washed, chilled
   and torn into small pieces
½ head red cabbage, shredded or
   finely sliced
6 celery stalks, thinly sliced
1 red or green pepper, slivered
2 small fresh cucumber pickles,
   peeled and diced

2 small raw zucchini, unpeeled
   and diced (optional)
3 cups mayonnaise
¼ cup chili sauce
¼ cup bottled creamy French
   dressing
Shredded Mozzarella cheese
   (optional)

Mix lettuce and cabbage with vegetables. Combine mayonnaise, chili sauce and French dressing. Chill salad and dressing separately until ready to serve. Before serving, toss salad with dressing; garnish with shredded Mozzarella cheese, if desired.

RASPBERRY MERINGUE PARFAITS

3 egg whites	1 teaspoon vinegar
3 tablespoons raspberry-flavored gelatin	1 cup miniature semi-sweet chocolate pieces
⅔ cup sugar	12 large scoops coffee ice cream

Beat egg whites until foamy; gradually add gelatin and sugar. Beat until sugar dissolves and whites form stiff peaks. Mix in vinegar; fold in chocolate pieces. Drop from a pastry tube or a large spoon onto a brown-paper-covered cookie sheet; form 12 individual meringue dessert shells. Bake in a preheated 250° oven for 30 minutes. Turn off oven and let meringues sit inside oven for 30 minutes longer. Cool completely. Fill each shell with ice cream and serve with Chocolate–Sour Cream Sauce.

Note: Store meringues in a tin until ready to use; will keep about one week. Meringues may be frozen.

CHOCOLATE–SOUR CREAM SAUCE

12 ounces semi-sweet chocolate pieces	¼ teaspoon salt
	½ cup milk
1 cup sour cream	½ teaspoon cinnamon (optional)

Fill the bottom of a double boiler half full of water and bring almost to the simmering point. Pour chocolate pieces into top of double boiler. Stir over the hot water until chocolate has melted. Blend in the other ingredients. If made early, refrigerate sauce and reheat over hot water when ready to use.

Informal Fun

(SERVES 24)

Choose any or many of the nine listed hamburgers. The basic recipe is the same for hamburger itself. Only the sauces vary.

Set up a long table, against a wall if possible. Write out a list below the title of the hamburger with "how to" instructions. Step-by-step information is fun and decorative. List instructions by number . . . and your guests will be busy and happy while creating something special.

Miniature Ribs   Curry Dip with Raw Vegetables

Hamburger Patties

South of the Border Burger

Down-Under Burger

Russian Burger

Burger à la Française

Double Decker Burger

Athenian Burger

Cantonese Burger

Burger Italiano

British Burger

Miniature Ice Cream Puffs

Chocolate Fondue Sauce

Assorted Soft Drinks and Beer

Freezer	Previous Day	Early Morning
Miniature Ribs	*Curry Dip*	*Prepare Raw Vegetables*
Cream Puffs	*Chocolate Fondue*	*Prepare hamburger fixings*
Hamburger Patties	*Sauce*	*in bowls or platters*
		Prepare all cooked vege-
		tables, dips, and sauces
		needed for hamburgers
		Remove Miniature Ribs
		and Hamburger Patties
		from freezer
		Place lists on wall

MINIATURE RIBS

6 pounds spareribs, cracked into thirds and cut into hors d'oeuvres–size pieces	Salt and pepper to taste
	Celery salt
	Bottled barbecue sauce
Garlic salt	

Ask butcher to crack ribs into hors d'oeuvres size and remove thin skin on back. Steam ribs in a large covered saucepan, in 1 cup hot water for 30 minutes. Turn occasionally while steaming. When meat is almost tender, remove, place in a large baking pan; season with salts and pepper and pour barbecue sauce over ribs. Marinate, refrigerated, for at least 1 hour or overnight. Place ribs in a shallow roasting pan, meaty side up, and roast in a preheated 350° oven for 20 minutes. Turn and cook for 20 minutes on other side, until cooked through and well glazed. May be cooked in advance and refrigerated or frozen.

CURRY DIP

3 cups mayonnaise	3 teaspoons tarragon vinegar
3 teaspoons curry powder	3 teaspoons grated onion
3 teaspoons garlic powder	3 teaspoons prepared horseradish

Mix all ingredients the night before serving and chill. Surround with assorted raw vegetables, such as cauliflower, carrots, celery and mushrooms.

HAMBURGER PATTIES

For Each Eight Servings:

2 pounds ground beef	1 teaspoon grated onion
2 egg whites	(optional)
2 tablespoons heavy cream	¼ teaspoon freshly ground pepper
2 teaspoons salt	

Blend all ingredients lightly with 2 forks and form into 8 patties. May be frozen. Place on barbecue and grill to desired doneness. Serve on buns.

SOUTH OF THE BORDER BURGER

1. Place hamburger on toasted bun.
2. Add hot canned chili con carne.
3. Add chopped onions.
4. Add shredded cheese—cheddar or Monterey Jack.
5. Add shredded lettuce.
6. Add sliced radishes.
7. Top with Guacamole (see Index).
8. Cover with top bun.

DOWN-UNDER BURGER

1. Place hamburger on toasted, buttered English muffin.
2. Top with fried egg.
3. Add sliced onions sautéed in butter.
4. Place top of English muffin—toasted and buttered—on hamburger.

RUSSIAN BURGER

1. Place hamburger on dark rye.
2. Top with sour cream.
3. Top with red or black caviar.
4. Place top slice of dark rye on burger.

BURGER A LA FRANÇAISE

1. Place hamburger on crusty warm slice of French bread.
2. Top with Béarnaise Sauce.
3. Top with watercress and sliced tomatoes and 1 tablespoon Vinaigrette (see Index).
4. Place French bread spread with a little Dijon mustard on top.

Béarnaise Sauce:

¼ cup white wine	1 teaspoon finely chopped or
¼ cup tarragon vinegar	grated onion
2 peppercorns	

Boil ingredients until reduced to 3 tablespoons. Add to Blender Lemon Hollandaise (see Index).

DOUBLE DECKER BURGER

Split hamburger bun in 3 slices.
1. Place lettuce on bun.
2. Add burger.
3. Add tomato slice.
4. Add mayonnaise, chili sauce, pickle relish, horseradish (optional).
5. Add another thin slice of bun.
6. Add another burger.
7. Top with slice of American cheese.
8. Add onion slices.
9. Top with more mayonnaise, chili sauce, relish, and horseradish.
10. Place top of bun on the whole thing and serve with French Fried Onions.

FRENCH FRIED ONIONS

1 large sweet onion, sliced into ¼ -inch slices	1 cup flour
2 eggs	1 teaspoon baking powder
½ cup milk	½ teaspoon salt
	Oil

Separate onions into rings. Mix eggs, milk and beat well. Add dry ingredients; stir just until well mixed. Heat at least 1½ inches oil in a deep saucepan; heat to 375° on a deep-fat-frying thermometer. Dip onion rings into batter and fry until crisp and golden, turning as needed. Total cooking time is about 4 minutes. Drain well, salt and serve. May be kept warm in oven.

ATHENIAN BURGER

1. Place burger on bun.
2. Top with grated feta cheese.
3. Add sliced Greek olives.
4. Add thin tomato slices.
5. Add diced scallions.
6. Add finely diced anchovies.
7. Top with lettuce.
8. Drizzle vinegar and oil over all.
9. Top with bun.

CANTONESE BURGER

1. Place hamburger on bun.
2. Sauté garlic clove and a thin slice of ginger, finely diced, in 2 tablespoons peanut oil.
3. Add 1 pound bean sprouts, 1 tablespoon light soy sauce, a pinch of salt and a few finely diced scallions. Sauté 3 minutes.
4. Top burger with bean sprouts and serve open-faced or topped with bun.

BURGER ITALIANO

1. Place hamburger on crusty Italian roll or bread.
2. Sauté strips of green peppers and onions in oil about ½ hour, until soft. Place on burger.
3. Top with slice of Mozzarella cheese.
4. Add a covering of hot tomato sauce (made with 8-ounce can of tomato sauce heated with 1 stick melted butter).
5. Top with a thin layer of cooked Italian sausage.
6. Top with roll or bread sprinkled with Parmesan cheese.

BRITISH BURGER

1. Place burger on bun.
2. Top with homemade, canned or frozen Welsh Rarebit cheese sauce.
3. Top with thin slices of tomatoes.
4. Add a few crisp bacon strips.
5. Top with bun.

WELSH RAREBIT

8 ounces shredded Cheddar cheese
2 teaspoons flour
½ cup beer
1 teaspoon Worcestershire sauce
¼ teaspoon English mustard

Mix cheese and flour. Heat beer, add other ingredients and stir until melted. Keep warm over hot water.

MINIATURE ICE CREAM PUFFS WITH CHOCOLATE FONDUE SAUCE

Miniature Cream Puffs:

1 cup water	½ teaspoon salt
½ cup butter	1 cup sifted all-purpose flour
4 eggs	

Slowly bring water, butter and salt to a boil. Lower heat; stir in flour all at once. Beat until mixture leaves sides of pan and becomes a small, compact ball. Remove from heat. One at a time, add eggs, beating smooth after each addition. Drop slightly rounded teaspoonfuls of dough, 2 inches apart, on ungreased cookie sheets. Bake in a preheated 375° oven for 25 to 30 minutes until puffed and golden. Cool. Makes 60 to 70 cream puffs.

Filling:

1 pint burgundy cherry ice cream   1 pint chocolate mint ice cream
1 pint jamoca ice cream

Filling and Assembling:

Cut tops off of cream puffs, and clean out insides to make a shell. Fill 6 puffs with 1 flavor of ice cream, using a melon baller. Fill next 6 puffs with a second flavor, and so on, until all puffs are filled. After filling every 6 puffs, press tops back onto puffs on top of ice cream, and place in freezer. To serve, arrange cream puffs on a serving platter. Serve with fondue forks. Let guests spear puffs on fondue forks and dip them into hot Chocolate Fondue Sauce. Serves 6. Multiply recipe according to number of guests.

Chocolate Fondue Sauce:

1 14-ounce can sweetened condensed milk	1 7-ounce jar marshmallow cream or 1 cup miniature marshmallows
1 12-ounce package semi-sweet chocolate pieces	½ cup milk
1 teaspoon vanilla	

Combine ingredients in a fondue pot or saucepan. Heat over medium heat, stirring, until mixture is smooth and heated through. May be made in advance and reheated. Add milk if sauce becomes too thick.

Barbecue Party

(SERVES 8)

Shrimp in Foil

French Bread

Hamburgers (see Index)   Barbecued Chicken

Fast Baked Potatoes

Gazpacho Salad

Fudge Brownies   Cherry Crunch Cake à la Mode

ADVANCE PREPARATION SCHEDULE

Freezer

Shrimp in Foil (uncooked)
Hamburgers (uncooked)
Fudge Brownies

Early Morning

Make sauce for Barbecued Chicken
Gazpacho Salad
Cherry Crunch Cake
Remove Shrimp in Foil and Hamburgers from freezer

SHRIMP IN FOIL

½ cup butter, softened
1 clove garlic, minced
½ cup chopped parsley
½ teaspoon salt

¼ teaspoon pepper
2 pounds raw medium-sized
  shrimp, peeled and deveined
Hot French bread

Cream butter with garlic, parsley, salt and pepper. Fold eight 9" x 9" squares of heavy foil in half. Divide shrimp evenly among pieces of foil and arrange in center of fold. Top with ⅛ of butter mixture. Close foil packets around shrimp and twist top tightly to seal. Grill over hot coals for 15 minutes or bake in a preheated 350° oven for 15 minutes; test for doneness. Serve with hot French bread.

BARBECUED CHICKEN

1 cup tomato purée or catsup
½ cup water
⅓ cup lemon juice
¼ cup butter, softened
1 medium onion, finely chopped
1 tablespoon Worcestershire
   sauce

1 tablespoon paprika
1 teaspoon sugar
1 teaspoon salt
½ teaspoon pepper
2 broiling chickens (1½ to 2½
   pounds each), cut up

Combine all ingredients except chicken, and heat to boiling. Brush chicken pieces with sauce or marinate in sauce while preparing charcoal fire. Brush grill with fat to keep chicken from sticking and set chicken on grill, 6 to 8 inches from hot coals. Turn every 5 minutes, basting often with sauce. Cook for 30 to 60 minutes, depending on size of chicken, and serve hot.

FAST BAKED POTATOES

6 large Idaho potatoes,
   scrubbed

½ cup butter
Salt

Slice each potato into eighths, lengthwise, with skins on. Place in a shallow baking pan, skin side down. Bake in a preheated 500° oven for 20 minutes. Brush with melted butter and sprinkle lightly with salt and serve.

GAZPACHO SALAD

4 large, very ripe tomatoes, peeled
   and chopped
1 large cucumber, peeled and
   diced
1 medium onion, finely minced
1 green pepper, seeded and finely
   minced

1 cup tomato juice
1 tablespoon wine vinegar
3 tablespoons olive oil
1 small clove garlic, minced or
   mashed
Salt and pepper to taste

Mix all ingredients, adding salt and pepper to taste. Chill until icy. Serve in small glasses or mugs, or spoon into bowls lined with lettuce leaves.

FUDGE BROWNIES

1 12-ounce package semi-sweet chocolate pieces
1 cup butter
4 eggs
Pinch of salt
1 cup sugar
1 cup sifted all-purpose flour
1 teaspoon baking powder
2 teaspoons vanilla
1 cup chopped nuts

Melt chocolate chips with butter over low heat. Beat eggs with salt and sugar and add to butter-chocolate mixture. Fold in remaining ingredients, mixing well. Pour into 2 greased 8″ x 8″ x 2″ pans or 1 9″ x 13″ pan. Bake in a preheated 375° oven for 25 minutes.

CHERRY CRUNCH CAKE A LA MODE

2 21-ounce cans cherry pie filling
1 large box yellow cake mix
Ice cream
1 3-ounce package walnuts
¾ cup butter, melted

Grease a 9″ x 12″ pan, and pour in cherry pie filling. If desired, sprinkle a bit of lemon juice over filling. On top, spread dry cake mix and walnuts and top with melted butter. Bake in a preheated 350° oven for 40 to 45 minutes. Cool and then cut into squares. Served topped with ice cream.

Indoor Barbecue

(SERVES 6)

Mushroom Consommé in Mugs

Parmesan Puffs   Hors d'Oeuvres Olives

Oven-Barbecued Spareribs   Corn-on-the-Cob

Applesauce (see Index)

Cherry Tomato Slaw

Spiked Fruit Sundae

Coffee

Freezer	Previous Day	Early Morning
Steamed Ribs	*Marinate olives*	*Mushroom Consommé*
Barbecue Sauce	*Applesauce*	*(ready to heat)*
	Prepare slaw for	*Prepare bread rounds*
	Cherry Tomato	*and cheese mixture*
	Slaw	*for Parmesan Puffs*
		Remove steamed ribs
		and Barbecue Sauce
		from freezer

MUSHROOM CONSOMME

3 10½-ounce cans consommé   1 tablespoon oil
1 10½-ounce can beef broth   1 tablespoon butter
1 cup water   Curry, a pinch to taste
½ pound fresh mushrooms   1 lemon, sliced thin
Chopped parsley

Combine consommé, beef broth and water for soup base. Wash mushrooms quickly in cold water; do not soak. Chop coarsely and sauté in oil and butter. Add drained mushrooms to broth and bring to a boil, then simmer 15 to 20 minutes. Add curry and serve in mugs, garnished with a slice of lemon and parsley.

PARMESAN PUFFS

1 1 pound loaf sliced white sand-   1 cup mayonnaise
   wich bread, crusts removed, cut   ¼ cup grated Parmesan cheese
   into 2-inch rounds   1 tablespoon finely grated onion
1 teaspoon prepared Dijon mustard

Toast bread rounds on one side only. Mix all other ingredients and spread 1 teaspoon on untoasted side of bread rounds. Place on a cookie sheet. Broil in preheated broiler for 2 minutes and serve. Bread may be toasted and mixture prepared in advance, but do not combine until just before broiling.

HORS D'OEUVRES OLIVES

1 4-ounce jar green pimiento olives
1 clove garlic
Pinch of black pepper
⅔ cup olive oil
1 tablespoon dried dill weed
½ cup cider vinegar

Drain olives and add remaining ingredients. Marinate for at least one day before serving. Olives improve upon standing.

OVEN-BARBECUED SPARERIBS

4 pounds spareribs
pepper
garlic salt
celery salt
Barbecue Sauce

Cut ribs into individual portions. Place meat side up in covered saucepan with 1 cup hot water. Steam for 30 minutes. Season steamed ribs with pepper, garlic salt and celery salt. Pour Barbecue Sauce over ribs and marinate for 1 hour. Bake in a preheated 350° oven for 1 hour, spooning sauce over ribs several times while baking. When ribs are tender, they are ready to serve.

BARBECUE SAUCE

1 large onion, chopped
½ cup water
1 cup chili sauce
¼ cup vinegar
2 tablespoons firmly packed brown sugar
1 tablespoon Worcestershire sauce
1 teaspoon dry mustard
1 teaspoon salt
1 teaspoon paprika
¼ teaspoon black pepper

Combine onion, water, chili sauce, vinegar, brown sugar, Worcestershire sauce, mustard, salt, paprika and black pepper and simmer 30 minutes.

CHERRY TOMATO SLAW

1 large head cabbage, coarsely shredded
¼ cup sugar
1 green pepper, diced

1 8-ounce bottle Italian salad dressing
1 pint cherry tomatoes, halved
Lemon pepper to taste

Sprinkle cabbage with sugar and add green pepper. Pour on dressing and marinate all day or overnight. Before serving, add tomatoes and lemon pepper and toss salad carefully.

SPIKED FRUIT SUNDAE

Bananas
At least 2 of the following fruits: sliced nectarines, sliced peaches, blueberries, strawberries, raspberries

Lemon
Sugar
Kirsch or Grand Marnier
Vanilla ice cream

Cut fruit into bite-size pieces, and sprinkle it with lemon and sugar to taste. Add a little bit of Kirsch or Grand Marnier and place a few tablespoons of fruit in bottom of parfait or wide bottomed glass. Cover fruit with 3 tablespoons ice cream, another layer of fruit, and top with ice cream.

Elegant Barbecue Dinner

(SERVES 8)

Seafood on the Half Shell
Chicken Yakitori
Brown Rice   Fresh Fruit Chunks on Skewers
Chinese Vegetable Salad
Overnight Chocolate Cream Cake
Coffee

ADVANCE PREPARATION SCHEDULE

Previous Day

Marinate chicken
Salad dressing
Overnight Chocolate
Cream Cake

Early Morning

Cook shrimp and prepare sauce
for Seafood on the Half Shell
Cook bacon and eggs and wash
spinach for salad

SEAFOOD ON THE HALF SHELL

Crushed ice
Cocktail Sauce, Russian Caviar
   Sauce or Mustard Mayonnaise
   (see Index)
8 oysters, on the half shell
8 clams, on the half shell
24 empty oyster or clam shells
   (ask fish market)

8 thin slices smoked salmon,
   rolled
4 ounces crabmeat
8 large shrimp, cooked, deveined
   and chilled
Parsley
Lemon wedges

Fill eight large soup dishes with crushed ice, just before serving.
Fill eight small glasses or cups with one of the suggested sauces and
nestle glasses in ice, in center of soup dishes. Surround each glass
of sauce with one oyster on the half shell, one clam on the half
shell and three empty half shells. Fill each of the empty half shells
with salmon, crabmeat and shrimp. Garnish each of the eight dishes
with parsley and lemon wedges.

COCKTAIL SAUCE

1 8-ounce bottle cocktail sauce
1 dash Tabasco, or to taste
   (optional)

1 tablespoon prepared horseradish, or to taste
Juice of ½ medium lemon

Combine cocktail sauce with other ingredients. Chill.

RUSSIAN CAVIAR SAUCE

2 cups mayonnaise
1 teaspoon dry mustard
2 tablespoons finely chopped onion

1 tablespoon Worcestershire sauce
2 ounces caviar
Squeeze of lemon, or to taste

Combine all ingredients and keep sauce chilled until served.

CHICKEN YAKITORI

3 pounds boneless chicken breasts, skin removed and cut into 1½-inch cubes
2 small bunches scallions
2 cloves garlic, minced
½ cup soy sauce
¼ cup lemon juice
¼ cup vegetable oil
2 teaspoons sugar
1 teaspoon salt
½ teaspoon ground ginger
¼ teaspoon pepper
Hot cooked brown rice

Remove skin from chicken and cut into 1½-inch cubes. Slice scallions thinly to make ½ cup; cut remaining scallions into 2-inch pieces. Combine thin scallion slices with remaining ingredients except rice. Mix thoroughly and pour marinade over chicken cubes. Marinate chicken, covered and refrigerated, for several hours or overnight, stirring occasionally. Alternately, thread chicken cubes and scallion pieces on skewers. Broil on rack in preheated broiler or outdoor grill over hot coals, turning to cook all sides; cook each skewer for 5 to 10 minutes, or until done to taste. Serve accompanied by hot brown rice.

Variation:

Chicken Yakitori may be accompanied by skewers of mixed chunks of fresh fruit (pineapple cubes, banana chunks and orange quarters). Brush skewered fruit with leftover marinade for Chicken Yakitori, grill for 5 minutes only.

CHINESE VEGETABLE SALAD

2 pounds fresh spinach, washed and crisped
½ pound bacon, crisply cooked and crumbled
3 hard-cooked eggs, grated
1 16-ounce can Chinese vegetables, drained
Dressing

Combine spinach, bacon, eggs and vegetables in a bowl. Shake Dressing and pour over salad. Toss well.

Dressing:

1 cup oil
½ cup sugar
⅓ cup ketchup
1 medium onion, grated
¼ cup vinegar
1 tablespoon Worcestershire sauce

Combine ingredients and refrigerate overnight.

OVERNIGHT CHOCOLATE CREAM CAKE

¾ pound sweet cooking chocolate
3 tablespoons sugar
3 tablespoons water
3 tablespoons Cointreau (or
   orange Curaçao)
6 egg yolks, well beaten
6 egg whites, stiffly beaten

3 packages ladyfingers, split in
   half lengthwise
½ cup cream sherry
½ cup sliced almonds
1 cup heavy cream, whipped
¼ cup confectioners' sugar
1 teaspoon vanilla

Sliced almonds

In a saucepan, melt chocolate over low heat. Add sugar, water and Cointreau; mix well and add egg yolk. Cook over low heat until thick and smooth, stirring constantly. Set aside to cool. When cool, add egg whites, folding them in carefully. Line sides and bottom of a 9-inch spring form pan with ladyfingers, flat side against sides and bottom of pan. With the fingers, moisten ladyfingers with sherry. Pour in half of chocolate mixture and sprinkle with almonds. Add another layer of split ladyfingers, flat side down, over filling. Moisten with sherry, pour in remaining chocolate filling, and sprinkle with sliced almonds. Cover almonds with ladyfingers, and moisten with sherry. Refrigerate cake overnight. Before serving, remove sides of pan from cake. Combine whipped cream with confectioners' sugar and vanilla. Top cake with whipped cream and sliced almonds.

Steak Sandwich Barbecue

(SERVES 6)

Onion Pie
Skirt Steak Sandwich
Hot Mushroom Garnish   French Bread
Cheese Lovers' Salad
Frosty Lemon Soufflé
Coffee

ADVANCE PREPARATION SCHEDULE

Early Morning

Onion Pie
Marinate Skirt Steak
Prepare Cheese Lovers' Salad
Frosty Lemon Soufflé

ONION PIE

½ cup butter, melted
1 cup unsalted cracker crumbs
4 cups thinly sliced onions
½ teaspoon salt
⅛ teaspoon freshly ground black pepper

1½ cups milk
4 eggs, lightly beaten
½ cup coarsely grated sharp Cheddar cheese

Mix half of melted butter with cracker crumbs and press firmly over bottom and sides of a 10-inch pie plate. Mix remaining butter with onions and sauté in a skillet until onions are soft, but not brown. Spread over crumb-crust in pie plate. Add salt, pepper and milk to eggs, gradually blending with a whisk. Pour mixture over onions. Sprinkle cheese on top and bake in a preheated 350° oven for 25 to 30 minutes. May be prepared and cooked ahead of time; reheat to serve.

SKIRT STEAK SANDWICH

3 tablespoons soy sauce
3 tablespoons vegetable oil
3 tablespoons sherry
2 crushed cloves garlic (optional)
3 pounds skirt steak

Combine soy sauce, oil, sherry and garlic. Marinate steak in mixture for at least 2 hours, turning frequently. Grill over hot coals or broil without any additional seasoning for 7 to 8 minutes on each side or until crusty on the outside and juicy-rare inside. Cut into individual servings and serve on French bread with Hot Mushroom Garnish spooned on top.

HOT MUSHROOM GARNISH

¾ pound mushrooms, washed and
    sliced
2 tablespoons butter
1 teaspoon lemon juice

¼ teaspoon dried oregano leaves
Salt
Pepper
1 cup sour cream

Sauté mushrooms in butter. Cover pan; cook 10 minutes. Season with lemon juice, oregano, salt and pepper. Add sour cream; heat gently.

CHEESE LOVERS' SALAD

1½ cups diagonally cut celery
2 15-ounce cans kidney
    beans, drained
1 12-ounce can whole-kernel
    corn, drained
2 tablespoons finely chopped
    onions

1 4-ounce can pimientos,
    chopped
½ cup finely chopped parsley
2 tablespoons drained capers
½ teaspoon salt
Cheese Dressing

Combine all salad ingredients. Add Cheese Dressing and blend well. Marinate salad in the refrigerator for several hours. Drain well before serving.

CHEESE DRESSING

½ cup grated Cheddar cheese
¼ cup crumbled blue cheese

2 tablespoons red wine
2 tablespoons wine vinegar

¼ cup oil (vegetable or olive)

Combine cheeses, wine, vinegar and oil. Shake well.

FROSTY LEMON SOUFFLE

2 tablespoons unflavored gelatine
2 tablespoons cold water
Grated peel of 4 lemons
½ to ¾ cup lemon juice (to taste)

1 cup sugar
8 egg whites
1 cup heavy cream
Thin lemon slices

Mint sprigs

Make a collar of oiled waxed paper to go around a 1-quart soufflé dish. Fasten with a paper clip or rubber band to secure waxed paper collar to dish. Collar should come up at least 3 inches above dish. Soften gelatine in water; place gelatine mixture in saucepan and add lemon juice, lemon peel and sugar. Stir over low heat until gelatine is dissolved. Remove from heat, cool slightly, then chill mixture until it is syrupy. When mixture reaches this stage, quickly beat egg .whites until stiff. Beat cream until stiff. Beat whites into lemon mixture; then fold whipped cream into all, folding until cream is thoroughly blended. Pour into the soufflé dish and chill until very cold—at least 6 hours. Decorate top with thin lemon slices with a sprig of mint pulled through center.

Equivalents and Measurements

Liquid measure volume equivalents

1 tablespoon = 3 teaspoons
2 tablespoons = 1 fluid ounce
4 tablespoons = ¼ cup
5⅓ tablespoons = ⅓ cup
8 tablespoons = 4 ounces

Dry measure volume equivalents

1 quart = 2 pints
8 quarts = 1 peck
4 pecks = 1 bushel

Sugar Equivalents

1 cup granulated sugar = 7 ounces
1 cup confectioners' sugar = 4½ ounces
1 cup firmly packed brown sugar = 7 ounces
1 cup molasses, honey or corn syrup = 12 ounces

Cups per pound

flour, sifted all-purpose	4 cups
cake flour, sifted	4¾ cups
rice	2¼ cups
butter	2 cups
cheese, grated	4 cups

Metric Conversions

WHEN USE of the Metric System in the United States becomes an actuality these are the units of measure the cook will need to know:

1 ounce	28 grams
1 pound	.45 kilograms
1 teaspoon	5 milliliters
1 tablespoon	15 milliliters
1 fluid ounce	30 milliliters
1 cup	.24 liters-rough-.25 liters, ¼ liter
1 pint	.47 liters-rough-.50 liters, ½ liter
1 quart	.95 liters-rough-1 liter
1 gallon	3.8 liters
1000 grams	1 kilogram
500 grams	½ kilogram
250 grams	¼ kilogram
100 grams	1/10 kilogram

Hints and Suggestions

I. *Substitutions*

If you run out—let there be no doubt!

1. No Bread Crumbs? Use crushed corn flakes or any other unsweetened flaked cereal.
2. No Butter? You can use margarine, 1 cup to 1 cup. Or you can use ⅞ cup of vegetable shortening plus ½ teaspoon salt.
3. No Buttermilk? Use 1 tablespoon vinegar or lemon juice to 1 cup milk. Let stand 10 minutes before using.
4. No Catsup? Combine 1 cup tomato sauce or mashed canned tomatoes, ¼ cup firmly packed brown sugar, 2 tablespoons vinegar, ¼ teaspoon cinnamon and a dash each ground cloves and allspice.
5. No Unsweetened Chocolate? For one square (1 ounce) use 3 tablespoons unsweetened cocoa plus 1 tablespoon shortening.
6. No Corn Syrup? Use 1 cup sugar plus ¼ cup water or liquid called for in recipe.
7. No All-Purpose Flour for gravies? If you need 2 tablespoons of flour for gravy, you can substitute 1 tablespoon cornstarch, rice, starch or arrowroot.
8. No Cake Flour? Sift all-purpose flour and use ⅞ cup for 1 cup of cake flour.

293

9. No Fresh Herbs or Spices? Substitute dried herbs and spices.

¼ cup chopped fresh = 1 tablespoon dried
1 teaspoon chopped fresh = ¼ teaspoon dried

10. No Hollandaise? For small quantities (for sauce or glaze) substitute mayonnaise.
11. No Honey? Use 1¼ cups sugar plus ¼ cup water.

II. *Rescues*

These should end some of the miseries that can happen.
1. Salty Soup or Stew? Add cut raw potato to the pot, discarding the potato when it is boiled.
2. Too Sharp? You can soften the taste by adding 1 or 2 teaspoons of sugar.
3. Too Sweet? Add vinegar to taste.
4. Curdled Hollandaise? Remove sauce from heat and beat in 1 teaspoon hot water, a few drops at a time. Do not return to heat. Serve warm or at room temperature.
5. Heavy Cream Won't Whip? Chill cream, bowl and beater or set bowl in a bowl of ice while you whip. If cream still does not stiffen, gradually whip in 3 or 4 drops of lemon juice.
6. Burnt Butter? When sautéing in butter it is wise to add a little vegetable oil to prevent the butter from browning.

III. *Speed-Ups*

1. Even-Cut Onion Rings. Cut before peeling. Slip the peel off each slice.
2. Cutting Sticky Foods. For moisturized prunes, dates, marshmallows, candied fruits, use kitchen shears dipped periodically in hot water.
3. Browning Meat. Avoid pot watching by browning meatballs, stew meat or pot roasts in the broiler or oven. Spread meat on rack in shallow pan and broil or bake at 450° until browned on top: turn and brown on other side. Then proceed with recipe.
4. Measuring Sticky Liquids. If you need to measure syrup or

honey, oil the cup with vegetable oil, or first use the cup to measure the oil or shortening needed for the recipe.

5. Quick-chill gelatin. Gelatin mixtures for molds or aspics can be poured in a metal pan and placed in freezer for 15 minutes. Stir occasionally.

6. Speedy Coffee. To make a large amount of instant coffee quickly, use your electric percolator (without basket or stem). Fill it with the correct amount of water and coffee and plug in.

iv. *Clean-Up*

1. Broken Egg. If you drop an egg on the floor, sprinkle it heavily with salt and leave for 5 to 10 minutes. Sweep up the dried egg into a dust pan.

2. Cleaning Blender. Put a few drops of detergent in it, fill partly with hot water, cover and turn it on for a few seconds. Rinse and drain dry.

3. Cleaning Glass, Ceramic and Porcelain Cookware. Use oven-cleaner.

4. Aluminum Stain. When you use an aluminum pan as the water bath for baking custard or pudding, add 1 teaspoon of cream of tartar to the water to avoid discoloring the pan.

v. *Miscellaneous*

1. At high altitudes be sure to check your baking recipes with local utility home economists.

2. For better results when making candies and meringues, wait for a cool sunny day, as rain and humidity can make this difficult.

3. To check the accuracy of cooking thermometers, place in boiling water and if the thermometer reads 212°, it is accurate.

4. When baking in heat-proof glass pans, lower oven temperature 25°.

Index